流畅美语会话系列

Fluent American English for Going Abroad
出国流畅美语

邱立志　编著
张道真　审订

北京大学出版社
PEKING UNIVERSITY PRESS

图书在版编目(CIP)数据

出国流畅美语 / 邱立志编著. —北京：北京大学出版社，2008.11
(流畅美语会话系列)
ISBN 978-7-301-14416-9

Ⅰ.出⋯　Ⅱ.邱⋯　Ⅲ.英语—口语—美国　Ⅳ.H319.9

中国版本图书馆 CIP 数据核字(2008)第 168665 号

书　　　名：出国流畅美语
著作责任者：邱立志　编著
责 任 编 辑：徐万丽
标 准 书 号：ISBN 978-7-301-14416-9/H·2101
出 版 发 行：北京大学出版社
地　　　址：北京市海淀区成府路 205 号　　100871
网　　　址：http://www.pup.cn
电　　　话：邮购部 62752015　发行部 62750672　编辑部 62765014
　　　　　　出版部 62754962
电 子 邮 箱：xuwanli50@yahoo.com.cn
印　刷　者：北京汇林印务有限公司
经　销　者：新华书店
　　　　　　650 毫米×980 毫米　16 开本　18.5 印张　311 千字
　　　　　　2008 年 11 月第 1 版　2010 年 5 月第 2 次印刷
定　　　价：36.00 元(配有光盘)

未经许可，不得以任何方式复制或抄袭本书之部分或全部内容。
版权所有，侵权必究　举报电话：010-62752024
　　　　　　　　　　电子邮箱：fd@pup.pku.edu.cn

Preface（前言）

说起来真是惭愧，教英语二十余年却教出了很多不会说英语的"哑巴"学生，他们会读会写，就是听不懂，说不出。有人将此归咎于学生的不勤奋和考试制度的弊病，对此，我觉得这只怪我们做老师的懒惰，惰在没有把英语这门外语当作一种交际技能和工具教给学生，而过分强调了考试和考试的成绩。语言是一种交际工具，学习一门外语就是要学会用这种语言去跟别人开展交际活动，对学生来说就是一种技能了。阅读和写作是书面的交际技能，而听说则是口头的交际技能。

检讨以往的过失，不能仍然停留在原来的状态，那是不思进取的表现。所以，笔者觉得要做一些事情，不为别的，就是为了使得有觉悟的英语学习者真正把英语当作一项全面的技能去培养，听、说、读、写四项技能同步发展。鉴于目前仍有相当多的读者在英语听说方面存在障碍，本套书编写重在口头交际技能的培养和训练。当然，市场上关于英语口语训练方面的书籍种类繁多，但是水平也良莠不齐，存在着这样或那样的问题，最明显的一点是落后于时代步伐，很多口语书使用的材料过于陈旧，说法也已经过时。而英语是有生命力的，随着时代的前进，英语也在发展、变化，口语表达习惯更是与时俱进、不断变化的。还有就是许多书中并没有能够反映英语口语的客观实际，一些编写者对英语日常交流用语并不是很了解，所谓的"典型句型"并不是人们经常使用的，而很多常用的表达方式却没有反映出来。因此，学习者只学到了皮毛，在肤浅的框架式英语结构中原地踏步，不能贴切或正确地运用到交流中去。

读者的选择往往是多方面的，不同的读者群有不同的偏好和需要，本系列力图覆盖以下几个方面。

出国之旅：出国的梦想是令人激动的，之所以激动是因为走出国门可以开阔眼界、感受异域风情；但是手续的繁杂、文化的差异，尤其是语言的障碍让很多人或者望而却步，或者倍感艰难，从而使许多人的出国梦想不得不搁浅。所以，这一专题细致入微地呈现了签证、登机等场景所需的习惯表达方式，让你从容踏上出国之旅。

日常交往：异域生活是新鲜的，同时也是琐碎的。我们每天都要面对：

衣食住行、购物买菜、朋友聚会、生日宴会、乔迁之喜、结婚晚宴,以至生病住院等各个生活场景,这些都是在海外生活的每个人必须亲历的。而作为一个新的参与者,要想生活惬意,能够无障碍地交流,避免文化冲突,你就必须做一个有准备的人。

校园生活:海外求学是很多有志青年追求的人生目标。海外校园生活是丰富多彩的,许多情况与国内迥然不同,如果你不了解,感到茫然是不可避免的,从申请入学、注册、选课、咨询教授、学分等级、奖学金到校内打工等具体问题是无法从教科书中得到答案的。

旅游参观:在今天,到国外旅游已是人们尤其是越来越多时尚年轻人假期的主题活动。入住酒店、景点参观、客房服务、餐厅服务、通讯服务等既是旅游六要素"行、住、食、购、娱、游"的具体表现,又是旅游中不可或缺的环节,此专题让你在旅游中克服语言的不便,充分享受游玩的乐趣。

求职工作:不管是在境外公司,或是在中国外资企业的蓝领、白领甚至金领,还是到外资公司跃跃欲试的求职者,你都必须跟"老外"打交道。在车间、办公室、会议等各个场景你想躲都躲不掉,不能够灵活地沟通交流,将会给工作带来极大的障碍。

本系列可读性强,语言地道,内容权威,因为书中70%的语言材料来自于笔者本人在美国生活、学习的语言记录,并加以整理和提炼,生动而不失规范;30%的语言材料来自于已经出版的书籍、文献和网络等媒体,并根据本系列书的需要而采取了改编、吸收和融合等手段,以采众家之所长;张道真教授多年以来对笔者关怀备至,对本系列书稿进行了校订,修改了不少错讹和疏漏之处,并把自己在美国生活十多年的感受和经验融合其中。

口头交际技能的培养,不能只是学会英语句子,学习者还必须了解英语国家的政治经济制度、文化习俗、教育体系、消费习惯、历史传统等多个方面的内容,才能把已经学到的句子应用到真实的交际环境中去。正是基于如上的考虑,本系列各书的主题框架设计如下:

话题导言(Topic Introduction)和背景知识(Background)是会话主题所在的文化氛围。一句话说出来是否得体,是要以其所在的文化背景来判断的。我们把这称作"交际的得体性(Communication Appropriateness)"。一句话说出来不得体,还不如不说,因为不得体的话轻则会让听者不知所云,或者会得罪人,或者会丧失生意机会,从而达不到交际的目的甚至起到相反的作用;重则可能影响国家之间的关系,造成不可挽回的损失或恶

Preface

果。所以,得体性意识的培养是口头交际训练中不能缺少的一个环节。

情景对话(Situational Dialogs)和典型句型(Typical Sentences)是语言的具体运用。任何一个句子只有存在于一定的语言环境(contexts)中才有确定的实际的交际意义。把话题置于情景和大的文化背景之下,就是想尽可能地展现语言的实际应用状态,让学习者在一定的实际状态下学习真实的交际技能。

难点注释(Notes)对情景对话和典型句型中的词语用法、特殊的语法现象、特别的含义以及理解困难的语句进行注解。

大道理谁都明白,归结到一点:掌握一种外语的口头交际技能,得体地有效地开展交际活动,最好的方式就是开口说出来!找到一切可能的机会与说英语的人保持交流!这样才能给书上死的句子赋予生命力!

邱立志
2008 年 5 月 5 日

Contents (目录)

1. Applying for a Visa ················· 1
   申请签证
2. Arranging the Itinerary ············· 8
   行程安排
3. Reserving Air Flights ··············· 16
   航班预订
4. Flying Abroad ······················ 22
   飞往国外
5. Transfer and Transit ················ 29
   转机与过境
6. Immigration Form ··················· 34
   入境申请表
7. International Quarantine ············ 40
   接受检疫
8. Entering a Foreign Country ·········· 45
   入境
9. Baggage Claim ······················ 53
   领取行李
10. Welcomed at Airport ··············· 58
    受到欢迎
11. Driven to Hotel ··················· 64
    前往酒店
12. Receiving Business Service ········ 70
    商务服务
13. Time Difference ··················· 76
    时差问题
14. Making Calls to China ············· 83
    打电话回中国
15. Shopping Alone ···················· 89
    独自逛街

16. At the Bookseller's ……………………………… 95
    逛书店
17. Business Luncheon ……………………………… 100
    公务聚餐
18. Recreation and Sports …………………………… 106
    文体活动
19. Sightseeing ………………………………………… 111
    观光游览
20. Buying Fruits ……………………………………… 116
    购买水果
21. Appointments with Friends ……………………… 121
    约会朋友
22. Presents and Gifts ………………………………… 127
    赠送礼品
23. Meeting New Friends …………………………… 133
    认识新朋友
24. Reception Dinner ………………………………… 139
    招待宴会
25. Visiting an Academia …………………………… 145
    访问学术机构
26. Visiting a University …………………………… 152
    参观大学
27. Attending a Dissertation ………………………… 159
    听学术演讲
28. About Research in Cooperation ………………… 166
    关于合作研究
29. About Students Exchange ……………………… 172
    关于学生交换
30. About English Training ………………………… 178
    关于英语培训
31. About Chinese Training ………………………… 184
    关于汉语培训
32. About Academic Cooperation …………………… 190
    关于合作办学

Contents

33. Attending an International Conference ········· 195
    出席国际会议
34. Paying a Visit to a Government Office ········· 201
    访问政府机构
35. A Visit to Law Courts ···················· 207
    参观法院
36. Visiting a Corporation ···················· 213
    到公司参观
37. Touring a Factory ······················· 219
    参观工厂
38. Visiting a Farm ························ 225
    参观农场
39. About China: Geography & History ·········· 232
    中国地理和历史
40. About China: Politics & Economy ············ 239
    中国政治和经济
41. About China: Population & the People ········ 245
    中国人口和人民
42. Chinese People's Life ···················· 251
    中国人的生活
43. Violating Traffic Rules ··················· 256
    交通违章
44. Baggage Damaged or Lost ················· 262
    行李损失
45. Robbed or Stolen ······················· 267
    被劫被窃
46. Something Lost ························ 272
    物品遗失
47. Suffering from Sickness ·················· 278
    罹患疾病

Acknowledgements (致谢) ···················· 283

Applying for a Visa
申请签证

Topic Introduction
话题导言

无论因公或因私，出国者都需要向所去的国家申请签证，除非两国之间有免签证协议。我国公民因公出国一般都是由单位通过当地外事办公室获得签证。因私出国，签证事宜必须自行办理，有的国家要求面谈，有的国家不要求面谈。

不需要面谈时，只需要准备齐所有的签证申请文件(visa application documents)就可以了。需要面谈时，有些情况下懂得一些英语对于获得签证是有利的，尽管签证官都会用中文与你交谈。

情景对话

丁唐(Ding Tang)出国前要办的最重要的事情就是申请签证。他要与签证官交谈，还要打电话去查询他的签证审批进程。

Dialog 1

Ding Tang: Could I have a business visa application form, please?
请给我一张商务访问签证申请表格好吗？

Officer:	Yes, of course. But please fill it out in English. 当然可以,但请你用英语填写。
Ding Tang:	How long will it take to process my application? 要多长时间受理我的申请?
Officer:	It will be processed within 14 workdays. 我们将在14个工作日内予以受理。
Ding Tang:	How will I be informed, madam? 女士,你们怎么通知我呢?
Officer:	Please tell us your telephone number so that we can let you know something. 请告诉我们你的电话号码,我们好通知你一些事情。
Ding Tang:	Besides this form and my passport, what else do I have to provide? 除了这个表格和我的护照以外,我还要提供别的什么材料?
Officer:	We need your marriage certificate and bank statement. If you think there is something important, you may bring them here. 我们需要你的结婚证明和银行证明。如果你觉得有东西特别重要的话,你也可以带来。
Ding Tang:	Thank you very much. 非常感谢。
Officer:	You are welcome[①]. 别客气。

Dialog 2

Officer:	How are you, Mr. Ding Tang? 丁唐先生,你好吗?
Ding Tang:	Pretty good, madam. And how are you? 很好,女士。你好吗?
Officer:	Good. You are going to the United States for a visit at Seattle, right? 很好。你将到美国西雅图去访问,对吧?
Ding Tang:	I am going to visit Microsoft Company there. 我要去参观微软公司。
Officer:	What's your job? 你的职业是什么?

Applying for a Visa

Ding Tang:	I am a Professor of Nanjing University.
	我是南京大学的教授。
Officer:	Can you give me your business card?
	能给我你的名片吗？
Ding Tang:	Sure, here you are. I am bringing all the copies of documents with me. You may check as well.
	当然，给你。我把所有文件都带来了，你可以看看。
Officer:	Okay. We need to verify if all the documents are true or not. Could you leave all this stuff here?
	好的，我们需要查证所有这些文件是否是真实的，你把这些东西都留下来吗？
Ding Tang:	Sure. When can I get the result of my application?
	当然，我什么时候能得到结果？
Officer:	It will be processed within 7 workdays. We will inform you as soon as we finish it.
	我们将在7个工作日内予以处理，一完成就通知你。
Ding Tang:	Thank you very much.
	非常感谢。

Dialog 3

Ding Tang:	Good morning, this is Ding Tang.
	早晨好，我是丁唐。
Officer:	Good morning, can I help you?
	早晨好，能帮你什么忙？
Ding Tang:	I'd like to know about[2] my visa application.
	我想了解一下我的签证申请情况。
Officer:	Let me see. Would you please tell me your application number?
	我看看，请告诉我你的申请序号，好吗？
Ding Tang:	All right. My number is 0920131.
	好的，我的申请号是0920131。
Officer:	It seems there is something fishy[3] in your passport.
	你的护照似乎有些问题。
Ding Tang:	I don't think so. I got it from the public security bureau by formalities.
	我认为不会这样，我是通过正式手续从公安局得到的。

Officer: Anyhow[4], we are going to look into[5] the matter. But first your visa application documents will be returned.
无论如何,我们会调查这件事,不过,我们要先返还你的申请材料。

Ding Tang: Well then, what shall I do?
那么,我该做什么?

Officer: Please wait until we verify your passport from related organs[6], and we'll inform you at once.
请等到我们向有关机关核实了你的护照,就会马上通知你。

Ding Tang: Thank you. I'll wait.
谢谢,我会等的。

Typical Sentences 典型句型

1) I am going to visit my uncle in the United States next month.
我要下个月去拜访在美国的叔叔。

2) I plan to attend a business meeting in the middle of next month.
我打算下个月中旬去参加一个商务会议。

3) We are planning to take up a cultural exchange program.
我们打算进行一个文化交流项目。

4) This is the invitation we got from the college last month.
这是我们上个月收到的该学院给我们的邀请函。

5) How long will it take to process my application?
要多长时间受理我的申请?

6) Your application is processed in turn.
你的申请将被按照顺序来受理。

7) It will be processed within 14 workdays
我们将在14个工作日内予以受理。

8) Your matter is receiving attention.
我们正在受理你的申请。

Applying for a Visa 申请签证

9) Calls are answered in turn.
请按照顺序等待叫号。

10) Please wait for a reply.
请等候回复。

11) Your visa application documents will be returned soon.
我们不久将返还你的申请材料。

12) It seems there is something fishy in this passport.
你的护照似乎有些问题。

13) Please quote our reference number in any correspondence.
以后照会请告知你的备案序号。

14) Please see further information overleaf.
请阅读背面的说明。

15) Are you bringing any dependant with you?
你是否随带家属?

16) Please show me your family photo?
请出示你的家庭合影?

17) Your visa application is granted.
你的签证申请被批准了。

背景知识

美国的签证:要进入美国,首先要获取签证,签证是入境证件,即美国驻外使领馆在申请签证者所持有效护照(valid passport)上贴的一张纸或者盖的一个印章。因而签证除了被称作 visa 外,人们也称为 sticker, stamp 等。去美国学习、工作、旅游的人要申请非移民签证(non-immigrant visas)。非移民签证种类繁多,有近 40 种,不同的目的签发不同的签证。签证均由一个英语字母加一个数字为代号,如 A-1, A-2 等。所有持非移民签证者要想在美国有永久居留权,必须获得绿卡(green card)。几种最常用的签证如下:

B-1:普通的商业性短期访问者签证。

B-2：普通的旅游性短期访问者签证。

F-1：读本科或研究生或进修语言的学生签证。

F-2：F-1 签证持有者的家庭成员签证。

H-1：具有特殊才能，赴美国做临时性特殊服务者签证，通常为演员、体育明星、演讲者。

H-2A：美国农业部所承认的短期的临时性农业工人签证。

H-3：赴美接受工作培训并在培训结束后归国者签证。

H-4：H-1，H-2，H-3 签证持有者的直系家庭成员。

J-1：美国新闻署承认的交流人员赴美国学习、工作或培训者签证。

J-2：J-1 签证持有者的直系家庭成员签证。

M-1：学习实用技术如飞行的学生签证。

M-2：M-1 签证持有者的家庭成员签证。

签证有关事宜：非移民签证持有者有可能成为纳税居民。如果 1 年之内在美国居住的时间达到 183 天以上，或者 3 年平均居住的时间每年超过 120 天，就会自动成为一个纳税居民。成为了纳税居民就必须申报个人收入，在每年 4 月 15 日之前提交美国税务申报表 1040 表。不遵守税法，可能被取消非移民签证，并且被驱逐出境。非移民签证没有额度限制，凡符合条件者均可取得签证。某些非移民签证需要有一个请求人（petitioner）替申请签证者申办。签证与权利是相应的，不同的签证附有不同的权利，如工作、学习、投资权等等，因此，签证不仅仅是入境证件。

注 释

① 英语中表示感谢的说法很多，Thank you. 是用得最多的一句话。其他的说法有：Thanks a lot. / Thank you so much. / It's very kind of you./ I appreciate your help. 等。对于别人的感谢，总要回应，You are welcome. 是美国人说得最多的一句话，英国人也开始用得多了。其他还

有:That's all right. / That's OK. / Don't mention it. / It's nothing.等。

② know about 的意思是"对……了解",例如:
She knows about antiques.(她对古董很在行。)
有时候,也在 know 之后加上一个词表示程度,如 know well about / know a little about / know a lot about / know everything about 等。

③ fishy 原意是"多鱼的",引申为"虚假的,可疑的,靠不住的"。

④ anyhow 口语中的常用表达,常放在句首表示"无论如何",也可写作"anyway"。

⑤ look into 是"调查"的意思。look 可以与很多介词搭配,如 look at / look after / look about / look like 等。

⑥ organ 在这里表示(官方)的机关、机构,也可译为"器官"。例如:
The eye is the organ of sight. (眼睛是视觉器官。)

Arranging the Itinerary
行程安排

Topic Introduction
话题导言

出国之前,为了稳妥起见,我们都会把行程安排妥当。这中间要和对方的接待单位(学校、政府机构、公司、旅行社等)就整个行程进行反复磋商,达到出国的真正目的,特别是出国访问、探亲、旅游、参加会议、商贸洽谈等活动,时间都是一分一秒计算好的。不然,来回的机票、境外的交通等都会产生衔接不上的问题。

就行程安排进行探讨,可以用传真、电话、电子邮件、在线讨论等形式进行联络,也有面对面的商讨。在这个时候就把所有可能涉及到的问题,如费用分担、接机安排、会谈细节等都提出来,出国的旅程才会顺顺当当。

Situational Dialogs
情景对话

丁唐(Ding Tang)出国前还要落实在美国几天的行程,这次他是以南京大学教授的名义去访问和参观几所大学。

Arranging the Itinerary

Dialog 1

Ding Tang: This is the Cross-Culture Research Center at Nanjing University. May I help you?
我这里是南京大学的跨文化研究中心,可以帮您吗?

Davis: May I speak to the director, Professor Ding Tang?
请找主任丁唐教授听电话。

Ding Tang: Yes, speaking. Who is that?[①]
我就是,您是哪位?

Davis: This is Dr. Davis from Asian Research Center at the University of Washington. I'd like to invite you and your colleagues to visit our university next month.
我是华盛顿大学亚洲研究中心的戴维斯博士。我想邀请您和您的同事们下个月访问我们大学。

Ding Tang: We're planning to do so. Besides UW, we'd like to visit Grays Harbor College at Aberdeen and Georgetown University at Washington D. C. Could you please harmonize the two schools?
我们正计划这样做,除了华盛顿大学,我们还想访问阿伯丁的格里斯港学院以及华盛顿特区的乔治城大学。您能协调一下这两个学校吗?

Davis: Yes, I can. How long altogether?
可以,总共多长时间?

Ding Tang: 14 days in the United States.
在美国一共 14 天。

Davis: OK, I'll get in touch with[②] them soon. Could you send me the names of persons you know in these two schools?
好的,我很快就和他们联系,能把您在这两所学校认识的人的名字告诉我吗?

Ding Tang: Yes, I'll send an email to you later.
可以,我晚一点发电子邮件给您。

Dialog 2

Davis: I'd like to confirm the itinerary of your visit.
我想确认一下你们访问的日程表。

Ding Tang: We're very pleased with the whole plan. But I hope we can visit some other places besides the three schools.
我们对于整个计划很满意，但是我们希望能访问这三个学校以外的其他地方。

Davis: What kind of places do you prefer, government, tourist attractions or companies?
你们喜欢什么样的地方呢，政府机构、旅游点还是公司？

Ding Tang: Better arrange us for a visit to Washington State Government, a City Hall and some tourist attractions.
最好安排我们参观华盛顿州政府、一个市政厅和一些旅游点。

Davis: That's easy to do. But how about financing for these trips? That'll be difficult for us to pay such kind of activities.
那很容易，但是费用怎么办呢？对我们来说负担这类活动的费用是很困难的。

Ding Tang: Don't worry about that. All the expenses of these visits are borne on our account.
别担心这个，所有这些访问的费用都由我们负担。

Davis: That's settled[3]. I'll fax a list of places. You may tick off what you're interested in.
那就解决了，我将把一些地方列出来传真给你们。你们可以把感兴趣的地方勾出来。

Ding Tang: OK, I'll make sure[4] as soon as possible.
好的，我将尽快确定。

Dialog 3

Ding Tang: This is Professor Ding Tang. I'd like to confirm the whole itinerary of our visit to the United States.
我是丁唐教授，我想确认我们到美国的整个行程。

Davis: I believe you've got everything ready.
我相信你已经做好一切准备了。

Ding Tang: Yes, we've got our B1/2 visa and have reserved our plane tickets.
是的，我们已经得到B1/2签证，也已经预订好了机票。

Arranging the Itinerary

行程安排

Davis:	What's the date of your arrival here? 你们到达的日期是哪一天？
Ding Tang:	September 20, 2008. That day is Saturday. The flight number is Northwest Airlines Flight 17. 2008年9月20日，那天是星期六，航班号是西北航空公司17号航班。
Davis:	Let me check... the time of arrival is 11 AM. What's your leaving date? 我来查一下，…… 到达时间是上午11点。哪一天离开？
Ding Tang:	October 2, Thursday. The time of flight is 10 AM at Dulles Int'l ⑤ Airport at Washington D.C. 10月2日，星期四。航班时间是上午10点，在华盛顿特区的杜勒斯国际机场。
Davis:	So, I'll make the final draft of your itinerary at once, and then send respectively to you, GHC and GU. 这样的话，我将马上制作一个你们访问行程表的定稿，然后分别发给你们，格里斯港学院和乔治城大学。
Ding Tang:	All right, thank you so much. 好的，非常感谢。

典型句型

1) I'd like to invite you and your colleagues to visit our university.
   我想邀请您和您的同事们访问我们大学。
2) How long altogether?
   总共多长时间？
3) I'd like to confirm the itinerary of your visit.
   我想确认一下你们访问的日程表。
4) We're very pleased with the whole plan.
   我们对于整个计划很满意。
5) I hope we can visit some other places besides the three schools.
   我们希望能参观这三个学校以外的其他地方。

6) Better arrange us for a visit to Washington State Government, a City Hall and some tourist attractions.
最好安排我们参观华盛顿州政府、一个市政厅和一些旅游点。

7) But how about financing for these trips?
但是费用怎么办呢?

8) That'll be difficult for us to pay such a kind of activities.
对我们来说负担这类活动的费用是很困难的。

9) All the expenses of these visits are borne on our account.
所有这些访问的费用都由我们负担。

10) I believe you've done everything ready.
我相信你们已经做好一切准备了。

11) What's the date of your arrival here?
你们到达的日期是哪一天?

12) What's your leaving date?
哪一天离开?

背景知识

访问日程安排：出国的行程安排一定要比较具体，同时要尽量留有余地，以备临时活动的需要。一般是接待方有一张接待表，出访人有一张出访日程表。下面是一张英语的日程安排表，可以了解一下。

The Itinerary for ××× Delegation USA Visit
Activities Arrangement

Date	Time	Activities
Day 1	11:00	Arriving at Honolulu Int'l Airport
	13:00	Visiting Pearl Harbor after Lunch
	16:00	Checking-in at Waikiki Surf Hotel
Day 2	08:00	Visiting Diamond Head
	10:00	Round-Island Trip

Arranging the Itinerary

	14:00	Sightseeing in Honolulu and Visiting Iolani Palace
	17:00	Visiting Waikiki Beach
Day 3	08:00	Visiting City Hall of Honolulu
	09:30	Sightseeing at Chinatown
	11:00	Checking-out at Hotel
	12:30	Leaving for Honolulu Int'l Airport after Lunch
	21:30	Arriving at San Francisco Int'l Airport
	22:00	Checking-in at Howard Johnson Inn
Day 4	08:00	Visiting Fisherman's Wharf
	13:00	Sightseeing at Chinatown
Day 5	08:30	Visiting UC-Berkley
	10:30	Touring Golden Gate Park
	14:00	Visiting Golden Gate Bridge
Day 6	08:30	Driving on Lombart Street
	10:00	Visiting Union Square and City Hall
	12:40	Leaving for Seattle after Lunch
	17:00	Arriving at Seattle-Tacoma Int'l Airport
	18:00	Dinner with GHC Presidents
	20:00	Checking-in at Holiday Inn Seattle
Day 7	08:00	Visiting Washington State Government (Olympia)
	10:00	Driving to GHC in Aberdeen and Checking-in at Grays Hotel
	13:00	Visiting the College after Lunch
	14:00	Meeting with GHC Presidents and Deans
	18:00	Dinner Party at Hong Kong Restaurant
	20:00	Visiting Vice-president Jane Johnson's Home
Day 8	08:30	Meeting with GHC Presidents and Deans
	14:00	Academic Seminar with GHC Professors
Day 9	08:00	Checking-out at GH and Driving back to Seattle
	10:30	Visiting the Museum of Flight in Seattle
	14:30	Visiting University of Washington
	18:00	Checking-in at Holiday Inn Seattle
Day 10	08:30	Academic Seminar with Professors at UW

	14:00	Meeting with Related Officials about Cooperation
	19:00	Hosting Dinner with GHC Presidents and UW Related Officials
Day 11	10:00	Flying to Washington D. C.
	16:00	Arriving at Dulles Int'l Airport
	17:30	Checking-in University Inn and then Having dinner with Georgetown University Officials
Day 12	08:00	Visiting White House
	10:30	Visiting Capitol
	14:00	Visiting Lincoln Memorial & Washington Monument
Day 13	08:00	Meeting with GU Related Officials
	10:30	Visiting National Air and Space Museum, & National Gallery of Art
	13:00	Arlington National Cemetery
Day 14	08:40	Back to China via Los Angeles and Tokyo

注 释

① 这是打电话常用的几个句子,注意不要照汉语的说法去"硬译"。
Who is that (speaking)? (您是哪位?)
This is Tom (speaking). (我是汤姆。)
May I speak to Tom? (请找汤姆听电话。)
Speaking. (我就是。)

② get in touch with 是"取得联系"的意思,如:
I'll get in touch with her as soon as possible. (我将尽可能快地和她取得联系。)
类似的还有 in touch with(有联系,对某事熟悉);lose touch with(失去联系,停止联系);out of touch with(无联系,生疏);get into touch with(和……取得联系)等。

③ settled 在这里是形容词"解决了的"的意思。
④ make sure 是"确定,使人确认"的意思,如:
You should make sure the first part of your plan before Monday.(你应该在星期一之前确定你计划的第一部分。)
⑤ 英语中,往往中对前面提到的名称或名称中的个别词语采用简写或缩写形式,如将 International 简写为 Int'l,将 Georgetown University 缩写为 GU,将 University of Washington 缩写为 UW,将 Grays Harbor College 缩写为 GHC,等等。

Reserving Air Flights
航班预订

Topic Introduction
话题导言

虽然纸质机票已停止使用，但预订电子机票的手续仍不可缺少。预订航班是出国征程的重要一环，因为没有预订就没法确定从头到尾的具体行程。目前，国际民航市场的竞争非常激烈，各个不同季节、各个不同航空公司、在不同的时间内预订机票，都有不同的价格政策。因此，出国之前最好把全程的所有航班都确定下来，那将会节约很多经费。

你既可以通过旅行社代订，也可以直接到航空公司的票务处去预订，并且各大航空都实行了代码共享（Code-Sharing），购买联程电子机票是非常方便的。电话预订、网上预订等都是可以采用的预订方式，预订的时候也可以货比三家，看看谁的便宜，谁的方便。

Situational Dialogs
情景对话

拿到了签证，安排好了行程，丁唐（Ding Tang）还要预定机票，要和航空公司的职员谈论航班、舱位、价格和航程，以及出发、到达时刻。

Reserving Air Flights 3

航班预订

Dialog 1

Airline: Northwest Airlines Ticketing Office. May I help you?
西北航空公司票务处,能帮您忙吗?

Ding Tang: I'd like to reserve economy class tickets for connecting flights of next month. And, we are six people altogether.
我想预订下个月的联程经济舱机票,我们一共是6个人。

Airline: Yes, sir. When do you want to start your journey?
好的,先生。你们想什么时候出发?

Ding Tang: May 24. We'd like to board your plane at Hong Kong Int'l Airport, better in the morning.
5月24日,我们想在香港国际机场上飞机,最好是上午。

Airline: What are the next stops and the dates, please?
请问,下面要停留的是哪几站,什么日期?

Ding Tang: Hong Kong to San Francisco May 24; San Francisco to Seattle May 28; Seattle to New York City June 3; Washington D.C. to Las Vegas June 6; Los Angeles to Hong Kong June 10.
5月24日香港到旧金山;5月28日旧金山到西雅图;6月3日西雅图到纽约;6月6日华盛顿特区到拉斯维加斯;6月10日洛杉矶到香港。

Airline: OK, let's check against① your reservations...
好的,我们来核对一下您的预订……

Ding Tang: Yes, quite right. What's the discount②?
对的,没错。折扣是多少?

Airline: 30% for economy class, sir. OK, I'll call you back as soon as I can get all seats on all the flights you required.
先生,经济舱的折扣是30%。好的,我一旦确定您要求的所有航班座位,我就给你回电话。

Ding Tang: All right, thanks a lot.
好的,非常感谢。

Dialog 2

Ding Tang: I'd like to reserve a flight to Washington D. C.
我想预订一个到华盛顿特区的航班。

Airline: Certainly. Please show me your passport.
当然可以，请出示您的护照。

Ding Tang: All right. Here you are.
好的，给您。

Airline: When are you going to leave, sir?
先生，您什么时间走？

Ding Tang: I'd like to leave on January 10.
我想1月10日出发。

Airline: That's fine. There is a flight at 10:30 that day. One way or round trip?
很好。那天10:30有个航班。要单程票还是往返票？

Ding Tang: One way please. How much is an economy ticket?
请买单程票，经济舱多少钱一张票？

Airline: Five hundred dollars.
500美元。

Ding Tang: Here you are. Is it a UA[3] flight?
给您钱。是美联航吗？

Airline: Yes, it will take 18 hours from Hong Kong to Washington D. C., and you'll have to change a plane at Guam.
是的，从香港到华盛顿特区要18个小时，您得在关岛转机。

Ding Tang: I see. Thank you.
我知道了，谢谢。

Airline: Wish you a nice trip.
祝您旅途愉快。

Typical Sentences
典型句型

1) I'd like to reserve a ticket to Washington D.C.
我想预订一张到华盛顿特区的机票。

2) I will have an economy class round trip ticket for Tuesday.
我要一张星期二的经济舱来回机票。

Reserving Air Flights 3

航班预订

3) I'd like to reserve economy class tickets for connecting flights of next month.
   我想预订下个月的联程经济舱机票。

4) I'd like to leave on January 10.
   我想1月10日出发。

5) We'd like to board your plane at Hong Kong Int'l Airport, better in the morning.
   我们想在香港国际机场上飞机,最好是上午。

6) There is a flight at 10:30 that day. One way or round trip?
   那天10:30有个航班。要单程票还是往返票?

7) Would you like a one-way ticket or a round-trip ticket?
   你要单程票还是往返票?

8) It is cheaper if you buy a round trip ticket.
   如果你买往返票,价钱会比较便宜。

9) Please check if the 7:15 will be all right.
   请看看有没有7:15的机票。

10) What's the discount?
    折扣是多少?

11) How much is an economy ticket?
    经济舱多少钱一张票?

12) It will take 18 hours from Hong Kong to Washington D. C.
    从香港到华盛顿特区要18个小时。

预订机票:国际电子机票的预订看来很简单,其实还是有很多学问的,有些问题需要特别注意。

(1) 国际机票的价格变动很大,提前预订更是可以得到各种优惠,同时优惠机票往往都有各种限制。比方说,正价票可以签转和更改,而特价票就不允许签转,有效期比较短。

(2) 票价也随着舱位的不同而不同。一般分为头等舱、公务舱和经济舱。头等舱最贵,公务舱居中,经济舱最便宜。不过也有航空公司将这三种票价进行细分,如经济舱可能划分为Y、M、L、K、T五种,每种代号代表不同的票价,分别拥有不同的座位数量,只要预定上了规定的舱位就使用规定的价格。所以,实际上,同等舱位的座位价格也可能不同。

(3) OPEN票是指往返票中的回程日期不事先确定的机票,机票上面标记为OPEN字样。购买机票时,如果没有确定回程日期,就可以预订这样的机票,用起来比较灵活,但一定要问清楚是否免费改期。在美国,确定回程日期的方法通常是给航空公司打电话订一个座位,有时候机位比较紧张,最好提前确定下来。

(4) 特惠机票的"三不"是指"不可签转、不可改期、不可退票"。"不可签转"指的是不准更改航空公司;"不可改期"是指不能更改出发或回程日期;"不可退票"是指不能退回程票或全程票。

(5) 出国旅行还要注意机票的再确认问题,就是在某地逗留超过72小时的情况下,要向航空公司确认后续航班的座位,否则机位有可能被取消。

(6) 乘坐国内航班往往要缴付机场建设费,国际航班则没有这一项,但购票时则要交纳机场税,税种和数额打印在机票上。

(7) 国际机票分为三个年龄层次:0至2岁的孩子要购买婴儿票;2至12岁的孩子要购买儿童票;12周岁以上者要购买全价票。航空公司不同,航线不同,票价的折扣也不同。

(8) 机票遗失的解决办法各航空公司不同,有的航空公司会收取少量手续费后补一张票;有的要求客人重新买票,以后确认未被盗用后再退钱。

Reserving Air Flights

注 释

① check against 是"查对,核对"的意思,如:
You should check against your answers before handing in your examination papers. (交试卷之前,要先查对一下答案。)
② discount 是"折扣"的意思。九折可以表示为 10 percent discount 或 discount of 10%。
③ UA 是 United Airlines(联合航空公司)的缩写词。

Flying Abroad
飞往国外

Topic Introduction
话题导言

  第一次乘坐国际航班出国是一件令人激动的事情，因为这对于平民百姓来说是一生中的大事，而从登上飞机到入境则是这件大事中的核心。有人很早就开始想到这一层，带些什么东西，飞机上吃什么，英语怎么说，外国的空姐是不是也很漂亮，诸如此类的问题。但临到上了飞机，可能除了激动还是激动。

  因而，学会一些在"飞往国外"旅程中的常用英语可能对你的旅行生活会有很多实际的帮助，也可以减少一些不必要的麻烦。首先是登机，能带多少行李，托运多少，手提多少；其次是机上饮食，吃什么，如何开口向空中服务员要饮料和食品；再次是到达哪个机场，如何通知你的亲友接你。说起来简单，真正临到自己头上，还是有问题的。

Situational Dialogs
情景对话

> 丁唐(Ding Tang)在乘国际航班飞往美国的过程中遇到了一些麻烦，如行李超重、葡萄酒要收费等。

Flying Abroad 4

Dialog 1

Clerk:	Your passport, sir? 请出示你的护照，先生。
Ding Tang:	Here you are. 给你。
Clerk:	OK. How many pieces of baggage would you like to check in? 好的，你要托运几件行李？
Ding Tang:	Two, this trunk and this bag. 两件，这个箱子和这个袋子。
Clerk:	Please put them over here one by one①, so I can know the weight. ... All right, thanks. ... I'm sorry to say this trunk is overweight. 请一个个地放在这个上面，我好知道重量……好的，谢谢……不好意思，这个箱子超重了。
Ding Tang:	What can I do now? 我该怎么办呢？
Clerk:	It's up to② you. You may throw some of your stuff away or you'll be fined according to the regulations. 由你决定。你可以扔掉一些东西，或者按照规定交纳罚款。
Ding Tang:	How much will you fine me? 你要罚我多少？
Clerk:	90 US dollars. 90美元。
Ding Tang:	That's too much. I'll throw something away to the trash bin. Could you wait a second? 那太多了。我要扔些东西到垃圾桶里，你能等我一会儿吗？
Clerk:	All right. Don't rush. You have thirty minutes left. 好的，别急。你还剩余30分钟。

Dialog 2

Ding Tang:	Excuse me, miss. Could you get me something to drink? 打搅一下，小姐。能给我拿些饮料来吗？
Hostess:	Sure, sir. What would you like to have? 当然可以，先生。你想要点儿什么呢？

Ding Tang: Do you have wine, red wine?
你有葡萄酒，红葡萄酒吗？

Hostess: Yes, we do. Four dollars, sir.
有，4美元，先生。

Ding Tang: Four dollars? But it was free when we took the plane from Hong Kong to New York.
4美元？但是我们乘坐从香港到纽约的飞机时是免费的。

Hostess: Alcoholic beverage is charged on domestic flights, but free on international flights.
酒精饮料在国内航班是要收费的，但国际航班是免费的。

Ding Tang: What's free, then?
那么，什么东西免费呢？

Hostess: All the soft drinks are free.
所有的非酒精饮料都免费。

Ding Tang: All right. Please give me a Coke, then.
好的，就请来一罐可乐吧。

Dialog 3

Hostess: What do you like to have for your lunch, sir?
先生，你午餐想吃点什么？

Ding Tang: What do you have?
你们有什么？

Hostess: We serve rice with chicken, rice with beef, and pastas.
我们供应鸡肉米饭、牛肉米饭和通心粉。

Ding Tang: Please give me chicken rice.
请给我鸡肉米饭。

Hostess: Sure, here you are.
好的，给你。

Ding Tang: Could you give me some drinks, please?
请你给我一些饮料，好吗？

Hostess: Just a minute. Another airhostess will be here later, and you may ask her for drinks.
等一会儿，另一个服务员会来这里，你可以向她要饮料。

Flying Abroad 4 飞往国外

Ding Tang: All right, thanks.
好的,谢谢。

Hostess: You're very welcome.
别客气。

Typical Sentences
典型句型

1) How many pieces of baggage would you like to check in?
你要托运几件行李?

2) I'm sorry to say this trunk is overweight.
不好意思,这个箱子超重了。

3) How much will you fine me?
你要罚我多少?

4) I'll throw something away to the trash bin. Could you wait a second?
我要扔些东西到垃圾桶里,你能等我一会儿吗?

5) Could you get me something to drink?
能给我拿些饮料来吗?

6) Please give me a cup of coffee.
请给我一杯咖啡。

7) Would you please bring me some hot water?
可以请您给我拿些开水吗?

8) Do you have wine, red wine?
你有葡萄酒,红葡萄酒吗?

9) Should I pay for the drinks?
我要给饮料付钱吗?

10) How long is it until today's dinner?
今天的晚餐还要等多久?

11) Please wake me up for lunch.
午餐时请把我叫醒。

12) What do you like to have for your lunch, sir?
先生,你午餐想吃点什么?

13) These earphones are not working properly.
    这些耳机有些问题。
14) When can I buy some duty-free goods?
    我什么时候可以买一些免税商品?

背景知识

登机(Boarding)：登机的规定各个航空公司不尽相同，下面以美国西北航空公司(Northwest Airlines)为例说明。

美国西北航空公司的机场值机柜台开启时间是在航班起飞前3小时，至少应该提前2.5小时到达机场以便办理登机、边防及安检手续，而关闭值机柜台的时间是在航班起飞前75分钟。如果没有在这个时间之前到达值机柜台，将不再为您办理登机手续。请在办理完登机手续后立刻前往边防柜台，办理边防和安检手续，以防延误。请务必在航班起飞前30分钟到达登机口，以免被拒绝登机及将托运的行李落下。

关于免费托运行李限额，各航空公司的规定也不同，美国西北航空公司国际航班的标准如下。

托运行李	件数限制	2
	重量限制	32公斤/件
	体积限制	三边之和不超过158厘米
	额外费用/件	美元 110—130
手提行李	件数限制	1
	体积限制	三边之和不超过118厘米

其他航空公司在美国、加拿大航线上一般也执行上述标准。但前往欧洲、大洋洲、亚洲其他国家的标准则低很多，一般只能免费托运一件行李和手提一件行李，重量一般为经济舱20公斤，公务舱30公斤，头等舱40公斤；而随身携带的行李不能超过5公斤。但各公司的规定也不一样，旅行之前查清楚为好，以免因为超重或者尺寸超大而受到处罚。

世界的主要机场如下：

巴黎： Charles De Gaulle Airport 戴高乐机场，在市区东北部
　　　Orly Airport 奥利机场，在市区南部
柏林： Schönefeld Airport 舍纳费尔德机场，在市区的东南
东京： Narita Airport 成田机场，在东京市区以东
　　　Haneda Airport 羽田机场，在东京市区以南
伦敦： Heathrow Airport 希思罗机场，在市区西部
　　　Gatwick Airport 盖德维克机场，在市区南部
　　　Stansted Airport 斯坦斯特德机场，在市区东北部
华盛顿：Ronald Reagan Airport 罗纳德·里根机场，在市区南部
　　　Dulles Airport 杜勒斯机场，在市区西部
纽约： Kennedy Airport 肯尼迪机场，在城市东南部
　　　Newark Airport 纽瓦克机场，在纽约附近
　　　LaGuardia Airport 拉瓜迪亚机场，在城市东北部
　　　White Plains Airport 白坪机场，在纽约附近
芝加哥：Midway Airport 中途机场，在城市西南部
　　　O-Hare Airport 奥黑尔机场，在城市西北部

注　释

① one by one 的意思是"一个一个地"。数词 one 有很多常用的说法，日常口语中使用很多，如：
one after another （一个接一个地，接连地）
one and all （每个人，全部）
one another （相互，互相）
one and only （唯一的，真正的；[美俚]情人）

one and the same (同一个,完全一回事)
one of those things (命中注定的事)
one or other (或者这个,或者那个,不管哪一个)
one or two (一两个,几个)

② up to 在这里是"由"的意思。up to 可以和很多词语连用,构成短语,如:
up to date (直到最近的,新式的,现代的)
up to now (到目前为止)
up to this time (到现在为止,到此刻为止)

Transfer and Transit
转机与过境

Topic Introduction
话题导言

跨国的长途旅行往往需要转机,即要从一架飞机上下来,然后转乘到另一架飞机上。这中间往往有一个等候的过程,一般仅仅为几个小时。但是,如果飞机的航班衔接不够紧密,中间间隔的时间比较长的时候,就要出机场了,这就是过境。

对于过境旅客,国际上的规定各不相同,有的国家或地区可以免签证停留一定的时间,如大陆旅客可以在香港过境停留7天,中国旅客可以在日本过境停留72小时,而不需要过境签证。但要过境美国,则需要事先取得过境签证,否则将不准离开机场区域。

转机和过境的时候,需要注意不要错过了航班,不要走错了候机楼或登机口,认真了解清楚,注意机场内的广播,不懂的时候要主动询问工作人员,时间紧的时候要请求帮助。

Situational Dialogs
情景对话

丁唐(Ding Tang)乘的航班并不能直接飞往要去的国家,中途还要转机,一般在东京、首尔或者温哥华转机。第一次国外转机,总有些担心的事情。

Dialog 1

Ding Tang: Excuse me, I'm transferring to Houston here. Which gate should I get on board①?
请问,我要转机去休斯敦,我要从哪个门登机?

Clerk: What's your flight number?
你的航班号码是什么?

Ding Tang: American Airlines No. 228.
美洲航空第 228 号。

Clerk: Please take the underground train and get off at No.3 Station, then go upstairs and you can find Gate N22. That's the very② place.
请乘坐地下火车在 3 号车站下车,然后上楼梯,就可以找到第 N22 号登机口。就在那儿登机了。

Ding Tang: Thank you.
谢谢你。

Dialog 2

Ding Tang: Excuse me, my flight is in two days' time. Can I get out of the airport boundaries?
请问,我的航班还要两天时间,我能离开机场吗?

Clerk: It depends. Are you a Chinese citizen?
这要看情况,你是中国公民吗?

Ding Tang: Yes, I'm going to Brazil, but there's one flight only per week.
是的,我要去巴西,但每周只有一个航班。

Clerk: All right. You may have a stopover for 72 hours here.
好的,你可以在这里过境停留 72 小时。

…… ……

Ding Tang: Can I leave my baggage in the Left-Baggage Room?
我可以把我的行李寄存在行李暂放室吗?

Clerk: Sure, you can. Are you on transit③ here?
当然可以,你是过境停留吗?

Ding Tang: I'm staying here for two days. How much do you charge?
我停留两天,多少钱?

Clerk: Eight dollars for that. Please keep this receipt.
8美元。请保管好收据。

Typical Sentences
典型句型

1) I'm a transit passenger for Washington D.C.
   我是前往华盛顿特区的过境旅客。
2) Does this flight fly directly to Spokane?
   这个航班直飞斯波坎吗？
3) You have to transfer at Tokyo, and that plane will take you to Seattle.
   你得在东京转机，然后将飞往西雅图。
4) You have to wait six hour at Tokyo and four hours at Seattle.
   你得在东京等候6个小时，在西雅图等候4个小时。
5) You must have three transfers altogether at Beijing, Seoul and Seattle.
   你总共得转机三次，北京、首尔和西雅图。
6) I'm transferring to New York here. Which gate should I get on board?
   我要转机去纽约，我要从哪个门登机？
7) Where do I go to board my connecting flight?
   我要在哪里转乘飞机？
8) When does the connecting flight to Osaka leave?
   去大阪的续航班机什么时候起飞？
9) Excuse me, my flight is in two days' time.
   我的航班还要两天时间。
10) Can I get out of the airport boundaries?
    我能离开机场吗？
11) You may have a stopover for 72 hours here.
    你可以在这里过境停留72小时。
12) Can I leave my baggage in the Left-Baggage Room?
    我可以把我的行李寄存在行李暂放室吗？

Background

背景知识

签证的种类(Types of Visas)：签证按其用途不同分为(1)入境签证,在有效期内,允许持护照者一次进入国境;(2)出境签证,在有效期内,允许持护照者一次出境;(3)入出境签证,在有效期内,允许持护照者一次入境并出境;(4)出入境签证,允许持护照者在有效期内一次出境并返回;(5)多次入出境签证,持照人在一定的有效期内多次入出国境;(6)过境签证,允许持照者在一定有效期内通过国境,并可作短期(一般为3—7天)停留。

签证按其等级分为外交签证、公务签证和普通签证。一般情况下分别发给外交护照、公务护照和普通护照的持有者。签证一般签在有效的护照上或其他旅行证件上。但有的国家不愿在未建交国家的护照上签证,便发给另纸签证,并注明需与所持护照同时使用方为有效。

出国前,一般均需先办妥所去国家的入境签证和过境停留国家的过境签证。如中途过境而不出机场,一般也可不必办理过境签证。各国签证都要规定有效期和居留期。如过境签证,有效期为一个月,居留期三天,则表示在一个月内可以过境,但只能在该国逗留三天。如入境签证,有效期为半年,居留期一个月,则表示半年之内可以入境,但只能在此地居留一个月,超过一个月者,需另行办理居留申请。

注 释

① board 虽拼写简单,但用起来却很不简单。这里 on board 是"在交通工具上"的意思,如:
We went on board the ship. (我们登上了轮船。)
这个词还可以作动词"搭乘(公共交通工具)",如:
He boarded the bus. (他上了公共汽车。)

② very 在这里翻译为"正是的,实在的,真正的",如:
You are the very man I want to see. (你就是我想见的人。)

③ on transit 是"中途停留",这里指"过境停留";而 in transit 是"在运输中"的意思。

Immigration Form
入境申请表

Topic Introduction
话题导言

在乘坐国际航班快要达到目的地时,机上乘务员都要派发到达国家或地区的入境申请卡(Immigration Form/Disembarkation Card)让旅客们填写。一般来说,入境卡是两种语言对照的,其中有一种是英语,但进入英语国家的入境卡则只用英语。填写入境卡应该说是一件小事情,但对于英语不怎么好的旅行者来说,也是一个困难。

入境卡上的内容一般有姓名、性别、出生日期、旅行目的、出发地、目的地、住址、国籍以及签名等。美国的入境卡被称为I-94表。在填写时要求用印刷体字母(block letters),不能用手写体。如果不懂入境卡上的内容,可以向旁边的人请教,甚至请人代为填写,然后自己签名就可以了。

Situational Dialogs
情景对话

丁唐(Ding Tang)搭乘的航班快要降落了,航空小姐要派发入境申请卡给各位乘客填写。可赴美探亲的李亚平(Yaping)却遇到了填写入境申请表的困难。

Immigration Form 6

入境申请表

Dialog 1

Hostess: Excuse me, sir. Is Japan your destination or are you just transferring in Tokyo?
打搅一下,先生。日本是你的目的地,还是你只是在东京转机?

Yaping: I beg your pardon①?
请你再说一遍?

Hostess: I mean if you will stay in Japan you need to fill in② this Immigration Form. If you are transferring to another country in Tokyo you don't need fill in this form.
我是说如果你要呆在日本,就需要填写这张入境申请表。如果你只是在东京转机去别的国家,就不需要填写这张表。

Yaping: My destination is Los Angeles, not Tokyo. I'll just have a stopover of six hours and I don't want to go out of the airport.
我的目的地是洛杉矶而不是东京,我只在东京停留6个小时,而不打算出机场。

Hostess: So don't worry about this form.
这样的话,你就别管这个表格了。

Yaping: Thank you anyhow.
还是谢谢你了。

Dialog 2

Hostess: Hello, do you need the Immigration Form?
你好,你需要入境申请表吗?

Yaping: Yes, I do. But can you do me a favor?
我要,但你能帮我一个忙吗?

Hostess: Sure if I can.
只要我能帮你。

Yaping: My hand hurts, and I can't write. Could you please fill in this form for me?
我的手受伤了,不能写字。你能帮我填这张表吗?

Hostess: Sure. Please open your passport for me, will you?
当然可以。请打开护照,好吗?

Yaping:	OK. 好的。
Hostess:	Your name ... date of birth ... place of birth ... nationality ... But where will you stay in the United States? 你的名字……出生日期……出生地……国籍……但是,你在美国要呆在哪里呢?
Yaping:	With my son, and this is the address he wrote on the envelope. I'm going to visit my son and daughter-in-law in Los Angeles. 和我儿子一起,这是信封上他写的地址。我去洛杉矶看我儿子和儿媳。
Hostess:	Okay, I got it. How long will you stay there? 好的,我知道了。你要呆上多久?
Yaping:	Two months. 两个月。
Hostess:	All right. It's finished. Please sign your name here. 好的,填好了。请在这里签上你的名字。
Yaping:	Thank you so much. 非常感谢。
Hostess:	You are welcome. 不用客气。

Typical Sentences
典型句型

1) Please read the instructions at the back before filling.
   填写之前请阅读背面的说明。
2) Please fill in the card in English.
   请用英语填写这个表格。
3) If you will stay in Japan you need to fill in this Immigration Form.
   如果你要呆在日本,就需要填写这张入境申请表。

4) My destination is Los Angeles, not Tokyo.
   我的目的地是洛杉矶而不是东京。
5) So don't worry about this form.
   这样的话，你就别管这个表格了。
6) Hello, do you need the Immigration Form?
   你好，你需要入境申请表吗？
7) Could you please fill in this form for me?
   你能帮我填这张表吗？
8) But where will you stay in the United States?
   但是，你在美国要呆在哪里呢？
9) I'm going to visit my son and daughter-in-law in Los Angeles.
   我去洛杉矶看我儿子和儿媳。
10) How long will you stay there?
    你要呆上多久？
11) Please sign your name here.
    请在这里签上你的名字。
12) US Immigration③ will keep the Entry Card.
    入境卡将由美国移民局保管。

背景知识

美国入境卡 (Immigration Card)：美国的入境卡被称作 I-94 表，是一张长条形的白色硬纸卡片。在进入美国前，机上乘务员会给你一份 I-94 (入境/出境记录) 表格，该表格需在下机前填妥。下机时，请把给移民官审查的护照、签证、I-20 表或其他证明文件及 I-94 证件备妥。入境时，移民官会收走上半部即入境记录 (Arrival Record)，而在下半部即离境记录 (Departure Record) 盖上你滞留美国时的身份证明。你可根据此份证明合法逗留在美国，并和你的护照订在一起。这张小白卡和你的护照一样，非常重要，绝对不要遗失，随时把他们和未过期的 I-20 或 IAP-66 证件或其他证件放在一起,妥善保存。

　　I-94卡在左上角有组数字,这是移民局(INS)用来了解你在美国的情况,包括入境、出境及许可等数字,可让你在美国合法访问,或是暂时在美合法工作。入境时,记得马上把I-94卡影印一份,包括卡的正、反面,然后和其它重要证件一起妥善保存,将来也许会用到。

　　下面是该卡正面的主要部分。

Form I-94(10-01-85)N	I-94 表格 (10-01-85)N
Admission Number 5527385031 01	登记号码 5527385031 01
Immigration and Naturalization Service	移民局
I-94	I-94
Arrival Record	入境记录
1. Family Name	1. 姓氏
2. First (Given) Name	2. 名字
3. Birth Date (Day/Month/Year)	3. 生日(日/月/年)
4. Country of Citizenship	4. 国籍
5. Sex (Male or Female)	5. 性别(男性或女性)
6. Passport Number	6. 护照号码
7. Airline & Flight Number	7. 航空公司和航班
8. Country Where You Live	8. 您在哪个国家居住
9. City Where You Boarded	9. 您在哪个城市搭乘飞机
10. City Where Visa Was Issued	10. 在哪个城市取得签证
11. Date Issued (Day/Month/Year)	11. 取得签证的日期(日/月/年)
12. Address While in the United State (Number and Street)	12. 美国住址(号码及街名)
13. City and State	13. 美国住址(城市及州名)
Departure Number 552738531 01	离境号码 552738531 01

Immigration Form 6

入境申请表

Immigration and Naturalization Service	移民局
I-94	I-94
Departure Record	离境记录
14. Family Name	14. 姓氏
15. First (Given) Name	15. 名字
16. Birth Date (Day/Month/Year)	16. 生日（日／月／年）
17. County of Citizenship	17. 国籍

注 释

① pardon 是"原谅，谅解"的意思，可以作动词，也可以作名词。如：
Pardon me—I didn't hear what you said. （对不起，我没听见你说的话。）
Pardon me for interrupting you. （对不起打扰了。）
要求对方重复还可以用下列说法：
Sorry, could you... （对不起，你能否……）
Could you repeat what you said, please? （你能重复下你说的吗？）
I didn't quite catch what you said. （我没全听懂你说什么？）
I missed that. （我没听到。）

② fill in 是"填写"的意思，fill out 也是这个意思。

③ 全称为 US Citizenship and Immigration Service（美国移民局），人们口头上往往只说 US Immigration， 其前身为 US Immigration and Naturalization Service (INS，美国移民归化局)。

International Quarantine
接受检疫

Topic Introduction
话题导言

普通的旅行者本来对于"检疫（quarantine）"一词并不熟悉，但2003年春夏之际的一场传染性非典型肺炎（Severe Acute Respiratory Syndrome，简称SARS）和此后几年反复出现的禽流感（Bird Flu）让国际旅客熟悉了对人的检疫。因为，我们以往一谈到检疫，就只是涉及动物和植物的检疫，我们所见到的新闻报道也只是说到某种水果、小麦或花卉带有某种病菌，入境之后可能给农业带来病虫害，云云。

其实，国际上对人的检疫历来都有规定，但只是针对一定的人群进行，普通的旅行者并不在其中，例如对艾滋病、黄热病、霍乱的检疫。由于SARS和禽流感的快速传播和病症的严重性，国际上对旅客的检疫加强了许多。

下了飞机，丁唐（Ding Tang）还要接受检疫部门的询问和检查。

International Quarantine 7

接受检疫

Dialog 1

Ding Tang: I hear that we have to fill in the Health Declaration Card①.
我听说我们要填写健康申明卡。

Friend: Yes, that's an accessorial item because of Bird Flu.
是的,那是因为禽流感而增加的一项。

Ding Tang: What if they find a person who catches bird flu? It's really a problem.
万一他们发现了一个感染禽流感的人,怎么办?真是个问题。

Friend: The person will be isolated in the intensive care unit② ward in a hospital until he gets recovered.
这个人将被隔离在医院的特护病房,直到康复。

Ding Tang: He has no choice but to stay there. Everyone's temperature should be taken, I think.
他就只好呆在那里,我想每个人都要量体温。

Friend: Yes, there're inductive thermometers where we get out of the Customs' gates. If you have a fever, the doctors will examine you carefully.
是的,我们出海关的地方有感应体温计,如果发烧的话,医生会仔细进行检查。

Ding Tang: That will benefit every traveler.
那对每个旅客都有好处。

Dialog 2

Inspectress: Excuse me, could you take your temperature③ here?
劳驾,请在这儿量体温,好吗?

Ding Tang: Oh, no problem ... something wrong?
哦,没问题,…… 有什么不对吗?

Inspectress: Yes, I'm afraid you've had a fever. Could you please go over there to have a careful check-up?
是的,恐怕你发烧了,你能到那边去进行一个仔细的检查吗?

Ding Tang: Sure.
当然可以。

....

Inspectress: Do you have your Health Certificate with you?
你带了健康证明书吗？

Ding Tang: Yes, it's issued by the Ministry of Public Health of China. I'm afraid I've caught a cold.
带了，这是中国卫生部颁发的，我恐怕是得了感冒。

Inspectress: I hope you're OK. Do you have a headache?
我希望你没有问题，你头痛吗？

Ding Tang: Yes, but not very serious.
是的，但不是很严重。

Inspectress: Do you cough or sneeze these days?
你这几天咳嗽或者打喷嚏吗？

Ding Tang: No, I just feel suffocated.
不，我只是感到憋气。

Dialog 3

Inspectress: Excuse me, please show me your Health Certificate for quarantine.
打搅一下，请你出示你的健康证明书以被检疫。

Ding Tang: Why?
怎么？

Inspectress: You may have been exposed to certain infectious diseases outside China. Did you stay in tropical areas recently, such as central Africa and Central America?
你可能在中国以外接触到某种危险的传染病，你最近在热带地区呆过吗，如中部非洲和中美洲？

Ding Tang: Did I?
是吗？

Inspectress: You visited Equatorial Guinea within the last three months, right?
你过去三个月以内访问过赤道几内亚，对吗？

Ding Tang: No, I went there the year before last[④]. The stamp is not very clear.
没有，我前年去了那里。这个印戳不是很清楚。

International Quarantine 7

接受检疫

Inspectress: Sorry, it's my mindlessness.
对不起,是我的粗心。

Typical Sentences
典型句型

1) The card is stamped by the Health and Quarantine Bureau.
这个卡片由卫生检疫局盖章。
2) I've been vaccinated against yellow fever.
我已经作了防止黄热病的接种。
3) I hear that we have to fill in the Health Declaration Card.
我听说我们要填写健康申明卡。
4) What if they find a person who catches Bird Flu?
万一他们发现了一个感染禽流感的人,怎么办?
5) Everyone's temperature should be taken.
每个人都要量体温。
6) If you have a fever, the doctors will examine you carefully.
如果发烧的话,医生会仔细进行检查。
7) Excuse me, could you take your temperature here?
劳驾,请在这儿量体温,好吗?
8) Do you have your Health Certificate with you?
你带了健康证明书吗?
9) I have a fever, but not very serious.
我发烧了,但不是很严重。
10) Please show me your Health Certificate for quarantine.
出于检疫的需要请出示你的健康证明书。
11) You may have been exposed to certain infectious diseases outside China.
你可能在中国以外接触到某种危险的传染病。
12) This is my record of physical check-up.
这是我的健康检查表。

Background 背景知识

美国检疫：为了防止传染病的传入、传染和传播，美国对来自国外或美国属地的人员实行规定范围内的留验、隔离、查验或限制性的放行，如对任何被认为感染上传染病的感染者要进行留验与查验。在查验时，一旦发现感染者即对其实行必要的隔离。同时，也可以为防止传染病，对来自特定地区的人员和货物暂禁入境和进口。

美国在主要的机场、港口设立了检疫站以控制和管理检疫工作，可以根据申请实行 24 小时或其中任何一段时间的检疫，检疫站可以根据要求延长服务时间。违反检疫法规者，要受到严厉的处罚，如对于未经检疫负责官员许可随意出入检疫站的人员应受到不超过 1000 美元的罚款，或不超过一年以下的监禁，或两者并罚。

与世界其他国家一样，美国也对境外输美的动植物实施严格的检疫，很多种类是根本不让带进美国领土的，并在农业部下面设立了动植物卫生检验署 (Animal and Plant Health Inspection Service) 负责这方面的工作。

注释

① 填写健康申明卡只是临时性措施，并不是每次都要填。在 2003 年 SARS 暴发和后来禽流感多发时才增加这一项，一旦疫情过后，又恢复常态而不用填写健康申明卡了。

② intensive care unit 是"特别护理组"的意思，一般用简称 ICU。

③ take one's temperature 是"量体温"，而 have a temperature 是"发烧"，不要混淆。

④ the year before last 是"前年"的意思。英语中表示时间的词语多由这种结构组成：the day after tomorrow (后天)，the day before yesterday (前天)。

Entering a Foreign Country
入境

Topic Introduction
话题导言

从国际航班上下来,还算不上进入了你要到的这个国家,还要办理一系列的入境手续,如接受移民局的询问、海关的检查甚至国家安全部门的检查。如果遇到不准入境的情形,还有可能因拒绝入境而被直接送回国。

其实,入境的手续很简单,只要持有合法的证件和签证,不违反该国的移民政策和海关的规定,就可以顺利入境。有些人办理入境手续时的紧张情绪是完全没有必要的,我们既不是恐怖分子,也不是偷渡客,光明正大地进入该国观光、旅游、探亲访友、学习进修,只管实事求是地回答问题,不卑不亢,大大方方,问什么答什么,就不会不让你入境。

Situational Dialogs
情景对话

李亚平(Li Yaping)还要接受移民局和海关的检查,总之要实事求是。同机的高卫平(Weiping)和李康(Li Kang)则分别是赴美进行学术交流和工作的。

Dialog 1

Inspectress: Hello, how are you?
嗨,你好吗?

Weiping: Fine, and how are you?
很好,你呢?

Inspectress: Pretty good. Please show me your passport and other documents.
很好,请出示你的护照和其他文件。

Weiping: All right. This is the invitation from the general manager of Century Drinks Corporation in Los Angeles.
好的,这是洛杉矶世纪饮料公司总经理给我们的邀请函。

Inspectress: So, you are going to do some technological exchange about drinks production, right?
这样的话,你们将要进行一些饮料生产的技术交流,对吗?

Weiping: Yes. They have very advanced technologies of extracting orange juice, and we'd like to introduce their new techniques.
对,他们拥有非常先进的橙汁榨取技术,我们想引进他们的新技术。

Inspectress: Good for you. How long will you stay here?
会对你们很有益处,你们打算逗留多久?

Weiping: Three days with this corporation, but later we'll visit Washington DC, New York and San Diego.
在这个公司呆上三天,但此后我们将访问华盛顿特区、纽约和圣地亚哥。

Inspectress: All right. Good luck to you.
好,祝你好运。

Dialog 2

Inspectress: Next please. Where are you from?
下一位请,你从哪里来?

Yaping: China, madam.
我来自中国,女士。

Inspectress: What's your purpose of coming to the United States?
你到美国来的目的是什么?

Entering a Foreign Country

Yaping: I'm here to visit my son and daughter-in-law. They're working for a branch of Microsoft Corporation in Los Angeles.
我来这儿看我的儿子和儿媳，他们在洛杉矶一家微软的分公司工作。

Inspectress: Do you have any letters they wrote to you?
你带有他们写给你的信吗？

Yaping: Yes, here you are.
有，这就是。

Inspectress: How long will you stay in this country?
你准备呆多久？

Yaping: Three months. I'll baby-sit for them, for they gave birth to[①] a child last month.
三个月，我要为他们看孩子，他们上个月刚生了个孩子。

Inspectress: Congratulations! All right, please go this way.
祝贺你！好的，请走这边。

Dialog 3

Inspectress: Hello, come to teach at Washington State University here?
你好，到这里的华盛顿州立大学教书？

Li Kang: Yes. I'm a visiting professor[②] from China.
是的，我是来自于中国的访问教授。

Inspectress: Then, what's in your trunk?
那么，箱子里面有些什么？

Li Kang: I've put inside my books, my clothes and personal stuffs. I'll be teaching here for a full year.
我把我的书、我的衣服和个人物品都放进去了，我将在这里教书一年。

Inspectress: Do you have any Chinese herbal medicine inside?
这里面有没有中草药？

Li Kang: No, madam.
没有，女士。

Inspectress: Anything prohibited, such as alcoholic drinks and tobacco products?
有没有违禁物品，如酒精饮料和烟草制品？

Li Kang: No, madam. And, this is my laptop computer.
没有，女士。这是我的笔记本电脑。

Inspectress: All right. Please put your baggage over there for transferring to your final destination.
好的，请把你的行李放到那边去，以便转运到你的最终目的地。

Li Kang: Yes, I will. Thanks.
好的，我会的。谢谢。

Typical Sentences
典型句型

1) Please show me your passport and other documents.
请出示你的护照和其他文件。

2) We are going to do some technological exchanges about drinks production.
我们将要进行一些饮料生产的技术交流。

3) This is the letter of invitation from my business partner.
这是我生意伙伴发给我的邀请函。

4) We'd like to introduce their new techniques.
我们想引进他们的新技术。

5) This is financial certification from the U.S. Company.
这是美国公司的资金证明。

6) How long will you stay here?
你们打算逗留多久？

7) What's your purpose of coming to the United States?
你到美国来的目的是什么？

8) I'm here to visit my son and daughter-in-law.
我来这儿看我的儿子和儿媳。

9) I'll baby-sit for them, for they gave birth to a child last month.
我要为他们看孩子，他们上个月刚生了个孩子。

10) I'm here to visit some places.
    我到几个地方游览。
11) I'm planning to visit Los Angeles and then Seattle.
    我打算游览洛杉矶和西雅图。
12) I'm a visiting professor from China.
    我是来自于中国的访问教授。
13) I'll be teaching here for a full year.
    我将在这里教书一年。
14) Do you have any Chinese herbal medicine inside?
    这里面有没有中草药?

背景知识

美国海关申报表(Custom Declaration): 进入美国,除了必须填写 I-94 表格以外,还要填写美国海关申报表。入关的主要规定或限制如下。

(1) 携带少于美金一百元的礼品入境不需付关税。

(2) 不可携带任何食物进入美国,尤其是易腐烂食物,包括水果、蔬菜、肉类或农作物。

(3) 衣物、专业设备及其他家庭物品,如果已经使用一段时间并不再出售的话,不需付关税,可带入美国。

(4) 以某些特定动物为原料的产品禁止带入美国。

(5) 带入美国的金钱数额不限多少,但如果超过一万美元,则必须填写海关申报表。

(6) 任何含有麻醉成份的药品或注射药物均须附上医生开的处方证明。走私麻醉药物入境美国,将受巨额罚款。

如果随旅行团到美国,有一些旅行社会事先将海关申报表基本资料都先打好或写好,您只要再填写某些问题即可,很方便。建议据实以报,因为美国海关人员有时候会抽查入境旅客的行李,如果被海关抽查到没有据实以报,海关可以没收财物,入境者也会留下不良纪录,以后再要进入美国,可能每次都会被翻箱倒柜地检查行李,得不偿失!

下面是美国海关申报表(Custom Declaration)的核心内容。

WELCOME TO THE UNITED STATES
DEPARTMENT OF THE TREASURY
UNITED STATES CUSTOMS SERVICE

欢迎来到美国
财政部
美国海关署

CUSTOM DECLARATION

海关申报表

Each arriving traveler or head of family must provide the following information (only ONE written declaration per family is required):

每位入关的旅游者或一家之主必须提供以下资料(一个家庭只须申报一份):

1. Family Name_____ First (Given)_____
   Middle_____
2. Birth date:
   _____Day_____Month_____Year
3. Number of family members traveling with you:
4. U.S. Address:
5. Passport issued by (country)
6. Passport Number
7. Country of Residence
8. Countries visited on this trip prior to U.S. arrival
9. Airline/Flight No:
10. The primary purpose of this trip is business.
    ○YES   ○NO
11. I am/we are bringing fruits, plants, meats, food, soil, birds, snails, other live animals, farm products, or I/we have been on a farm or ranch outside the U.S.
    ○YES   ○NO
12. I am/we are carrying currency or monetary instruments over $10000 U.S. or the foreign equivalent.

1. 姓氏_____名字_____
   中间名_____
2. 出生日期:
   _____日_____月_____年
3. 与你同行的家庭成员人数:
4. 在美地址:
5. 护照发照(国家)
6. 护照号码
7. 居住国家
8. 到美国前造访过的国家
9. 航空公司/航班号:
10. 此次旅程的主要目的是商务。
    ○是   ○否
11. 您携带水果、植物、肉类、食品、土壤、鸟类、蜗牛、其他动物和农产品,或您一直居住在美国以外的农村或牧场吗?
    ○是   ○否
12. 您携带现金或珍贵物品,其价值超过一万美金或相当于一万美金的外币吗?

Entering a Foreign Country

○YES   ○NO

13. I have (We have) commercial merchandise? (articles for sale, samples used for soliciting orders, or goods that are not considered personal effects.)

○YES   ○NO

14. The total value of all goods I/we purchased or acquired abroad and am/are bringing to the U.S. is (see instructions under Merchandise on reverse side; visitors should report value of gifts only):

$_____U.S. Dollars

I have read the important information on the reverse side of this form and have made a truthful declaration.

SIGNATURE_____

Date_____

○是 ○否

13. 您有携带任何商品？(贩卖之商品、订购之样本等任何非属私人之物品)

○是 ○否

14. 您境外购买或获得并带入美国所有物品总价值(参看背面商品栏目；访问者只须申报礼品价值)：

$_____美元

我已阅读过这表格背面之重要须知，并据实以报。

签名_____

日期_____

美国海关申报表正面(来源：US Dept. of Homeland Security)

注 释

① **give birth to** 是"生、产生、引起、造成"的意思。**birth** 是名词"生产、产生"的意思,如 a still birth(死产,死胎);a person of noble birth(出身高贵的人);birth control(节制生育);The child's birth occurred at 2 a.m.(这孩子凌晨两点出生。) 而 give birth to a child 就是"生孩子",如 She gave birth to a girl last night.(昨晚她生了一个女孩。)

② **visiting professor** 是"访问教授",类似的说法还有 guest professor, exchange professor 等。

Baggage Claim
领取行李

Topic Introduction
话题导言

　　到达入境的国际机场，领取托运行李的时间是在移民官员检查之后海关官员检查之前。行李是通过传送带(Conveyor Belt)把行李送到旅客面前，由旅客自己从传送带上拿下来。所以，一定要找到正确的领取区域，下飞机前要注意机上广播，下飞机后要注意机场广播，注意看行李领取区的电子显示牌。如果不清楚，可以询问在场的服务人员，由他们带领你去领取行李。

　　大型的国际机场旅客多，行李的外观有时候看起来也没有多大区别，因此很容易拿错。中途转机时行李也可能因上错飞机而把行李弄丢了，这时就要向机场报告，具体说明行李的外观特征并留下联系电话或地址，一般来说都可以找回来。万一找不回来，也可按照规定得到赔偿。

Situational Dialogs
情景对话

　　乘坐联程航班的丁唐(Ding Tang)要在两个目的地领取行李，一是入境机场，一是最终目的地机场。

Dialog 1

Ding Tang: Excuse me, is this the baggage claim area for United Airlines Flight 18?
请问,这是美国联合航空公司 18 号航班的行李领取处吗?

Clerk: Yes. What can I do for you?
是的,我能为您做点什么吗?

Ding Tang: I'm going to transfer to Reno, Nevada. I'm wondering if I can make it①.
我要转机到内华达州的里诺,不知道是否来得及。

Clerk: When is your flight?
几点的航班?

Ding Tang: There's one hour left. I have to carry my baggage to the transfer check-in counter.
还有一个小时,我必须把行李拿到转机柜台。

Clerk: Don't rush. It's very fast to go through② the Customs.
别急,过海关很快的。

Ding Tang: Where can I get a baggage cart?
我到哪里可以得到行李车?

Clerk: Look, over there.
看,在那边。

Ding Tang: All right. Thanks.
好的,谢谢。

Dialog 2

Ding Tang: I'm sorry, perhaps this case is mine.
对不起,也许这是我的箱子。

Judy: Oh, I am sorry. Mine looks almost the same as this one.
哦,不好意思,我的看起来和这个几乎一样。

Ding Tang: I have another one. ... Here it is. Excuse me, could you keep an eye on③ these two suitcases for me a little while?
我还有一个……来了。请问,你能帮我照看一下这两个箱子吗?

Judy: No problem, but don't let me wait too long.
没问题,但别让我等太久。

Baggage Claim 9 领取行李

Ding Tang: No, it won't take me long. I'll be back soon, for I've got to fetch a baggage cart to carry them.
不会的，要不了多少时间，很快就回来，我要到那边拿一个行李车。

Judy: All right. Could you help me incidentally?
好的，能顺便帮我一个忙吗？

Ding Tang: Sure.
当然可以。

Judy: Please get a city map from the information desk near the carts.
请帮我到行李车附近的咨询台取一张市区地图。

Ding Tang: OK, no problem. I'll be back in a second.
好的，没问题。我马上就回来。

Typical Sentences 典型句型

1) Could you take out my baggage?
你能帮我拿出行李吗？

2) Is this the baggage claim area for United Airlines Flight 18?
这是美国联合航空公司 18 号航班的行李领取处吗？

3) I have to carry my baggage to the transfer check-in counter.
我必须把行李拿到转机柜台。

4) Where can I get a baggage cart?
我到哪里可以得到行李车？

5) Mine looks almost the same as this one.
我的看起来和这个几乎一样。

6) Can I help you with your baggage?
我能帮你拿行李吗？

7) Could you keep an eye on these two suitcases for me a little while?
你能帮我照看一下这两个箱子吗？

8) I can't find my baggage in the baggage claim area.
我在行李区找不到我的行李。

9) I discovered that several things were missing.

我发现几件东西丢了。

10) What goods do you have in your baggage?

你的行李里面有些什么东西？

11) The trunk is about 90 inches long, 60 inches wide and 30 inches thick.

大箱子大约90英寸长，60英寸宽，30英寸厚。

12) What's the brand of the trunk?

你的箱子是什么牌子？

13) It's a Polo House with three tags with my name and phone number.

是马球屋牌，上面有三个标签，标签上有我的名字和电话号码。

乘客到达后的手续：乘坐国际航班到达了别的国家，要办理一定的手续才能走出机场，许多偷渡客就是走不出这道门而被重新送回原来的地方。这些手续通常包括：

(1) 检疫(arrival quarantine)：一般有检疫官员查看健康证明书(Health Certificate / Immunization Record Book)，如果遇到非常时期还要进行体温检测、验血等，以防止某种传染病流入国内。

(2) 移民管理(Immigration)：一般由移民局的官员检查护照、签证、其他文件，主要目的是看你是否为正当进入该国的，也要问一些问题，诸如国籍、旅行目的、停留时间等等。这道手续之后，旅客就要到行李领取区领取行李了。

(3) 海关检查(Customs Clearance)：海关的通道一般分为红色和绿色两种，也有个别国家还有第三种。需要报关的旅客应该走红色通道，拿出在飞机上填好的报关单交由海关官员检查，也有的实行口头报关；不需要报关的旅客就可以走绿色通道，但也要经过海关的检查，有时候只是询问一下就算了,也可能抽查行李。究竟可以携带什么东西入境,事先要弄清楚才行。

注　释

① make it 是口头说法,意思是"达到预定目标,及时抵达,走完路程,病痛等好转"等,如:
I have to finish the job this week, but I don't know if I can make it.(我这周必须完成这件工作,但不知能否做到。)

② go through 是"经历,遭受,完成,通过"的意思,如:
These countries have gone/been through too many wars.(这些国家饱经战火。)
You should go through the official channels to get help instead of through private relationship.(你应该通过官方渠道而不是通过私人关系寻求帮助。)

③ keep an eye on 是"留心,照看"的意思,类似的表达法很多,如:
keep a jealous eye on (担心地注视着)
keep a close eye on (照看,留心瞧着,注意)
keep an eye out for (当心,警惕)
keep one's eyes off (不去看,不眼馋)
keep one's eyes open (密切注视,留意)
keep one's eyes skinned (时刻警惕,留心)
keep both eyes peeled (警惕,留心)
keep a weather eye on (密切注视,时刻警惕)

Welcomed at Airport
受到欢迎

Topic Introduction
话题导言

出国旅行之前,一般都先安排好了境外的行程和接待方。接待方也会安排人到机场去迎接,如旅游由旅行社接待,学术访问由组织机构接待,探亲访友由亲友接待。受到欢迎,对于初次踏入该国的人来说当然感到欣慰和高兴,觉得心中有了底。

走出海关检查站,有很多人在迎接客人的到来。如果接待方的人和你相互之间并不认识,对方往往会打出牌子,这时候就要注意辨别接你的人。尤其要注意的是,姓名的书写形式不同可能会导致你找不到人,英语中的姓名书写是"名+姓"的格式;还有就是有人特别喜欢把所有字母都写成大写或小写字母。

如果下飞机的时间正是用餐时间,对方有可能请你吃饭,但是如果此行是正式的学术、商业活动,一般自己解决吃饭问题比较好。过后的招待宴会则是事先商定的。

丁唐(Ding Tang)和高卫平(Weiping)分别出了机场,立刻就有人来接他们了,这时候要向对方介绍自己的身份,也要确认对方的身份。

10 Welcomed at Airport

受到欢迎

Dialog 1

Weiping: Hello, my name is Weiping. Are you meeting me here?
你好,我叫卫平,你是来接我的吗?

Alice: It's nice to meet you. I'm Alice from Century Drinks Corporation.
很高兴见到你,我是世纪饮料公司的爱丽丝。

Weiping: Nice to meet you, too. You wrote my name as Weiping Gao, and I felt confused at first glance①.
也很高兴见到你,你把我的名字写成卫平高,我第一眼看上去的时候还不敢肯定。

Alice: We write first name first and last name last. Did you have a good flight?
我们是名字在前、姓在后,旅途还好吧?

Weiping: Yes, there were only a few turbulences during the journey, but they didn't bother us.
还好,只是有几次颠簸,但没有问题。

Alice: Probably it's much colder here than your area.
也许这里比你们那里要冷很多。

Weiping: Yes. I should put on my coat.
是的,我应该穿上外套。

Dialog 2

Belinda: Hello, are you Professor Ding from China?
你好,你是从中国来的丁教授吗?

Ding Tang: Yes. But, are you from Grays Harbor College?
是的,但是,你是从格里斯港学院来的吗?

Belinda: No, I'm not. The Professor Ding I'm waiting for is from Fujian Normal University. Are you?
不是。我要接的丁教授是福建师范大学的,你是吗?

Ding Tang: Sorry, I'm not. I'm from Nanjing University and I'm going to Grays Harbor College.
对不起,我不是。我是南京大学的,我要去格里斯港学院。

Belinda: Sorry, I've made a mistake.
对不起,我弄错了。

Ding Tang: It doesn't matter. There's a sign for me.
没有关系,那里有个牌子是接我的。

…… ……

Ding Tang: Hello, I'm Professor Ding from Nanjing University, China.
你好,我是中国南京大学的丁教授。

Jane: Very pleased to meet you, Professor Ding. Our car is outside. Could I help you with your baggage?
非常高兴见到你,丁教授。我们的车在外面,我可以帮你拿一下行李吗?

Ding Tang: Yes, please. Thank you very much.
好的,非常感谢。

Dialog 3

Alice: Welcome to the United States. Welcome to our city.
欢迎到美国来,欢迎到这个城市。

Weiping: Thank you very much. We are looking forward to[2] visiting your country. Thank you for your warm welcome.
非常感谢,我们一直盼望访问你们国家,谢谢你们的热情迎接。

Alice: It's high time[3] for lunch. How about having your first meal here with us today?
正好是吃午饭的时间,和我们一起吃你们在这里的第一餐饭,好吗?

Weiping: It's OK for us. But your reception plan doesn't include this lunch.
我们没有问题,但你们的接待计划不包括今天的中餐。

Alice: That's easy, and we can go Dutch[4].
那好办,我们可以各付各的账。

Weiping: Yes, that's a good solution.
好的,那是一个好办法。

Welcomed at Airport 10

Typical Sentences 典型句型

1) Aren't you Mr. Smith from Washington State University?
   你是华盛顿州立大学的史密斯先生吗？

2) Are you from Grays Harbor College?
   你是从格里斯港学院来的吗？

3) It's nice to meet you. I'm Peter from Anderson Company.
   很高兴见到你，我是安德逊公司的彼得。

4) Did you have a good flight?
   旅途还好吧？

5) There were only a few turbulences during the journey.
   只是有几次颠簸。

6) I'm Professor Chen from Nanjing University, China.
   我是中国南京大学的陈教授。

7) Let me introduce all the members of our delegation.
   我来介绍我们代表团的所有成员吧。

8) We are looking forward to visiting your country.
   我们一直盼望访问你们国家。

9) Thank you for your warm welcome.
   谢谢你们的热情迎接。

10) How about having your first meal here with us today?
    和我们一起吃你们在这里的第一餐饭，好吗？

11) But your reception plan doesn't include this lunch.
    但你们的接待计划不包括今天的中餐。

12) Thank you for coming to meet us.
    谢谢你来接我们。

Background

背景知识

出入境常用词语：从上飞机到受到欢迎的整个过程都是出国行程的最初环节，这中间要接触到如下许多相关的词语：

animal quarantine 动物免疫
check-in counter 登记处，机场检票处
customs declaration 海关申报单
customs duty 关税
customs inspection 海关检查
dutiable articles 需要上税的物品
duty receipt 税单
duty-free allowance 免税定额
duty-free shop 免税店
duty-free/tax-free 免税
Flight Information Board 航班通知一览表
Green Pass 绿色通道
immunization card 免疫卡
in quarantine 隔离检疫
indecent publications 黄色/色情出版物
inoculation against plague 注射预防鼠疫的预防针
inoculation certificate 注射预防针证明
joint inspection 联合检查
oral declaration 口头申报
out of quarantine 解除检疫
passenger lounge 候机室
passport control 护照检查
plant quarantine 植物免疫
pornographic pictures/books/CDs/films 淫秽图片/书刊/光盘/电影
quarantine regulations 检疫管制条例

10 Welcomed at Airport 受到欢迎

quarantine 检疫
Red Pass 红色通道
release upon registration 登记后放行
release without examination 免检放行
smallpox vaccination certificate 接种牛痘证书
smuggle cocaine/marijuana 走私可卡因／大麻
tariff rate 税率
valuables declaration 贵重物品申报
written declaration 笔头申报
yellow[5] book 黄皮书（健康证明）

注 释

① at first glance 的意思是 "乍一看"，如 At first glance the plan seemed unworkable.（乍一看此计划好像不可行。）还可以说 at a glance 等，类似的短语很多，如 take a glance to（对……匆匆一看，一瞥）；give a glance of（对……匆匆一看，一瞥）；steal a glance at（偷偷一看）；tell at a glance（一看就看见）。

② look forward to 是 "盼望，期待" 的意思，如：
We are all looking forward to our holiday.（我们都盼望着假期。）
I'm looking forward to seeing you this summer vacation.（我盼望今年暑假见到你。）

③ high time 的意思是 "正是干什么的时间"，后面可以接介词短语、从句和动词不定式，如：
It's high time for class.（是上课的时间了。）
It's high time to go to school.（是上学时间了。）
It's high time that you started working.（你早该开始工作了。）

④ go Dutch 是美国口语，意思是 "聚餐时各人付各人的账"，如：
Shall we go Dutch?（我们各人付各人的账吗？）

⑤ 英语中有很多由颜色构成的短语，在翻译时不能直译，而应视具体情况而定。如：blue jeans（工装裤），blue moon（极为罕见的），yellow boy（金币），red letter day（重要的日子）。

Driven to Hotel
前往酒店

Topic Introduction
话题导言

西方人和中国人一样地"好客",过去常常会留宿远道而来的客人,就是现在也偶尔会这样。但随着酒店业的发展和人们卫生习惯的养成,越来越多的人家都安排客人到酒店住宿。

不论是探亲访友、学术交流,还是商贸往来、工作移民,接待方都会把客人从机场、码头等处用车接到酒店安顿下来。沿途会介绍自然风光、历史遗迹、农田村舍,让客人熟悉这个地方,更多的人喜欢把他们引以为豪的一面向客人大加宣传。

作为客人,你对于这种热情的接待,要表示感谢,对于当地的名胜美景,要加以称赞。入住酒店时,要按照双方事先的约定办理,不要争着抢着付钱。主人一般也不会进入客人在酒店的房间,除非经过请求并得到允许,因为在西方人的眼里这就是你临时的"家"。

Situational Dialogs
情景对话

到机场来迎接丁唐(Ding Tang)的 Linda 为他安排好了一切,丁唐很感激她。有人迎接和安排,当然省去了不少麻烦。

Driven to Hotel 11

Dialog 1

Linda: All right, follow me please. Our van is over there.
好的，请跟我来。我们的车在那边。

Ding Tang: OK. I didn't expect the airport could have such a beautiful view.
好的，我没有想到机场的风景这么优美。

Linda: Yes, now it is the most beautiful season here. All flowers are in full blossom①, and even we can smell the fragrance of the wheat.
是的，现在是这里最美的季节，所有的花都开得正旺，你甚至可以闻到小麦的清香。

Ding Tang: Yes. Though this is a hilly area, people found a very good place to build this airport. It's just in the valley.
是啊，虽然这是丘陵地区，人们却找到这么好的一个地方建了这个机场，就在山谷里。

Linda: The airport is small, but very convenient for people here to go to big cities. Ah, let me help you to carry the trunk. ... It's so heavy.
机场虽小，但对人们到大城市去很方便。啊，让我来帮你拿这个箱子，……这么重。

Ding Tang: Yes, it's heavy. I put my books in it.
是很重，我把书放进去了。

Linda: It seems we have to push it to the parking lot.
看来我们只好推到停车场了。

Dialog 2

Linda: OK, let's go!
好的，我们走吧！

Ding Tang: How long will it take us to go to the hotel?
到酒店要多长时间？

Linda: Not very long, twenty minutes, I suppose. Is this your first time to visit the United States?
不要很久，我想20分钟吧。这是你第一次到美国来吗？

Ding Tang: Yes, it is. I have been expecting such a chance to exchange our points of view about our research.
是的，我一直盼望着有这么一个机会能就我们的研究交流一下。

Linda: You have done a very good job. Look, this is the ancient battlefield relic, where the Native Americans and the white fought volcanically.
你们做得很不错。瞧，这是古战场遗址，美洲土著和白人在这里进行了激烈的战斗。

Ding Tang: When did the battle happen?
这场战斗发生在什么时候？

Linda: Around two hundred years ago. The white defeated the Native Americans that time.
大约200年以前，当时白人把美洲土著人打败了。

Ding Tang: Where do the Native Americans' offspring[②] live now?
美洲土著的后代现在生活在哪里？

Linda: In the reserves of this state.
在这个州的保留地。

Dialog 3

Linda: Here we are at the hotel.
我们到了酒店了。

Ding Tang: Thank you for your driving us here. This is a quiet place.
谢谢你送我们来这里，这是个安静的地方。

Linda: Yes, I hope you can have a sound[③] sleep at night after long journey. Please go to check in there, and I'll carry your baggage off the van.
是啊，我希望你们在长途旅行之后能在夜晚睡个好觉。请到那里去登记，我来把行李从车上拿下来。

Ding Tang: Thank you very much. In whose name[④] did you book the room?
非常感谢，你是以什么名字预订的房间？

Linda: In the name of Mr. James Wilson. You may tell the desk clerk about it.
我是以詹姆斯·威尔逊的名字预订的，你可以告诉前台服务员。

11 Driven to Hotel
前往酒店

Ding Tang: All right, thanks a lot.
好的，多谢。

Typical Sentences
典型句型

1) Leave the baggage here first.
   先把行李留在这儿吧。
2) Could you drive the car here to carry the baggage?
   你能把车开到这儿来装行李吗？
3) I didn't expect the airport could have such a beautiful view.
   我没有想到机场的风景这么优美。
4) Now it is the most beautiful season here.
   现在是这里最美的季节。
5) We can smell the fragrance of the wheat.
   我们可以闻到小麦的清香。
6) Let me help you to carry the trunk.
   我来帮你拿这个箱子吧。
7) How long will it take us to go to the hotel?
   到酒店要多长时间？
8) Is this your first time to visit the United States?
   这是你第一次到美国来吗？
9) When did the battle happen?
   这场战斗发生在什么时候？
10) Where do the Native Americans' offspring live now?
    美洲土著的后代现在生活在哪里？
11) Thank you for your driving us here.
    谢谢你送我们来这里。
12) In whose name did you book the room?
    你是以什么名字预订的房间？

Background
背景知识

交际礼仪(I): 与西方人打交道,有些礼仪问题值得注意,否则就会获罪于人,或者自身的利益受到损害。

(1) 注意称呼:英美国家的普遍称呼是"先生"(Mr.—mister)、"太太"(Mrs.—mistress)、"小姐"(Miss)。一般来说,男士为某某(姓氏)先生;对有学位或学衔者称呼博士或教授等;对未婚女子称"小姐",已婚的称"太太",弄不清的时候称"女士"(Madam)为上策。

(2) 多用礼貌语言:"谢谢你"(Thank you)、"请"(please)和"对不起"(Excuse me / I'm sorry) 是英美人在日常生活中最常见的礼貌用语,多说客气话有利于双方气氛融洽,有益于交际。凡为你服务,对你的帮助无论大小,都要说声"谢谢";请求帮助,要说"请";如果打扰对方,则一定要说声"对不起"。

(3) 打招呼别忘了孩子:当你拜访英美人家时,常常会有孩子出来向你打招呼问好,你也必须礼貌向孩子问好,千万不要认为对方是孩子而加以怠慢,或根本不放在眼里。如果是这样的话,不仅使孩子受到伤害,而且还通常被认为是对主人的不尊敬。

(4) 谈话勿涉及隐私:不涉及对方隐私是一种礼貌,隐私包括婚姻、收入、年龄、宗教信仰、政治派别、衣服价钱等,如"你的脸色不大好,是不是身体不舒服?"(You look pale. What's wrong with you?)或"你的年龄这么大了,为什么不结婚呢?"(You are so old. Why are you not married?)等问题都侵害了对方的隐私权,是很不礼貌的。

(5) 过分客气会被误解:过分客气和谦虚,在美国人的眼里不是彬彬有礼,而是虚伪。如果一个中国人在同美国人谈话时说"我的英语讲得不好",而在之后又说出一连串流利的英语,这在美国人眼里是自打嘴巴的欺骗行为,或是另有目的,居心叵测。所以在美国,坦率爽快也是一种礼貌。

(6) 注意小节:英美人比较讲究仪表礼貌。不随地吐痰,不在人面前抠鼻子、挖耳朵、擤鼻涕、打喷嚏、打嗝、抓头、瘙痒、用牙签剔牙、打呵欠、伸懒腰、伸舌头、咳嗽等。如不能控制咳嗽,要用手帕捂

Driven to Hotel

嘴,轻声咳嗽,并表示歉意。

(7) 入室先叩门,入室后脱帽:在英美,无论是私人拜访或因公拜访,以及出席各种社交活动,入室前均需轻声叩门,经主人允许方可进入,男人进屋需脱帽和脱去外套。

注 释

① in blossom 是"开花"的意思,如 a friendship in full blossom(深厚的友谊)。
② offspring 是"后代"的意思,这个词的单数和复数形式是一样的。
③ have a sound sleep 是"睡个好觉"的意思,亦可用 sleep a sound sleep。sound 在这里做形容词,是"好的,充分的"的意思,如:sound fruit(完好的水果)。
④ in one's name 或者 in the name of 是"以某人的名义"的意思,如:This diploma is awarded in the name of the president.(这个奖状是以总统的名义颁发的。)

Receiving Business Service
商务服务

Topic Introduction
话题导言

商务服务这个词语的意思很广,这里说的是酒店、会议中心提供的商务服务,包括电讯、网络、邮政、问讯、文件处理等项目。出过国的人,特别是因商务出访、学术交流、友好访问而出国的人都知道这些服务有时显得异常重要。身在异乡,信息的交流是一件不可忽视的事情,有时候关系到生意成败、荣誉得失。

一般的大酒店都有商务中心,专门为客人提供这些服务。如果需要打电话、发传真、邮寄信函、上网、打印文件、了解交通信息等,都可以到商务中心接受这样的服务。有要求都可以直接提出来,即使是酒店不提供的服务项目,他们也会很热情地告诉你如何解决这样的问题。

Situational Dialogs
情景对话

入住后,丁唐(Ding Tang)当然不能忘记同国内的亲戚保持联系。朋友们通过打电话、发电邮等方式保持联系,幸好酒店的商务中心都提供这些服务项目。

Receiving Business Service 12

商务服务

Dialog 1

Clerk: Can I help you, sir?
先生,我能帮您什么忙?

Ding Tang: May I get on the Internet here, miss?
小姐,我可以在这里上网吗?

Clerk: Certainly, please register your name here.
当然,请登记一下您的姓名。

Ding Tang: How much is it for me to be on the Internet?
我上网要多少钱?

Clerk: You are free to get on the Internet in our hotel, but you have to show your room card.
在我们酒店您上网是免费的,但要出示您的房卡。

Ding Tang: Fantastic! I may e-mail my friends here and check my e-mail.
好极了!我可以在这里给我的朋友发电子邮件,也可以查阅我的电子邮件。
…………

Clerk: Thank you for using the computer and welcome again.
谢谢您使用电脑,欢迎下次光临。

Ding Tang: Thank you, good-bye.
谢谢您,再见。

Dialog 2

Clerk: What can I do for you, sir?
先生,我能帮您什么忙?

Ding Tang: I would like to send a fax to Guangzhou, China. Can you help me?
我要发一个传真到中国广州,您能帮我吗?

Clerk: Certainly, sir.
当然可以,先生。

Ding Tang: How much shall I pay then?
我要付多少钱?

Clerk: Two dollars for each page plus an extra of five dollars as service fee.
每页两美元,另加五美元服务费。

Ding Tang:	Thank you very much. Here is the money.	
	非常感谢您,给您钱。	
Clerk:	Here is your change and the receipt, sir.	
	这是找您的钱和收据,先生。	
Ding Tang:	Thanks. Good-bye.	
	多谢。再见。	
Clerk:	Have a nice day, sir	
	先生,再见。	

Dialog 3

Clerk:	May I help you, sir?
	先生,要我帮什么忙吗?
Ding Tang:	Yes, I've got some documents to be photocopied①. Can you help me?
	是,我有文件要复印,您能帮我吗?
Clerk:	Sure, sir. We've a very good photocopier here.
	当然可以,先生。我们这里有一台非常好的复印机。
Ding Tang:	Great! I want to have the document copied②.
	好极了!我想把这个文件复印一下。
Clerk:	What size of paper do you like, sir?
	先生,您要什么型号的纸?
Ding Tang:	Size A4, please. How much do you charge for it?
	请用 A4 的纸,您怎么收费?
Clerk:	Ten cents each page. And what color do you prefer, sir?
	每页 10 美分,先生,您要什么颜色的纸?
Ding Tang:	Pink paper if you have.
	如果有,就用粉红色的。
Clerk:	Well, it's finished. It's 12 dollars altogether.
	好了,复印完了。总共 12 美元。
Ding Tang:	You have done a very good job. Here's twenty dollars.
	您复印得很好。这是 20 美元。
Clerk:	Thank you, sir. Please keep the receipt.
	谢谢,先生。请保存好收据。

Receiving Business Service

Typical Sentences 典型句型

1) May I get on the Internet here, miss?
   小姐,我可以在这里上网吗?

2) I may e-mail my friends here and check my e-mail.
   我可以在这里给我的朋友发电子邮件,也可以查阅我的电子邮件。

3) How much is it for me to be on the Internet?
   我上网要多少钱?

4) I would like to send a fax to Guangzhou, China. Can you help me?
   我要发一个传真到中国广州,您能帮我吗?

5) I've got some documents to be photocopied. Can you help me?
   我有文件要复印,您能帮我吗?

6) I want to have the document copied.
   我想把这个文件复印一下。

7) How much do you charge for it?
   您怎么收费?

8) How much shall I pay then?
   我要付多少钱?

9) I've got the conference agenda here to be typed out as soon as possible.
   我有一个会议日程表要尽快打印出来。

Background
背景知识

　　英文 E-mail 的写作要领：Internet(互联网)连接了世界各地，信息传递就成为一件非常轻松惬意的事情。人们之间的交流又多了一个工具，就是电子邮件(electronic mail，常缩略为 E-mail，e-mail 或 email)，使用方便，传播快捷。

　　(1) 必须填写标题(Heading)栏的"收件人(To)"框中的收信人的 E-mail 地址。"主题(Subject)"框的内容应简明地概括信的内容，短的可以是一个单词，如 greetings；长的可以是一个名词性短语，也可以是个完整的句子，如 Tomorrow's meeting canceled(明天的会议取消)。较为规范的格式是实词的首字母大写，如：New E-mail Address Notification(新电子邮件地址通知)。也可以加上 URGENT (紧急)或者 FYI(For Your Information，供参考)。

　　(2) 正文(Body)的称呼可以简单化。因为 E-mail 一般使用非正式文体，称呼(Salutation)通常无须使用诸如 Dear Mr. Steve Smith 之类的表达，熟悉的人之间、同辈的亲朋好友之间，或同事之间可以直呼其名，但对长辈或上级最好使用头衔加上姓，如 Prof. Smith 等。

　　(3) E-mail 文体特点是简单明了。电子邮件为便于阅读都比较简短，太长的内容可以以附件的方式发出，相应的段落也是比较短。信尾通常也很简明，如 Thanks / Best / Cheers 等。称呼和正文之间、段落之间、正文和信尾客套话之间一般空一行，开头无须空格。

　　(4) 在电子邮件的使用者中还流行使用一些由首字母或读音组成的缩略词，如：

　　asap: As soon as possible. (越快越好。)

　　brb: I'll be right back. (我很快回来。)

　　btw: By the way (顺便提一下)

　　cu 2morrow: See you tomorrow. (明天见。)

　　du wnt 2 go out 2nite: Do you want to go out tonight?(今晚你想出去吗？)

　　fanx 4 ur elp: Thanks for your help. (多谢帮忙。)

Receiving Business Service 12

商务服务

imho: In my humble opinion（以我的鄙见）
lol: Laughing out loud（笑出声来了）
mte: My thoughts exactly.（就是我所想的。）
oic: Oh, I see.（哦，我明白了。）

上述缩略词要视具体情况而定，不宜滥用。

（5）严肃认真的态度。E-mail 的非正式的文体特点并不意味它的撰写可以马虎行事，特别是给长辈或上级写信，或者撰写业务信函更是如此。写完信后，一定要认真检查有无拼写、语法和标点符号的错误。当然 Outlook Express 等软件的"拼写检查"功能可以助你一臂之力。

注　释

① get something to be done 是"要把某事做了"的意思，往往是这件事情还没有做而要让别人去做，如：
I'll get the paper to be written by someone.（我要找人把这篇文章写了。）
注意 get someone to do something 是"让某人做某事"，如：
The teacher got the students to move the desks and chairs into the next classroom.（老师让学生们把桌椅搬到隔壁的教室里去。）

② have something done 是"要让人做某事"，该事是否做了，要看前面的动词时态，如：
I need to have my hair cut.（我需要理发了。）
I went to have my hair cut yesterday.（我昨天去理发了。）

Time Difference
时差问题

Topic Introduction
话题导言

中国位于东半球,而欧美各国位于西半球,地球的自转引起了各地日落日出的时间差异,从而产生了时差问题。上午从广州乘坐飞机赴美国,感觉白天过得很快,不知不觉天就黑了下来;而从美国洛杉矶乘坐飞机返回的时候,又感觉到白天特别长,飞机老是在追赶太阳,明明空中飞行了15个小时,中午出发下午晚些时候就到了。这就是时差造成的。

对于旅行者来说,时差打乱了生物钟,比方说,美国的白天正是中国的黑夜,在这个时间睡觉的习惯往往会使人觉得昏昏沉沉,而到了晚上又觉得头脑格外清醒,这叫做"时差综合症(Jet Lag)"。说到底,这是个习惯问题,只要注意调整就不是问题了,如出国之前就试着改改习惯,或者在航班上有意无意地睡觉或不睡觉,并且头一两天一定要控制自己的睡眠习惯。

Situational Dialogs
情景对话

对于旅行者来说,总是会因为时差问题出现状况。丁唐(Ding Tang)就碰到了时差综合症的问题,于是跟朋友April讨论了起来。

Time Difference 13

时差问题

Dialog 1

April: Feeling dizzy?
感到头昏吗?

Ding Tang: Yes, perhaps it's the jet lag. I was used to[①] sleeping this time every day before I came here.
是的,可能是时差综合症。我来这里之前习惯于每天这个时间睡觉的。

April: You should adjust your life habits so as to be seasoned with[②] all the daily activities here. Cheer up, and try to keep yourself awake.
你要调整你的生活习惯,好适应这里的日常事务。振作起来,努力使自己保持清醒。

Ding Tang: I hope to find such kind of medicine to cure or release the jet lag symptoms.
我希望找到这样一种药来治疗或解除时差综合症的症状。

April: I hope so, too. Scientists hope to develop so-called chronobiotics, medications that can quickly reset the human body's biological rhythms.
我也希望这样。科学家们希望找到所谓的时间抗菌素之类的药物,能很快地调节人体的生物节奏。

Ding Tang: I must make my biological clock reset more quickly than usual, for I have a lot of things to deal with[③].
我必须使得我的生物钟调节得比平时要快,因为我有很多事情要处理。

April: You need at least two or three days.
你至少需要两三天。

Dialog 2

Ding Tang: What time is it here?
现在这里是几点钟?

April: It's four in the afternoon. You'd adjust your watch to the local time.
是下午4点,你最好把你的手表调到当地时间。

77

Ding Tang:	All right. Is it the Pacific Time or Mountain Time? 好的，这里是太平洋时间还是山地时间？
April:	We use the Pacific Standard Time in Northern Idaho. 爱达荷州北部使用太平洋时间。
Ding Tang:	How do you calculate the time in Beijing? 如何计算北京是几点钟？
April:	It's easy. You may add four to the Pacific Time and make it inverted. 很简单，在太平洋时间上加 4，再倒过来。
Ding Tang:	Inverted? What does it mean? 倒过来？什么意思？
April:	Shall we say④, now it's eight in the morning, plus four, and you get twelve, but not twelve o'clock at noon in Beijing, and it's already midnight there. 可以这么说吧，现在是上午 8 点，加上 4，等于 12，但这不是北京的中午 12 点，而已经是午夜了。
Ding Tang:	Oh, I see. 哦，我明白了。

典型句型

1) What's the time in New York when we get there?
   我们到的时候，纽约是几点钟？
2) What time is it here?
   现在这里是几点钟？
3) Do you have any idea what time it is in Paris now?
   你知道巴黎现在是几点吗？
4) What's the time difference between Beijing and New York?
   北京和纽约的时差是多少？
5) New York's local time is thirteen hours behind Beijing.
   纽约的当地时间比北京晚 13 个小时。

Time Difference 13
时差问题

6) Possibly it's the jet lag.
   可能是时差综合症。
7) You'd adjust your watch to the local time.
   你最好把你的手表调到当地时间。
8) Is it the Pacific Time or Mountain Time?
   这里是太平洋时间还是山地时间？
9) Is it still the same day?
   还是同一天吗？
10) How do you calculate the time in Beijing?
    如何计算北京是几点钟？
11) You may add four to the Pacific Time and make it inverted.
    在太平洋时间上加4,再倒过来。
12) We are crossing the International Date Line.
    我们就要穿过国际日期变更线。

背景知识

时差问题(Time Difference)：由于地球的自转，世界上的24个时区中,东边的时区总比西边的时区时间早。但是许多国家并没有按照时区来计算时间，而是人为地采用某个时区的时间作为全国或某一区域的标准时间，如中国采用东八区的时间作为全国统一的时间，称作北京时间。美国则把全国分为几个时区。

这里有两个重要的概念，一个是格林威治标准时间(Greenwich Mean Time)，即以零度经线通过的中时区的标准时间作为世界上统一采用的标准时间，称为世界时。另一个是国际日期变更线(International Date Line)，这是一条沿着东西经180度线的日期分界线。该线的东边是"今天"，而西边是"昨天"，凡是越过这条线的时候都要变更日期，向西越过就增加一天，反之就减少一天。我们假定日界线东边是3月22日晚上10点的时候，而日界线西边却已经是3月23日的晚上10点了。两个地方都位于东西十二区，但一个东、一个西就隔了一天。下面是世界重要城市时差表。

城市	与北京时差	北京8点时
美国旧金山	-16	昨天16点
墨西哥墨西哥城	-15	昨天17点
美国纽约，加拿大蒙特利尔	-13	昨天19点
法国巴黎，英国伦敦	-8	今天0点
意大利罗马，德国柏林，瑞士日内瓦	-7	今天1点
捷克布拉格，匈牙利布达佩斯	-7	今天1点
罗马尼亚布加勒斯特，埃及开罗	-6	今天2点
俄罗斯莫斯科	-5	今天3点
澳大利亚悉尼	+2	今天10点

时差综合症(Jet Lag)：研究表明，90%的长途飞行乘客有时会出现时差综合症的症状。一般认为，由西面飞向东面时，受时差影响会较大，由东面向西面飞行受时差影响较小。有些人需要较长时间才可以克服时差问题，一些乘客的时差症状可能维持长达两个星期。

这一症状的主要表现为疲倦、注意力下降、晚上不能入睡、腹泻或便秘、眼睛感到干涸、肌肉痛等。这主要是由于我们体内昼夜性节律(Circadian)的激素(Cortisol)受到干扰，令身体节奏失调。一个人年纪越大，受时差影响也越大。

克服时差综合症要从很多方面着手，主要是：

(1) 启程前，安排好所有东西，以减少焦虑，在旅程中可以保持轻松。

(2) 行前数日，应避免疯狂聚会和过度饮酒，还要睡眠充足。

(3) 尽量安排白天抵达目的地，可以更容易融入当地的活动。另外，尽可能挑选合适的航班时间，好让自己在一些重要会议或活动前有足够的时间休息。

(4) 旅途中避免进食油腻食物，或吃得太饱。

(5) 尽量争取在机舱内做些活动，如在机舱过道来回行走，或在座位做手脚伸展运动，可减轻手脚肿胀情况，并防止血液循环不畅，可在上机前服食阿斯匹灵。

(6) 眼罩、颈垫、充气枕头及耳塞有利于旅途中入睡，这时要确

Time Difference 13

时差问题

保双脚没有任何压力。

（7）乘搭飞机应穿着宽松的衣物,透气或由天然纤维做成的衣物可令您在长途旅程中感觉较舒服,也可保持身体干爽。在飞行途中也可把鞋脱下,增加血液循环。

（8）调整手表时间,适应当地时间。

（9）选择自己喜爱的音乐收听,帮助身体放松,消除疲劳。

（10）若白天到达目的地,尽量不要在白天睡觉,最好坚持到当地人的睡眠时间,这样可让身体尽快适应当地时间。

注 释

① **be used to** 是"习惯于"的意思,这里 **used** 是形容词,如:
Are you used to the life here? (你习惯这里的生活吗？)

② **be seasoned with** 是"适应"的意思,如:
I'm not seasoned with the food here. (我吃不惯这里的食物。)

③ **deal with** 是"处理,对付,研究,安排"等意思,宾语可以是人,也可以是物,如:
The teacher deals fairly with his pupils. (这个教师公平地对待他的学生。)
The book deals with this problem. (这本书论述了这个问题。)
As his secretary, you should deal with the daily affairs for him. (你作为他的秘书,就要为他处理日常事务。)

④ **shall we say** 在这里是插入语,表示语气。英语中这类词语、短语、短句很多,往往可以表示说话的态度、口气、补充等,下面是一些含有 **say** 的短语、短句:
so say I (我也是这么说的)
as much as to say (等于说,仿佛说)
I couldn't say! (我不知道！/ 我说不上！)
I dare say (我想,大概)

I should say(我想,大概,也许)
let us say (=say)(比方说,例如,假定,姑且说)
needless to say(不用说,不出意料)
that is to say(即,就是,换句话说,就是说,更确切地说)
they say(人家说,据说)
You can say that again!(我完全同意!/你说对了!)

Making Calls to China
打电话回中国

Topic Introduction 话题导言

出门在外,家里人难免惦记,打个电话报个平安是非常必要的。不管是因私出国探亲访友、留学、移民,还是因公出访、学术交流、商务谈判,时刻同自己家里人和单位领导保持联系,既是心理上的一种慰籍,又是交流思想、集思广益的一种方法。

其实,从国外打电话回中国的学问很多,如打电话的方法、如何打才便宜、什么时间打比较好,都是打电话前要想的问题。比方说,从美国打电话回来是否也像从中国打到美国一样在国际代码之前加拨00,是否也可以直接拨号就可以打通,究竟应该购买哪一种电话卡,网上的电话卡是否安全……都是问题。最容易了解这些问题的方法,就是多听听老移民、老留学生的意见,因为他们在打电话回中国这方面"经验丰富"。

Situational Dialogs 情景对话

丁唐(Ding Tang)离开家有些日子了,难免有些想家了。他想给家人打个电话,但国际长途的费用对他来说也太贵了。幸好朋友Juliet提供了不少好意见。

Dialog 1

Ding Tang: By the way, do you know which is the cheapest way to make calls back to China?
顺便问一下,你知道打电话回中国最便宜的方法吗?

Juliet: Using a kind of phone cards for Internet Phone service is the cheapest way, I guess.
我想,用一种互联网电话卡是最便宜的方法。

Ding Tang: Where can I buy this kind of card?
我在哪里可以买到这种电话卡呢?

Juliet: On the Internet, and you should have a credit card. The rate is around four cents per minute.
在互联网上,而且你应该有信用卡。费率大概是每分钟4美分。

Ding Tang: Ah, that's much cheaper than IDD① phone. But, could you tell me the Internet address?
啊,那比国际直拨电话要便宜很多,但是,你能告诉我互联网地址吗?

Juliet: Very easy to remember. It's www.firstphonecards.com and you should choose China from the country list.
很好记,是 www.firstphonecards.com,你从国家的列表中选择中国就可以了。

Ding Tang: Thanks a lot.
多谢。

Dialog 2

Ding Tang: Can you tell me how to use this card?
你能告诉我如何使用这个电话卡吗?

Juliet: You see, this number is the access number, so you should dial this number first and then this PIN② number.
你看,这个号码是接入号,你应该先拨这个号,然后是这个密码。

Ding Tang: It's so complex. After this long cluster of digitals, can I dial my phone number?
这么复杂,在这一长串数字之后,我可以拨我要打的号码了?

Making Calls to China   14

打电话回中国

Juliet: Yes, the country code plus your area code plus your home number is what you need to dial.
是的,国家代号和地区代号加上家中的号码是必须拨的。

Ding Tang: So, I should dial the access number 1-800-235-8768, the PIN 93208752180, the country code 86, the area code 25, and my home number 8765-4321, right?
这样的话,我就要拨接入号 1-800-235-8768,密码 93208752180,国家代码 86,地区号码 25,以及我家里的号码 8765-4321,对吗?

Juliet: If so, they can't put you through[③]. There is a preceding number 011 before the country number.
如果这样,你还是接不通。在国家代号之前还有一个国际冠字 011。

Ding Tang: I see. It's so troublesome to make an international call.
我明白了,打一个国际电话这么复杂。

Juliet: But it's cheap enough.
但是却很便宜。

Typical Sentences
典型句型

1) Could you tell me how to call to China?
请告诉我如何往中国打电话吗?

2) Do I need to apply for an IDD service to AT&T?
我需要向电话电报公司申请国际直拨服务吗?

3) I don't know how to dial the number.
我不知道如何拨号码。

4) You should dial 011 before the country code of China.
在中国的国家代码前拨 011。

5) What's the rate?
费率是多少?

6) By the way, do you know which is the cheapest way to make calls back to China?

顺便问一下,你知道打电话回中国最便宜的方法吗?

7) Where can I buy this kind of card?

我在哪里可以买到这种电话卡呢?

8) You may buy this kind of card in the super market or any other store.

你可以在超市或任何别的商店买到这种电话卡。

9) That's much cheaper than IDD phone.

那比国际直拨电话要便宜很多。

10) If no one picks up the phone, there's no charge.

如果没有人接电话,就不扣钱。

11) Can you tell me how to use this card?

你能告诉我如何使用这个电话卡吗?

背景知识

电话机上的英文符号:电话机的基本功能是通话,但美国的很多电话机都有录音、自动应答、显示号码、显示通话时间等很多其他功能,认识它们也许有用。

ANSWER	应答,留守
AUTO	自动拨号
CH / CHARGE	(无绳电话机上的)充电指示灯
CLR	清除记存的电话号码
FLASH	代替叉簧挂机,使话机重新处于拨号状态
FOLLOW / ONCALL	不挂机,继续听拨号音进行拨叫
HANDFREE	免提扬声开关,不提起话筒进行拨号和通话
HI	振铃声大的位置
IN-USE	话机正在使用的指示灯
LCD	液晶显示

LO	振铃声小的位置或电池处于低电压状态
MAX	受话音量大的位置
MEM / MEMO	显示记忆存储电话号码键
MIN	音量小的位置
MUTE	静音
OGM	录音电话录制主人应答留言内容
ON	话机处于开机状态
P	脉冲拨号方式
P→T	脉冲拨号转换到双音频拨号
PLAY / PLAYBACK	录音电话放音
POWER	电源指示灯
PS	无绳电话的副机
R/P	重拨和暂停共用键
RD/P	重拨、暂停共用键
RDL	重拨最后一次拨出的号码
REC	录音电话双方通话录音
RELEASE	解除和释放键
REW	录音电话机的快速卷退
RINGER	振铃声音或音调的调节
SAVE	双方通话时记录对方的号码
STOP	录音电话机取消录音状态
STORE	存储电话号码键
TIM	计时
T / Tone	双音频拨号方式
VOL / VOLUME	受话音量调节旋钮

① IDD 是 International Direct Dial 的缩写,意思是"国际直拨"。
② PIN 是 personal information number(个人信息码)的缩写,也常指服务密码。
③ put through 是"接通电话"的意思,如:
Can you put me through to this number?(你能给我接通这个电话号码吗?)
还有"使……表现能力或技术接受考验"的意思,如:
The drama coach put her students through their paces before the first performance.(这位戏剧老师要她的学生们表演前接受考查。)

Shopping Alone
独自逛街

Topic Introduction
话题导言

到了国外，难免要去逛街。旅游团都是集体逛街，而其他情况下则多半是独自一人闯荡。逛街目的主要有二，一是希望能够买到在国内买不到的商品，二是希望看看街景，以求对异国市民生活有所了解。出发之前，最好取一张所住酒店的地址卡，买一张地图；走到大街上，要注意方向，不然很容易迷路；为安全起见，晚上不要独自逛街。

独自一人逛街也不可能不说话，也会遇到迷路、饮食、购物等问题，需要向周围的行人请教，涉及到的情景很多。本话题以商店购物、大街上闲谈两个情景来展示基本的会话语言。

Situational Dialogs
情景对话

到了国外，当然要到处走走，除了要了解风土民情，还可以帮家人、朋友带些国内买不到的东西。丁唐(Ding Tang)去了丹佛(Denver)并和路人 Helen 聊了起来。

Dialog 1

Assistant: May I help you, sir?
先生，要买点什么？

Ding Tang: I'd like to buy two pairs of shoes. Do you have Nike?
我想买两双鞋，有耐克鞋吗？

Assistant: Yes, we do. For yourself or someone else?
有，你自己穿还是给别人买？

Ding Tang: My daughter likes Nike sports shoes very much. I'd like to buy two pairs for her.
我女儿非常喜欢耐克运动鞋，我想给她买两双。

Assistant: Look, these Nike shoes are for girls. What size?①
瞧，这些耐克鞋是女孩子穿的。多大号码？

Ding Tang: 23 centimeters, I think.
我想是 23 公分。

Assistant: That's Size 4. What color?
那就是 4 号，什么颜色呢？

Ding Tang: I think this black/white-varsity red and this white/midnight navy-black are the very ones for her.
我想这双黑白相间运动红，以及这双白色和深海军蓝正适合她。

Assistant: Yes, they are very beautiful. Also, we have preferential price these days.
是啊，真的很漂亮。而且，我们这些天有优惠价。

Ding Tang: How?
怎么优惠？

Assistant: For the first pair you can get 10% discount and for the second pair just half price.
第一双优惠 10%，第二双半价。

Ding Tang: Cool! Thank you very much.
好极了，非常感谢。

Dialog 2

Ding Tang: Hi, fine weather, isn't it?②
你好，天气不错，是吧？

Shopping Alone 15
独自逛街

Helen: Yes, it's always fine weather here, and almost no bad weather.
是的,这里的天气总是不错的,几乎没有坏天气。

Ding Tang: I agree. Is this street the busiest at Denver?
我同意你的说法。这条大街是丹佛最繁华的吗?

Helen: Sure, this is the famous Sixteenth Street Mall, and you can buy everything you need at the Tabor Center.
当然,这是著名的十六街购物区,你可以在塔博尔中心买到你需要的一切。

Ding Tang: Can I take this bus there?
我可以乘这公共汽车到那儿吗?

Helen: Without any question, this bus is toll free going up and down③ the Sixteenth Street. May I know if you are a tourist here?
毫无问题,这车是免费来往于十六街的。能否告诉我你是个旅游者吗?

Ding Tang: No, madam. I'm attending an international academic conference at the University of Colorado here, and I'm from China.
我不是,女士。我来这里的科罗拉多大学参加一个国际学术会议。我从中国来。

Helen: Welcome to Denver. A friend of mine is a Chinese restaurant boss.
欢迎你到丹佛来。我有一个朋友就是中国餐馆的老板。

Ding Tang: You must be a kind person. I've got to buy something at the Tabor Center. It's nice talking with you.④
你一定是个友善的人。我得去塔博尔中心买东西了。很高兴和你交谈。

Helen: Nice talking with you, too. See you later.
我也是,再见。

典型句型

1) Do you have something special to eat?
有什么特别的东西可以吃吗?

2) Can you tell me how to go back to my hotel?
   你能告诉我如何返回酒店吗?

3) I'd like to buy two pairs of shoes.
   我想买两双鞋。

4) Do you have Nike sports shoes?
   有耐克运动鞋吗?

5) My daughter likes Nike sports shoes very much.
   我女儿非常喜欢耐克运动鞋。

6) Are these shirts made in China?
   这些衬衫是中国生产的吗?

7) For the first pair you can get 10% discount and for the second pair just half price.
   第一双优惠10%,第二双半价。

8) It's always fine weather here, and almost no bad weather.
   这里的天气总是不错的,几乎没有坏天气。

9) Is this street the busiest at Denver?
   这条大街是丹佛最繁华的吗?

10) Can I take this bus there?
    我可以乘这公共汽车到那儿吗?

11) This bus is toll free going up and down the Sixteenth Street.
    这车是免费来往于十六街的。

12) Does this bus go to the city library?
    这趟车到城市图书馆吗?

背景知识

公共标志和说明:大街上有各种各样的标志,有的以图形表示,更多的配有文字说明,将主要的列举如下。

Business Hours 营业时间　　SOS 紧急求救信号
Office Hours 办公时间　　　Hands Wanted 招聘

Shopping Alone 15 独自逛街

Entrance 入口
Exit 出口
Push 推
Pull 拉
Dead End 此路不通
Open 营业
Closed 停止营业
One Way 单行道
Keep Right/Left 靠右/左
Buses Only 只准公共汽车通过
Wet Paint 油漆未干
Danger 危险
Lost and Found 失物招领处
Filling Station 加油站
No Smoking 禁止吸烟
No Photos 请勿拍照
No Visitors 游人止步
No Entry 禁止入内
No Admittance 闲人免进
No Honking 禁止鸣喇叭
Parking 停车处
Toll Free 免费通行
Mechanical Help 车辆修理
Do Not Pass 禁止超车
No Cycling in the School 校内禁止骑车
Men's/Gentlemen/Gents Room 男厕所
Road Up, Detour 马路施工,请绕行
Women's/Ladies' Room 女厕所

Staff Only 本处职工专用
No Littering 勿乱扔杂物
Hands Off 请勿用手摸
Keep Silence 保持安静
On Sale 削价出售
Not for Sale 恕不出售
Cafe 咖啡馆,小餐馆
Bar 酒吧
Laundry 洗衣店
Beware of Pickpocket 谨防扒手
Information 问讯处
No Passing 禁止通行
Ticket Office 售票处
Booking Office 售票处
Visitors Please Register 来宾登记
No U Turn 禁止掉头
U Turn OK 可以U形转弯
Occupied (厕所)有人
Vacant (厕所)无人
Admission Free 免费入场
Dogs Not Allowed 禁止携犬入内
Keep Away From Fire 切勿近火
Reduced Speed Now 减速行驶
Luggage Depository 行李存放处

注释

① 鞋子号码各国的单位不同,现在中国多用厘米(公分),而美国用编号,同一号码的也分下宽、下窄、上紧、上松等等。

② 和陌生人说话,可以从谈论天气开始,这是一个好的话题。当然,也可以从社会新闻、世界形势谈起。

③ up and down 可以作为短语介词使用,也可以作为短语副词,意思是"来来回回",如:

His eyes moved up and down the rows. (他的眼睛对着一排排人转来转去。)

He is walking up and down at the bus-stop waiting for his wife back from work. (他在公共汽车站来回走动,等他的妻子下班回家。)

④ 有些说法看起来一样,但用起来不同。例如,下面两句的中文意思都是"很高兴见到你",但场合不同:

It's very nice to meet you. (见面时说的话)

It's very nice meeting you. (分手时说的话)

At the Bookseller's
逛书店

Topic Introduction
话题导言

逛书店可以说是某些人的嗜好,闲来无事就喜欢到书店去看看最近有什么新书,也不一定买书,可能就只是翻翻而已。美国的书店很多,但多半不是大型的购书中心且门脸不大。超级市场也有图书专柜,多半是卖些故事、小说之类的消遣读物。书店不仅出售新书,而且也出售旧书。如果想买到便宜的专业经典著作,可以到书店多看看,旧的版本文字一个不差,并且确实便宜许多。

在大城市的商业区及小城镇的商业街都能找到书店(bookseller's, bookstore, bookshop),主要出售各个学科比较畅销的书;而大学书店以出售大学教材为主。美国人称书店为 bookstore,而英国人则称之为 bookshop,如果找不到书店在哪里,就可以问路人 Where's the bookstore?(书店在哪儿?)。如果心中已有目标,在书店也可以直接问店员 Do you have the book named *American Government*?(你们有书名叫做《美国政府》的书吗?),可以节省很多找书的时间。

Situational Dialogs
情景对话

要想好好游览当地的风土民情,最好的方法莫过于买上一本当地的旅游指南,这样一来既省时,又省力。李亚平(Yaping)决定去书店逛逛。

Dialog 1

At the Bookseller's 16

Assistant:	It has been out of print①. But we have a revised edition of *Tour Over the U.S.*
	它已经绝版了。但我们有修订版的《游遍美国》。
Yaping:	Would you let me have a look?
	让我看看,好吗?
Assistant:	Here you are. Please take your time②.
	给您,慢慢看看吧。
Yaping:	Very good. Can you recommend me the latest novel that is being most widely read?
	很好。你能给我推荐一本最受欢迎的最新小说吗?
Assistant:	The bestseller of novels is *Red Rose* by Samuel Jones, but you can't get one until the day after tomorrow for it's sold out here.
	小说的最畅销书是塞缪尔·琼斯的《红玫瑰》,但因为已经卖完,您后天才能买到。
Yaping:	Sorry to hear that. My son wants to read it very much.
	那真遗憾。我儿子很想读这本书。
Assistant:	We'll send one to your house the day after tomorrow if you like.
	如果您愿意,我们可以后天送一本到您家。
Yaping:	All right. I'll leave you my address and phone number.
	好的,我会把我的地址和电话号码留给你的。

典型句型

1) What can I show you?
   请问要什么?
2) I wish to buy a guidebook of Los Angeles.
   我要买一本洛杉矶指南。
3) Is this a reliable one?
   这本是可靠的吗?

4) I assure you it's the most reliable one.
   我保证这本是最可靠的了。
5) I don't think you can get a better one.
   我想再没有更好的了。
6) I want A's *English-Chinese Conversation Book*.
   我要A氏的《英汉会话读本》。
7) Have you got *How to See America*?
   你有《美国导游》卖吗?
8) It is out of print.
   它已经绝版了。
9) Can you recommend me the latest novel that is being most widely read?
   你能推荐给我一本最受欢迎的最新的小说吗?
10) I would recommend you to provide yourself with a copy.
    我劝你买一本。
11) I should like to subscribe for Mr. B's complete works.
    我很想买B先生的全集。
12) It is now being offered to the public.
    现在正在出售呢!

背景知识

买书的学问：出国买书多半是学术研究的需要,也有的是为了能够阅读原著,这就要对英语原著的结构有一定了解。所以,买书的时候要注意:

(1) 书名：英语书的书名一般能够反映全书的内容,如 *Research Design: Qualitative, Quantitative, and Mixed Methods Approaches* (研究设计：定性定量以及混合方法)就是一本关于三种研究设计方法的书。如果你手头上原来就有了中文版,而希望找到英文版的原著,就不能再把标题倒译过来,因为书名的翻译有音译、直译、意

At the Bookseller's 16 逛书店

译和编译等多种情况，有时候根本看不出原文是什么，如《乱世佳人》的原文是 *Gone with the Wind*，根本看不出什么来。

（2）内容提要：一般地说，每本书在扉页之后都有一个叫做 Abstract 的内容提要，概括地说明了全书的内容和主要观点，但买书的时候仅看内容提要是不够的。

（3）目录：买书一定要看目录，我们都有这方面的经验。英语书的目录，尤其是学术专著的目录，往往有三到四种，即主要目录（Brief Contents）、详细目录（Detailed Contents）、插图目录（Contents of Illustrations）、图表目录（Contents of Charts and Forms）。

（4）版权页：只要是正式出版物，目录之前都有一个版权内容，说明是由哪一个出版机构什么时间出版的，不然有可能买到过时的版本，所以要注意这里的时间。

（5）主体部分：买书时不可能把书读完了再决定是否购买，但可以根据目录的指引挑出一个章节详细看看文字风格、写作逻辑、布局谋篇、语言难易，就知道了全书的概貌了。

（6）索引：我们买书时可能只是看中了书中的某个部分，可以通过书末的索引查阅出是否有你所感兴趣的内容。英文的学术原著几乎都有这样的索引列表，是一个很好的工具。

注　释

① out of print 是"已经绝版,已经售完"的意思，如：
The book published five years ago is out of print.（五年前出版的这本书已经绝版了。）
out of ... 的基本意思是"在……之外"，搭配很多，如 out of proportion（不成比例）、out of press（绝版）、out of range（在射程外）、out of question（毫无疑问）等。

② take your time 的字面意思是"花你的时间"，引申为"别急，慢慢来，从容不迫"等。

Business Luncheon
公务聚餐

Topic Introduction 话题导言

赴国外从事商业合作、学术交流、政府访问、文化活动等往往只有在接待、签约和告别的时候要举行比较盛大的正式宴会,而整个活动的过程中多半只是公务聚餐。这种饭局都是比较随便和自由的招待活动,就像主人平时吃饭一样,可能菜式略微好一些。

例如,在美国去参加学术会议时,接待单位多半在大学食堂、饭店餐厅为参加人员预订业务午餐和晚餐,到时候凭票进餐,一般都是自助式的,食品和饮料都不限量,只不过每天都是那几种菜式。西方国家的这种业务招待方式,可能让人觉得不够热情。其实,这种公务聚餐的方式是值得提倡的。

Situational Dialogs 情景对话

美国的聚餐比较随意,和中国有很大不同,这次丁唐(Ding Tang)对美国的饮食文化又加深了了解。

Business Luncheon 17

Dialog 1

Anne: We've arranged for you to dine in the Richard's Cafeteria during the time fixed for the conference①, three meals a day.
会议期间我们安排你们在理查德餐厅吃饭，一天三餐都是。

Ding Tang: Thank you so much. Should we pay for the meals?
谢谢了，我们要付钱吗？

Anne: No, sir. These are your meal tickets with date and time stamped. Just give the waiter your corresponding ticket.
不用了，先生。这些是就餐券，上面盖上了日期和时间。只要把相应的餐券交给服务员就可以了。

Ding Tang: Oh, I see. Blue ones for breakfast, yellow ones for lunch and red ones for dinner.
哦，我明白了。蓝色的是早餐，黄色的是午餐，红色的是晚餐。

Anne: Correct. If you have any complaints, tell the boss there or let me know.
正确，如果有什么意见，就告诉老板，或者跟我说。

Ding Tang: Thank you very much.
非常感谢。

Dialog 2

Anne: How do you like the food here?
你们觉得这里的饭菜如何？

Ding Tang: Quite good. Your university has a very good cafeteria②. Do all the students and teachers eat here?
很好，你们大学有这么好一个食堂。所有的学生和老师都在这里吃饭吗？

Anne: Most students but few③ teachers do. Now, I'd like to introduce you to the new members of the project group....
多数学生在这里吃，很少教师在这里吃。哦，对了，我想给你介绍我们项目组的新成员……

Ding Tang: Nice to meet you. Can we talk a little bit④ about the project?
很高兴见到你们。我们可以谈谈有关的工作计划吗？

Anne:	Sure, but don't forget to eat more. 可以，但别忘了多吃些。
Ding Tang:	Thanks. I hope to adjust the rate of progress. Can we finish the whole plan ahead of two days? 谢谢，我希望调整进度。我们可以提前两天完成吗？
Anne:	No problem, I believe. 我相信没问题。

Dialog 3

Anne:	Welcome to our business luncheon. What would you like to drink? 欢迎光临我们的工作午餐，想喝点什么？
Ding Tang:	Beer is good for me... Thanks. 那就要些啤酒吧，……谢谢。
Anne:	Allow me to propose a toast to[5] our friendship and success of our talks. 请让我提议，为我们的友谊和谈判成功干杯！
All:	Cheers! 干杯！
Anne:	Please help yourself to some chicken. Would you like to use chopsticks? 请随便吃一些鸡。您愿意用筷子吗？
Ding Tang:	The fork and knife is OK. I can manage, I think. 刀叉也可以，我想我对付得了。
Anne:	I like Chinese food very much and I think Chinese cooking is the best in the world. 我很喜欢中餐，并且我认为中国的烹饪是世界上最好的。
Ding Tang:	The food here is also very good. Thank you very much for preparing such a splendid luncheon especially for us. 这里的饭菜也不错，谢谢您为我们特意准备如此丰盛的午餐。
Anne:	You're very welcome. 别客气。

Business Luncheon

Typical Sentences 典型句型

1) We've arranged for you to dine in the university cafeteria.
   我们安排你们在大学食堂就餐。

2) Should we pay for the meals?
   我们要付钱吗？

3) Your university has a very good cafeteria.
   你们大学有这么好一个食堂。

4) How do you like the food here?
   你们觉得这里的饭菜如何？

5) What would you like to drink?
   想喝点什么？

6) Allow me to propose a toast to our friendship and success of our talks.
   请让我提议，为我们的友谊和谈判成功干杯！

7) I'd like to introduce you to the new members of the project group...
   我想给你介绍我们项目组的新成员……

8) Can we talk a little bit about the project?
   我们可以谈谈有关的工作计划吗？

9) I hope to adjust the rate of progress.
   我希望调整进度。

10) I think Chinese cooking is the best in the world.
    我认为中国的烹饪是世界上最好的。

11) Thank you very much for preparing such a splendid luncheon.
    谢谢您准备如此丰盛的午餐。

Background
背景知识

各国公务聚餐(business luncheon/dinner)：因公出访，并不总是招待宴会，多数时候只是简单的公务聚餐会，或者是中餐，或者是晚餐。但世界各地的聚餐会因为各国文化不同，连饭局也有很大的差别。

(1) 美国：单调的饭局。美国人吃饭很单调，早餐喝牛奶煮麦片，吃些面包抹果酱；中餐吃个夹肉的三明治或夹香肠的热狗，喝杯咖啡就算了事。一年四季，总是那几种饭菜。即使设饭局请客吃饭，也无非是咖啡、牛奶、可口可乐、面包、热狗、三明治、汉堡包、煎牛排之类。饭局开始时，美国人通常先要喝一杯冰水或者一碗汤，然后是一盘沙拉，接着才开始吃一道主菜牛排或牛肉饼。主菜吃完后吃西瓜或水果，不饱的话，再吃块甜点心。

(2) 俄罗斯：酒的代名词。伏特加酒是俄罗斯的名酒，俄罗斯人在饭局上首先要给每人倒上一杯伏特加，第一杯通常是一齐干，然后各人按自己的酒量随意酌饮。不过，俄罗斯人在饭局上喝酒都极为诚实，一般不劝酒，能喝多少就喝多少。俄罗斯人的饭局不太讲究菜的质量和多少，只要有酒喝就行。喝口酒，吃口面包，再来一小口奶酪，就是一桌绝佳的饭局。

(3) 日本：吃不饱的饭局。日本饭局上气氛随和且轻松，饭前都互相为对方倒酒，第一杯一起饮过后，大家就可以随意开吃了。日本人自称为"彻底的食鱼民族"，每年人均吃鱼100多公斤，超过大米的消耗量。生鱼片在日本的饭局上象征着最高礼节，但客人不能放开肚皮吃，因为菜的数量相对较少。日本人的饭局虽简单，但他们对待饭局的态度却是最真诚的，此外他们一贯很守时。

(4) 新加坡：最谨慎的饭局。新加坡人对饭局持非常谨慎的态度，他们一般不会邀请初次见面的客人吃饭。新加坡人喜欢清淡、微甜味道，饭局主食是米饭，常有炸虾、香酥鸡、番茄白菜卷、鸡丝豌豆等风味菜肴。客人赴饭局时通常要随身携带一份礼物，因为新加坡人有赠送礼物的习惯。

Business Luncheon 17

公务聚餐

（5）德国：肉和啤酒的天下。德国人的饭局是名副其实的"大块吃肉、大口喝酒"，饭局上的菜大部分都是肉制品，主菜就是在酸卷心菜上铺满各式香肠及火腿。此外，德国美食还有著名的德式清豆汤、德式烤杂肉、德式苹果酥、煎甜饼等。

① the time fixed for a conference 是"会议期限"的意思，fix 是"安排"的意思，如：
We can fix you up for the night.（我们可以给你安排今晚的住处。）
② cafeteria 指(美国自取菜饭的)自助食堂。
③ few 是否定用法，意思是"很少数，几乎没有"，如：a man of few words（沉默寡言的人）。a few 表示肯定，意思是"少数，几个"。如：
A few of them come.（他们来了几个人。）
同样用法的还有 little, a little。
④ a little bit 是"有点，些许"的意思。
⑤ propose a toast to 是"提议干杯"的意思，如：
May I propose a drink for your health?（我可以提议为你的健康干杯吗？）

Recreation and Sports
文体活动

Topic Introduction
话题导言

人们在紧张的工作之余,总是争取最大量的时间参加一些文娱体育活动。现代生活节奏日益加快,文体活动能够使人们的神经放松,得到足够的休息。出国参加会议、访问或者是学术交流活动,抽空参加文体活动不仅有利于身心健康,更是一个交朋结友的好时机,说不定还能为以后的合作打下一个良好的基础呢。

文体活动多种多样,舞会、看戏、看电影、看体育比赛、参加运动等都是经常性的活动。一般来说,既可以参加事先安排好的活动,也可以邀集有共同兴趣的人进行自己的文体活动,如打网球、下国际象棋、去夜总会等,主要的目的是达到相互交流。

Situational Dialogs
情景对话

工作之余,当然少不了休闲娱乐,丁唐(Ding Tang)正和他的朋友讨论着一些休闲娱乐活动。

Recreation and Sports 18

Dialog 1

Anne: What's your favorite sport?
你最喜爱的运动是什么？

Ding Tang: I like high-pressure workout in a gym, for example, weight lifting. It'll build arm and shoulder muscles, won't it?
我喜欢在体育馆里进行高强度的锻炼，比如举重。举重可以锻炼手臂和肩膀的肌肉，不是吗？

Anne: Yes, but I don't think I would care for① that kind of activity. My favorite sport is jogging. I run late afternoon every day for half an hour along the trail.
是的，但我不喜欢那一类的运动。我最喜欢的运动是慢跑。我每天傍晚都沿着这条小路跑半个小时。

Ding Tang: Jogging is a good hobby. Have you ever been on a track-and-filed team?
慢跑是个好习惯。你以前参加过田径队吗？

Anne: Yes. I used to be a runner when I was in Yale.
是的，我在耶鲁上学时，我就是赛跑运动员。

Ding Tang: I was on the swimming team when I was in college. I enjoyed that very much.
读大学时，我是游泳队的成员。我很喜欢游泳。

Anne: I don't like swimming.
我不喜欢游泳。

Dialog 2

Anne: This dance hall is magnificent and the music is wonderful.
这舞厅很豪华，音乐也很美妙。

Ding Tang: Yes, it's a great place. The band is also excellent. I love to dance to② fast music.
是的，是个很不错的地方，乐队也很棒。我喜欢随着快节拍的音乐跳舞。

Anne: Then you must be interested in disco.
那么，你一定对迪斯科感兴趣。

Ding Tang: Quite right. Disco is my favorite, full of③ fun and a great exercise as well.
很对，那是我最喜欢的，很有意思，也是一个充分的锻炼。

107

Anne:	Oh, the disco music is beginning. Let's start.
	哦，迪斯科音乐开始了，我们跳吧。
Ding Tang:	Wow, you're a good dancer.
	哇，你跳得很棒。
Anne:	Thanks. Do you like dancing tango?
	谢谢，你喜欢跳探戈吗？
Ding Tang:	Yes, I like it.
	喜欢，我很喜欢。

典型句型

1) Volleyball is my favorite sport. What's yours?
   排球是我最喜欢的运动，你最喜欢的运动是什么？

2) What's your favorite sport?
   你最喜爱的运动是什么？

3) Do you play sports regularly?
   你定期做运动吗？

4) I like running and swimming, but I don't like hunting.
   我喜欢跑步和游泳，但不喜欢打猎。

5) The hardest thing to learn is to be a good loser.
   最难学的是要做一个输得起的运动员。

6) I like high-pressure workout in a gym, for example, weight lifting.
   我喜欢在体育馆里进行高强度的锻炼，比如举重。

7) My favorite sport is jogging.
   我最喜欢的运动是慢跑。

8) I run late afternoon every day for half an hour along the trail.
   我每天傍晚都沿着这条小路跑半个小时。

9) Have you ever been on a track-and-filed team?
   你以前参加过田径队吗？

10) I prefer something more exciting.
    我偏爱那些更刺激些的活动。

Recreation and Sports

11) Who do you think is the best pitcher of all time?
你认为谁是有史以来最好的投手？
12) Who is the umpire in this basketball game?
这场篮球赛的裁判是谁？
13) This is really a very exciting game!
真是一场激动人心的比赛！
14) Do you like dancing?
你喜欢跳舞吗？

背景知识

美国大学的竞技体育：竞技运动已经成为美国高等教育的重要组成部分，这是与其自身特有的价值以及美国高等教育的特点密不可分的。竞技运动不仅能够丰富学校课余文化生活，还能培养学生的公平竞争意识和顽强拼搏精神，这正符合美国的价值观体系。

竞技运动是高校招揽生源的重要途径之一。竞技运动深受美国大中学生的喜爱，上大学除了挑选有学术声望的大学外，就是选择具有优良运动传统的大学。竞技运动是一个重要的财源，它可以通过出售比赛门票和电视转播权为学校带来可观的收入。规模较大的大学，一般都有两三个体育馆，可容纳3万至8万观众不等。一半以上的大学都有田径馆、游泳馆，经常举办各种比赛。电视转播的费用因比赛项目和水平不同有所差别，一般每场转播费在5万至25万不等。全国转播出场费可达50万美元。另外一个重要的收入来源是参加全国大学联赛，像参加篮球、橄榄球、冰球以及曲棍球等，比赛收入相当可观。正是由于能够带来利润，一些较大的大学每年的竞技运动预算就高达1200万美元。一般大学也达到300—400万美元。另外竞技运动比赛的胜利往往还能够引来校友以及地方企业的无偿捐赠，多者往往达到几十万美元。竞技运动的胜利还能为学校带来政治上的影响。弗吉尼亚特切学院院长曾说过这样一句话：随

着锦标赛的胜利,毕业生社团以及州议会将倾向于学院,并为学院提供各方面的便利条件。

美国奥委会直接管理大学生竞技运动的全美大学生体育联合会,简称NCAA。据统计资料,NCAA所属会员约700个,管理着18个运动项目,每年约有27万大学生参加校际竞技运动。NCAA管辖的竞技运动分为三个等级,即甲级、乙级和丙级。甲级是最高水平的比赛,如今已成为事实上的职业运动,这类学校通常提供数量可观的运动奖学金。丙级则属于传统的业余性学校竞技运动,旨在丰富学生的课余文化生活,禁止提供运动奖学金。

美国大学运动员基本来源于中学,许多大学都设立奖学金以吸引有运动天赋的中学生。一名优秀的篮球或橄榄球运动员可能同时收到来自五十多所大学的邀请函和奖学金。奖学金的数量一般在5500美元左右,但学校还为运动员免费提供住宿,并免除学费。有的学校还提供交通工具。这对于一般大学生而言是极具吸引力的。

为确保运动员学习和训练两不误,NCAA对运动员参加比赛的资格也有严格要求,参加校际竞技比赛的运动员必须是在校全日制学生,每学期必须修得12个学分。每学期学习成绩必须达到全体学生成绩的平均值,否则将失去参赛资格。

注 释

① care for 在这里是"喜欢"的意思,如:
I don't care for tea. (我不喜欢喝茶。)
该词组也有"关怀,关心"的意思,如:care for her health(挂念她的健康)。

② dance to...是"随着……跳舞"的意思,下文还有 sing to...(随着……唱歌)。如:
She began to dance to the music. (她开始随着音乐跳起舞来。)

③ full of 是"充满"的意思,如:
Her eyes were full of tears. (她的眼里充满泪水。)

Sightseeing
观光游览

Topic Introduction
话题导言

欧美国家有一句脍炙人口的名言："Traveling is learning."（旅游就是学习。）由此可见他们热爱旅游的程度。几乎人人都知道，不管是外出开会、访问、学术交流、生意商谈、短期培训，也不管是在国内还是出国，主办方都会安排短距离的旅游，到附近的风景点或名胜古迹去看看。这种活动是主体活动之外的一种补充，是一种放松和休息，也增进了人们之间的了解和感情。

因此，如果出国的时候有这样的旅游活动，参加进去是很有好处的，可以增长见识，了解社会。因为这属于集体活动，所以要听从接待方的安排，切忌自由行事，以免掉队，给个人和整个团队带来烦恼，也给同伴们一个不好的印象。

Situational Dialogs
情景对话

李康(Li Kang)在教学之余，也要周游美国。

Dialog 1

Patricia: How do you like the National Gallery of Art?
你们认为国家美术馆怎么样?

Li Kang: This is the first time I've ever seen so many pictures by celebrities. Where is the next place to visit?
这是我第一次看到这么多名家的画作。我们要看的下一个地方是哪里?

Patricia: It's easy to get there. Look, that's the National Air and Space Museum. Please walk in and take a look.
很容易就到了,瞧,那个就是国家航空和航天博物馆。请走进去看看。

Li Kang: Great. How long can we stay inside?
好极了,我们可以在里面呆多久?

Patricia: How about 90 minutes? Eleven thirty, I'll be picking① all you up in front of that museum.
90分钟如何? 11点30分,我在博物馆前面接你们。

Li Kang: Who's accompanying us? Is there a guide for us?
谁会陪我们? 有导游吗?

Patricia: Yes, Miss Swift is with you all the time. She'll arrange everything for you. OK, see you eleven thirty.
有的,斯威夫特小姐将一直陪你们,她会安排一切。好的,11点30分再见。

Dialog 2

Patricia: Have you visited Niagara Falls before?
你以前游览过尼亚加拉瀑布吗?

Li Kang: Yes, several times. It has become a tiring old tourist sight. I came here every year when I was studying at New York State University at Buffalo.
游览过好几次了,已经成了一个老掉牙的旅游景点了。我在纽约州立大学水牛城分校读书时,每年都来。

Patricia: You used to be a student here, no wonder. But today we're looking it over in an airplane.
你曾经是这里的学生,难怪呢。但今天我们是从飞机上看。

Sightseeing 19

观光游览

Li Kang: That's fantastic.
那好极了。

…… ……

Li Kang: Oh, it's really great! We can see Niagara Falls all at once④ at altitude.
哦,真是壮观!我们可以从高处一下子就看到尼亚加拉瀑布了。

Patricia: The waters are thundering down. It's so fascinating, in a stupefying way.
水在滚滚流下,让人惊奇,令人陶醉。

Li Kang: It fills my mind.
我心潮澎湃。

Patricia: Is Niagara a tiring old tourist sight?
尼亚加拉瀑布是老掉牙了吗?

Li Kang: Of course not. It's a completely new sight watching at altitude.
当然不是,从高处看完全是一个新的景色。

Typical Sentences 典型句型

1) Please tell me some of the places I should visit.
请告诉我一些我应该去游览的地方。
2) What're the famous places in this city?
这个城市有哪些名胜?
3) Can you tell me where we're going to look around?
能告诉我咱们将要到哪些地方去看看吗?
4) I'm afraid we cannot visit so many places in one day.
我恐怕一天之内也看不了那么多地方吧。
5) Where can I get information on sightseeing?
在哪里可以得到观光的资料?
6) I need a tourist map of this city.
我想要一份城市的游览图。
7) Do you mean you want to take a good look at the Museum?
你是说你要好好地看看博物馆吗?

8) How do you like the National Gallery of Art?
你们认为国家美术馆怎么样？

9) Where is the next place to visit?
我们要看的下一个地方是哪里？

10) Great. How long can we stay inside?
好极了，我们可以在里面呆多久？

11) Have you visited Niagara Falls before?
你以前游览过尼亚加拉瀑布了吗？

12) It's a completely new sight watching at altitude.
从高处看完全是一个新的景色。

背景知识

　　观光游览：想在有限的时间内，多看些地方，还要看仔细，就要对这种游览有个最好的安排。随团游览，以服从大局为重，而在此之外，还是有些事情需要准备的。

　　(1) 准备观光资料：到达目的地，首先要了解当地的风景名胜，可以在各处的旅游信息中心(Tourist Information Center)或酒店索取观光手册，做到有的放矢。

　　(2) 买一张地图：事先最好买一张当地的游览地图，即使单独行动也不会迷路。

　　(3) 多听多问：集体游览往往都会安排导游随团，中途遇到问题都可以向导游询问，既学到了知识，又练习了英语口语。

　　(4) 以防万一：如果你在某个景点错过了车，或者迷路了，可以乘坐出租车返回酒店或者赶上团队车辆。因此出发前就要在住宿的酒店取一张地址卡片，或者记下接待人员的手机号码。

Sightseeing 19 观光游览

注 释

① 这是将来进行时态的表达方法，强调将来某个确切的时间正在发生的事情，如：
We'll be waiting for him at the harbor tomorrow noon.(明天正午我们在码头等他。)

② all at once 是"突然、一下子"的意思，如：
The bus-driver braked the bus all at once, and some passengers standing tumbled.(公共汽车司机突然刹车,一些站着的乘客跌倒了。)

Buying Fruits
购买水果

Topic Introduction
话题导言

人们普遍认为，水果中含有大量人体所需要的各种维生素，多吃水果就能补充足量的维生素。不管为了什么而出国，购买水果是不可少的事情，可以到超市去买，也可以在周末的农民市场买，如果遇到水果收获季节还可以开车直接到果园去买。

美国是水果出产大国，其价格一定会令你大吃一惊，很多换算成人民币之后比在中国购买还要便宜一些，这时候就不会再去算经济账了。长住美国的人最喜欢在秋末时节开车到果园去，因为那里的水果不仅便宜、新鲜，而且可以随便吃、随便挑，不少人一买就是几箱。

美国使用的重量计量单位是磅，一磅大约是 470 克，比一市斤略微少一点。不管在哪里购买，都要对称量放心，不要像在国内买菜一样盯着秤看，那样会引起反感，因为这被认为是不信任的表现。一般也没有讨价还价的习惯，人们已经形成了这样的观念。

Situational Dialogs
情景对话

新鲜的水果是很多人的最爱，特别是自己亲手摘下来的水果，就更加有意义了。李康(Li Kang)和他的朋友们相约去摘又便宜又新鲜的水果。

Buying Fruits 20

购买水果

Dialog 1

Della: Some of us will drive to the Columbia Basin[①] to pick apples tomorrow morning. Will you go with me?
我们几个明天上午要开车去哥伦比亚盆地去摘苹果，你跟我一起去吗？

Li Kang: Is it very far?
很远吗？

Della: Not far, about two hours' drive. We can leave early in the morning.
不远,大约两个小时车程。我们可以一早出发。

Li Kang: Why not buy in the supermarkets in town?
怎么不在城里的超市买呢？

Della: Now it is the apple-harvesting season. Apples there are very fresh, high quality and the most important, very cheap.
现在是苹果收获季节,那里的苹果很新鲜,质量很好,最重要的是很便宜。

Li Kang: That sounds very attractive. How much is a pound?
那听起来很诱人,多少钱一磅？

Della: Around 30 cents, perhaps more inexpensive.
大约30美分,也许更便宜些。

Li Kang: All right. I'll go with you. When are you leaving here?
好的,我可以跟你去,你什么时候出发？

Della: I'll pick you up at your place at seven. Remember to get up early enough.
我7点钟到你那里去接你,记住要起床早些。

Li Kang: I won't miss the alarm clock.
我不会听不到闹钟的。

Dialog 2

Li Kang: Excuse me, madam. How can I get to the Morison's Farm?
请问女士,我怎么可以到莫里森农场呢？

Stranger: You are going to pick cherries, I guess. Please drive forward about ten minutes, and you'll see a sign on your right.
你要去摘樱桃,是吧。请往前开大约10分钟,你就可以看到右手边的招牌。

Li Kang:	Thank you.
	谢谢你了。
	…… ……
Farmer:	Hello, everyone, I have baskets for you.
	大家好,我为你们准备了篮子。
Li Kang:	Thank you so much. You have a very good yield this year.
	非常感谢,你今年的收成不错。
Farmer:	Yes, we've worked on② these trees quite a few years. Today this side is open for you.
	是的,这些树我们花了好几年的工夫了。今天这一边对你们开放。
Li Kang:	Thanks a lot. Can we eat?
	谢谢,我们能吃吗?
Farmer:	Yes, please. You should wash them here before eating. But, remember to pick those dark red cherries, for they are mature.
	请吃吧,你要洗了再吃。但记住摘那些深红色的,那些是成熟的。
Li Kang:	I will. Thank you.
	会的,谢谢。

Typical Sentences
典型句型

1) Will you go with me to buy apples tomorrow morning?
   你明天上午要跟我一起去买苹果吗?
2) Some fruits are cheaper here than in China.
   这里的一些水果比你在中国买还要便宜。
3) Why not buy in the supermarkets in town?
   怎么不在城里的超市买呢?
4) Now it is the apple-harvesting season.
   现在是苹果收获季节。
5) That sounds very attractive. How much is a pound?
   那听起来很诱人,多少钱一磅?

6) Is this kind of orange yielded in California?
   这种橙子是加州产的吗?
7) How about picking cherries on the Morison's Farm?
   到莫里森农场去摘樱桃怎么样呢?
8) You are going to pick cherries, I guess.
   你要去摘樱桃,是吧。
9) This sounds much cheaper than in the supermarkets.
   这听起来比超市要便宜多了。
10) You have a very good yield this year.
    你今年的收成不错。
11) Can we buy some fruit on the farmers' market Saturday?
    我们周六能在农民市场买一些水果吗?
12) You can buy apples, pears, cherries, strawberries and bananas.
    你可以买到苹果、梨、樱桃、草莓和香蕉。

背景知识

美国水果简介:美国地理位置优越,生产多种水果,并出口到世界上的很多国家。

据美国农业部国家农业统计局(NASS)统计,2007年美国苹果产量约为422.2万吨,比2006年(447万吨)低7%。几个苹果主产区,如华盛顿州、密歇根州、宾夕法尼亚州、加利福尼亚州和弗吉尼亚州的苹果都有不同程度的减产。

2007年美国柑橘产量为1377万吨,主要产区为佛罗里达、加利福尼亚、得克萨斯和亚利桑那等州,其中佛罗里达的柑橘比较闻名。除鲜果出售以外,每年要产出14.56亿加仑冷冻浓缩果汁(FCOJ)。鲜果和果汁主要出口日本和欧盟国家。

2007年美国梨产量为79.9万吨,略高于2006年。在美国三大梨主产区中,加利福尼亚州和华盛顿州梨产量增加,俄勒冈州梨产量下降。

2007年美国葡萄产量可达635.6万吨。比上年增长9%。其中,加利福尼亚州葡萄产量预计为563万吨,同比增长7%。

樱桃的主产要区为密歇根州、犹他州、华盛顿州、纽约州和宾夕法尼亚州等,其中密歇根州生产全美70%的樱桃。威斯康星州和俄勒冈州也能生产一些樱桃。

猕猴桃主要产区在加利福尼亚州,既从智利、新西兰、意大利、法国和希腊等进口,也向加拿大、韩国等地出口。

注 释

① Columbia Basin(哥伦比亚盆地)位于华盛顿州中部,属于半干旱地区,但哥伦比亚河(Columbia River)横贯其间,盛产苹果等水果。
② work on 在这里是"对……下工夫,致力于"的意思,如:
They've been working on the project for more than ten years.(他们过去十年一直在做这个工程。)

Appointments with Friends
约会朋友

Topic Introduction
话题导言

　　短期出国,总想见见以前结识的外国朋友,回顾过去的友谊和畅谈对未来的理想。约会以前的朋友,可以到朋友家里聚会,也可以到酒店见面,还可以到酒吧、餐馆、咖啡厅、公园等处碰头,但事先都要用电话约定时间和地点。即使知道朋友家的地址,也不能贸然前往拜访。

　　和朋友约会一定要遵守时间,按照约定的时间到约定的地方是对别人的尊重;双方交谈的话题也要看关系的亲疏,来往是否密切,切不可死死追问一些隐私问题;如果是在餐饮场所见面,除非对方明确表示请客,否则最好是各自付账。

　　如果在国内就准备去见以前的朋友,可以准备一件小礼物,如一条围巾、自己写的一本书、有特色的小工艺品,但不要送贵重的礼品,以免被误解你要求他办事。

Situational Dialogs
情景对话

　　短期出国,总是要探望一下以前的朋友,丁唐(Ding Tang)打算去拜访很久不见的一个外国朋友迪金森教授(Prof. Dickinson)。

Dialog 1

Miss Dickinson: Hello, this is Miss Dickinson.
你好,我是迪金森小姐。

Ding Tang: Hello, Miss Dickinson. This is Ding Tang speaking. May I speak to Prof. Dickinson?
你好,迪金森小姐。我是丁唐,可以找迪金森教授听电话吗?

Miss Dickinson: I'm sorry my mother is out. May I take a message for her?
对不起,我妈妈不在家。需要留个口信给她吗?

Ding Tang: Yes. I'm one of her friends from China and staying in the Holiday Inn Seattle. I came here to attend an international meeting.
可以,我是中国来的她的一个朋友,住在西雅图假日酒店。我是来参加一个国际会议的。

Miss Dickinson: Do you need me to tell her to call you back?
你需要我告诉她给你回电话吗?

Ding Tang: Yes. My phone number is 232-8766, and the extension① is 2016. Please tell her I'd like to meet her today or tomorrow.
是的,我的电话号码是232-8766,分机是2016。请告诉她,我想和她在今天或明天见面。

Miss Dickinson: Okay. I think she'll be back in an hour, and possibly I may ask her to meet you in the hotel.
好的,我想她一个小时以后就回来了,也许我可以告诉她到酒店去见你的。

Ding Tang: That's better. Thank you so much.
那样更好,非常感谢。

Dialog 2

Prof. Dickinson: Ding Tang, isn't it really you? Simply unexpected!
丁唐,真的是你吗?简直想不到!

Ding Tang: I hadn't thought that I could have seen② you here ten years later, Prof. Dickinson.
迪金森教授,我也没有想到十年之后能在这里见到你。

Appointments with Friends

Prof. Dickinson:	How have you been these years? 你这些年过得怎么样？
Ding Tang:	Pretty good, and I have done several research projects successfully. How about you? 很好，我几个项目都做成功了。你呢？
Prof. Dickinson:	Very well. We have lived happily, but I'm always busy. Er ... how is your wife? 很好。我们生活得很幸福，但就是很忙。呃……你妻子如何？
Ding Tang:	She's fine, and still working with the hospital. Now she is the head of the hospital. 她很好，还在那个医院工作，现在是院长了。
Prof. Dickinson:	Congratulations! How about having a dinner with my family tomorrow evening? 恭喜了！明天晚上与我们一家人一起吃晚饭，好吗？
Ding Tang:	Great. I'm happy to stay with you. 好极了，我很高兴和你们在一起。

Dialog 3

Prof. Dickinson:	Welcome to my house, Ding Tang. 丁唐，欢迎到我家来。
Ding Tang:	I'm very glad to come to dinner with you. 我非常高兴和你们一起吃晚饭。
Prof. Dickinson:	Please just make yourself at home③. Jack, this is Ding Tang from China, and he was my main assistant when I worked in China ten years ago. 请不要客气。杰克，这是中国来的丁唐，他是我十年前在中国工作时的主要助手。
Mr. Dickinson:	Very nice to meet you, Ding Tang. 丁唐，很高兴见到你。
Prof. Dickinson:	Tang, this is my husband Jack. He works with an accounting office in this city. 唐，这是我的丈夫杰克，他在本市的一家会计师事务所工作。
Ding Tang:	Glad to meet you. Prof. Dickinson talked about you with

	me yesterday. 很高兴认识你。迪金森教授昨天还和我谈到你。
Mr. Dickinson:	Please be seated. Would you like something to drink? 请坐吧,要喝些什么?
Ding Tang:	Yes, please. How about orange juice if you have? 要的,如果有橙汁,就来些橙汁。
Mr. Dickinson:	All right, just a second. 好的,稍等。

1) I'm wondering if we can meet somewhere today or tomorrow.
   我想我们能否今天或明天在哪里见个面。

2) Do you need me to tell him to call you back?
   你需要我告诉他给你回电话吗?

3) Please tell him I'd like to meet him today or tomorrow.
   请告诉他我想和他在今天或明天见面。

4) Possibly I may ask him to meet you in the hotel.
   也许我可以告诉他到酒店去见你的。

5) Please come to the hotel at seven this evening.
   请今晚7点到酒店来。

6) I hadn't thought that I could have seen you here ten years later.
   我没有想到十年之后能在这里见到你。

7) How have you been these years?
   你这些年过得怎么样?

8) We have lived happily, but I'm always busy.
   我们生活得很幸福,但就是很忙。

9) You may take a taxi to my house.
   你可以乘坐出租车到我家。

10) How about having a dinner with my family tomorrow evening?

Appointments with Friends

明天晚上与我们一家人一起吃晚饭,好吗?

11) I'm sure you'll have great expectations.
我确信你会有远大的前程。

背景知识

交际礼仪(Ⅱ):

(8) 坐要有坐相:交谈时,要坐端正,不要翘着二郎腿,连摇带抖。对于长者,以正襟危坐为尊敬。入座后,双腿要并拢,女子尤须注意。

(9) 注意边幅:英美男人喜欢每天早晨要把胡子刮得光光的,不刮胡子,被视为失礼。即使是有留胡子的习惯,也要打理得整整齐齐,千万别弄得像一片乱草。

(10) 走路不能啪啪响:在美国,在人行道上走路时,绝不能把脚踏得啪啪响。如果有人那样做,会被认为是在咒骂自己的母亲。

(11) 不能穿睡衣外出:在美国,绝不能穿睡衣上街或外出买东西。

(12) 说"不"要干脆:到英美国家去,无论同什么人说话,说"不"字(No)一定要清楚,绝不可含糊其辞。回答问题简洁清晰,肯定地说出 Yes 或 No,这是说话的礼貌。

(13) 人前当面脱鞋是粗野行为:在英美,无论男人还是女人,绝不可在人面前脱鞋,这是一种粗野的行为。此外,也不可在人前当面扯下袜子或调整袜带,即使鞋带松了也不可在人前紧带子,应到一旁没人的地方,否则很不雅观。

(14) 不要三句话不离本行:同英美人谈话,切忌总是谈论自己的专业,或与专业有关的事。这在英美人的眼里很俗气。他们认为你是一个只懂得本行专业的人,而在其他方面一无所知。交谈在人的交际中占非常重要的地位,所以平时注意积累各方面的知识,切勿在交谈中三句话不离本行。

(15) 不可与同性跳舞:在英美同性不可一起跳舞,同性共舞不仅违反礼仪,还会被误认为是同性恋者,甚至还会惹出许多麻烦来。

(16) 同性面前大方更衣：通常，中国人有一种习惯，无论是同性还是异性，脱衣服时身体总要背过面前的人，这是一种礼貌。可英美人脱衣服却恰恰相反。他们认为，既然在场的全是同性，那就没有隐瞒的必要，大大方方的更衣，不要拘束。如果羞羞答答转过身去，反而会弄巧成拙，被视为有问题。

(17) 礼尚往来：在英美各国，最好的礼物莫过于花，但是生日礼物和圣诞礼物例外，应送给一些对方喜欢的东西，如高级香水、花露水或香气扑鼻的爽身粉等，但最好不要送室内装饰品。在英美，如果有人送你圣诞礼物，就是过了圣诞期了，你也应回送一份礼物给对方。

注 释

① extension 原意为"伸展，延长"，如 an extension of a loan（借款的延期偿还），这里引申为"分机"。

② 对于已经做过的事情，可以用"情态动词＋完成式"构成，这和不定式的完成式是一样的功能。如：

I hadn't expected that you would have been here.（我没有想到你已经来了。）

She must have finished the task last week.（她一定在上个星期就完成了任务。）

③ make oneself at home 的字面意思就是"使某人像在家里一样"，喻指"不要客气、不要拘束"。类似的表达法还有：

be at home（觉得安适，无拘束）

feel at home（觉得安适，无拘束）

be at home in some place（在某处觉得安适自在）

feel at home in some place（在某处觉得安适自在）

Presents and Gifts
赠送礼品

Topic Introduction
话题导言

中国有句话说得好:礼尚往来。来而不往,非礼也。这是说,人们之间的交往是相互的,而不是单向的。其实西方人也如此,如果你请美国人到你家吃饭,他们必定带来一些小礼物,如一瓶酒、一束花、一本书,并不是说他们用礼物来交换你的一顿饭,而是说人们之间的来往强调相互性。

我们出国访问、学术交流、留学移民、探亲访友,从国内带一些小礼物去馈赠给接待你或者为你服务的人,是很有必要的。但如果送大礼、重礼,可能会被误解你在贿赂他们,一条丝织围巾、一盒中国茶叶或者一件工艺品就是很好的礼物。西方人对于接到的礼物都要当面打开,并称赞漂亮及表示感谢,赠送人也可以做些简单的介绍,并可以说 I'm glad you like it.(你喜欢我很高兴。)之类的话。

Situational Dialogs
情景对话

不管是探亲访友还是去朋友家做客,馈赠一些小礼物都是必要的,但是送什么样的礼物好呢?丁唐(Ding Tang)、李康(Li Kang)和高卫平(Weiping)他们碰到了令他们头痛的问题。

Dialog 1

Susan: What's up for next weekend, Li Kang?
李康，下周末干什么事？

Li Kang: My research associate has invited me to his house for dinner party this coming Saturday evening.
我的研究伙伴邀请我到他家参加周六晚上的宴会。

Susan: That's a good chance for you to know more about American people.
那是一个更多了解美国人的好机会。

Li Kang: What kind of present or gift should I bring with me?
我应该带什么样的礼物去呢？

Susan: It's absolutely unnecessary to send anything. But, if you really want to bring something, it should be a small, inexpensive item. My idea is to bring a nice "token" gift that says "I thought of you" not a gift that says "look how much money I spent".
绝对不必要送什么东西。但是，你要是真是想送礼物，应该送一个小的便宜的东西。我的意思是礼物应具有"象征"意义，表示"我想着你"，而不是一件显示"我花了多少钱"的礼物。

Li Kang: I think I have understood what you said. Thank you so much.
我想我已经理解了你说的话。非常感谢你。

Dialog 2

Alice: We're very glad you've come to visit our company. This is a souvenir for you each. I hope you'll like it.
你们到我们公司参观，我们非常高兴。这是给你们每个人的纪念品。我希望你们喜欢。

Weiping: It's so beautiful. Thank you very much. Is this one of the models of your company's products?
真是漂亮，非常感谢。这是你们公司的产品模型吗？

Alice: Yes, we've made some as gifts especially for visitors to our company.
是的，我们制作了一些专门用作来访者的礼物。

Presents and Gifts 22

赠送礼品

Weiping:	Good, very good. And, we've prepared some small items for you, too. They were typically Chinese manufactures, and it has a history of① more than 1000 years. 好,很好。而且,我们也准备了一些小东西给你们。这些可是地道的中国产品,有一千多年的历史了。
Alice:	Oh, wonderful things! Are they cloisonné? 哦,好漂亮的东西!是景泰蓝制作的吗?
Weiping:	Yes, quite right. 是的,很对。
Alice:	Thank you so much. Our products don't have so long a history as② yours, but we hope our friendship will last forever. 非常感谢。虽然我们的产品没有你们的历史那么长,但是我希望我们之间的友谊永存。
Weiping:	We hope so, too. 我也这样希望。

Dialog 3

Ding Tang:	Hello, Adriana. I brought a present from China for you. 你好,阿德里安娜,我从中国给你带了件礼物来。
Adriana:	Thank you very much. ...Oh, it's a silk scarf, beautiful indeed. 非常谢谢你,……哦,是一条丝巾,漂亮极了。
Ding Tang:	You like it? 喜欢吗?
Adriana:	Of course. You're so nice, smart guy. 当然。聪明的家伙,你真好。
Ding Tang:	This is made of pure silk. Look, the label says 100% silk. I think girls like bright colors. 这是纯丝制作的。看,标签上说是100%的丝。我想女孩子们喜欢明亮的色彩。
Adriana:	You're so considerate. Thank you very much again. 你考虑得真周到,再次谢谢你。
Ding Tang:	I feel glad you like the scarf. 你喜欢这条丝巾,我感到高兴。

129

Typical Sentences
典型句型

1) What kind of present or gift should I bring with me?
   我应该带什么样的礼物去呢？

2) It's absolutely unnecessary to send any gift.
   绝对不必要送什么礼物。

3) A present should be a small, inexpensive item.
   应该送一个小的不贵的礼物。

4) This is a souvenir for you each. I hope you'll like it.
   这是给你们每个人的纪念品。我希望你们喜欢。

5) We've made some as gifts especially for visitors to our company.
   我们制作了一些专门用作来访者的礼物。

6) And, we've prepared some small items for you, too.
   而且，我们也准备了一些小东西给你们。

7) I brought a present from China for you.
   我从中国给你带了件礼物来。

8) I feel glad you like the scarf.
   你喜欢这条丝巾，我感到高兴。

9) This is for your baby, Nancy.
   南茜，这是送给你的小宝宝的。

10) I hope you haven't bought them yet.
    我希望你还没有买这些东西。

11) This is a small gift for your son.
    这是给你儿子买的小礼物。

Presents and Gifts

Background 背景知识

送礼礼节：在国际交往中，人们经常通过赠送礼品来表达谢意和祝贺，以增进友谊。由于各国习俗不同，赠礼的种类和方式也有差异。

(1) 送什么礼品：馈赠礼品时要尽可能考虑受礼人的喜好，"投其所好"是赠送礼品最基本的原则。如不了解对方喜好，稳妥的办法是选择具有民族特色的工艺品，因为送别人没有的东西，最易于被对方接受。礼不在重而在于合适，正所谓"千里送鹅毛，礼轻情意重"，有时送太贵重的礼品反而会使受礼者不安。因此在选择礼品时，往往是挑选一些物美价廉，具有一定纪念意义、民族特色，或具有某些艺术价值，或为受礼人所喜爱的小艺术品、小纪念品、食品、花束、书籍、画册、一般日用品等。

(2) 以什么方式送：赠礼的方式一般以面交为好。西方人在送礼时十分看重礼品的包装，多数国家的人们习惯用彩色包装纸和丝带包扎，西欧国家则喜欢用淡色包装纸。与中国人的习俗不同，在西方国家接受礼物后应即刻表示感谢，并当面拆看，不论其价值大小，都应对礼物表示赞赏。

(3) 什么时间送：赠礼要适时。在有的国家(如日本)，要选择人不多的场合送礼；而在阿拉伯国家，必须有其他人在场，送礼才不会有贿赂的嫌疑。在英国，合适的送礼时机是请别人用完晚餐或在剧院看完演出之后。在法国，不能向初次结识的朋友送礼，应等下次相逢的适当时机再送。

(4) 什么场合送：赠礼要分清场合。去友人家做客，不要带在宴会上吃的食品作为礼物。出席酒会、招待会不必送礼，必要时可送花篮或花束等。

在不同的国家，赠送礼品也应有所不同，如中国人讲究送烟送酒，而日本人却送酒不送烟。给德国人送礼时忌讳用白色、棕色或黑色的纸包装礼品，而向南美国家的人送礼，千万不能送刀或手绢，因为刀意味着双方关系一刀两断，手绢则总与眼泪、悲伤联系在一起。

注释

① a history of 是"多长时间的历史",如:
This city has a history of 2000 years. (这座城市有2000年的历史。)

② so long a history as 这个结构是将形容词提前了,说 such a long history as 也行,如:
She is so beautiful a girl that everyone likes her.(她是这么漂亮的一个姑娘,人人都喜欢她。)

Meeting New Friends
认识新朋友

Topic Introduction
话题导言

从小时候算起，我们认识的人真是不少，但并不是在同一天认识的，而是不断有新朋友加入进来。出国的旅程也是认识新朋友的机会，别人介绍的，自己认识的，偶然碰上的，各种情况都有。

这其中也有一些礼节，如别人介绍新朋友给你，你要热情地打一句招呼"Very nice to meet you."或者是"How do you do?"以表示接受别人的介绍；自己想认识别人时，更是要礼貌地寒暄，当面交谈要运用一定的交谈技巧，如谈论天气等；别人想认识你时，也要客气地回应才能成为朋友。不管哪种情况，如果对方有意，就可以伸出手同对方握一握。同时，由于是新朋友，注意称呼要比较正式，不可以随意问长问短，以免被认为没有教养。

Situational Dialogs
情景对话

"朋友多了好办事"，多认识些朋友总是件好事情，丁唐(Ding Tang)和刘杭(Liu Hang)都认识了很多新朋友。

Dialog 1

Liu Hang: Hey, Dr. Baldwin, I feel I have met you before. Didn't you teach in Wuhan University, China?
嗨,鲍德温博士,我感到我以前见过你。你以前没有在中国的武汉大学教过书吗?

Dr. Baldwin: No, I didn't. Are you from that university?
没有。你是从那个大学来的吗?

Liu Hang: I graduated there in 1997. You look like an English teacher who once gave a lecture① in our auditorium.
我1997年毕业于那所大学。你看起来很像一个曾在我们的大礼堂做过讲座的英语老师。

Dr. Baldwin: That must be my twin brother. He taught in China from 1994 to 1998, perhaps in Wuhan University.
那一定是我的双胞胎兄弟,他从1994年到1998年在中国教书,可能就是在武汉大学。

Liu Hang: It's a small world, isn't it? You look alike as two peas②. How is he?
这是个很小的世界,是吧?你们看起来一模一样,他好吗?

Dr. Baldwin: He's pretty good. He is now teaching at the University of California at Los Angeles. I'll tell him about you.
他很好,他现在在加利福尼亚大学洛杉矶分校教书。我会和他说起你的。

Liu Hang: Please remember me to him and his family.
请代我问他和他的家人好。

Dialog 2

Larry: Hi, Liu Hang. May I introduce you to John? John, this is Liu Hang from China, and she is a master's program student in Tourism.
嗨,刘杭,我可以把你介绍给约翰吗?约翰,这是从中国来的刘杭,她是旅游学专业的硕士学位研究生。

Liu Hang: Very nice to meet you. Larry has mentioned you several times.
很高兴见到你,拉瑞多次提到过你。

Larry: And, Liu Hang, this is John, my best friend.
刘杭,这是我最好的朋友约翰。

Meeting New Friends 23

认识新朋友

John: Very pleased to meet you, too. How do you think of the town?
也很高兴见到你。你觉得这个小镇怎么样？

Liu Hang: It's a very good place, quiet, beautiful and safe. What's your major?
是个非常好的地方，安静、漂亮、安全。你是什么专业？

John: Double E.
我学双 E。

Liu Hang: What's that? Electronic Engineering?
那是什么专业？电子工程吗？

John: Quite right. I'm fond of automatic electronic apparatuses.
很对。我很喜欢自动电子仪器。

Liu Hang: That's very applicable. Are you a graduate or undergraduate?
那很实用，你是研究生还是本科生？

John: I'm a senior undergraduate[3], and I should be a graduate next semester.
我是四年级本科生，下学期就应该读研究生了。

Liu Hang: I've got to go now. See you later, Larry and John.
我得走了。拉瑞、约翰，再见了。

Dialog 3

Danielle: Lovely weather, isn't it?
天气不错，是不是？

Ding Tang: Yes, I like the weather here, not cold and not hot.
是啊，我喜欢这里的天气，不冷又不热。

Danielle: I agree. Especially the gentle breeze makes people comfortable.
我也这样想，特别是这微风使人感到舒服。

Ding Tang: By the way, are you a representative of this congress?
顺便问你一下，你是这个会议的代表吗？

Danielle: Yes, I'm from Holland, the University of Amsterdam.
是的，我来自于荷兰的阿姆斯特丹大学。

Ding Tang: How do you do? That's a very famous university. I'm from China, and this is my name card.
幸会！那是个很有名的大学。我从中国来，这是我的名片。

135

Danielle: Very glad to meet you, Dr. Ding. Are you going to make a presentation tomorrow?
很高兴认识你,丁博士。你明天要做发言吗?

Ding Tang: Yes. I'll talk about our research program.
是的,我要谈谈我们的研究项目。

Danielle: Wish you success.
祝你成功。

Ding Tang: Thanks a lot.
多谢。

Typical Sentences 典型句型

1) Lovely weather, isn't it?
天气不错,是不是?
2) I like the weather here, not cold and not hot.
我喜欢这里的天气,不冷又不热。
3) May I introduce you to John?
我可以把你介绍给约翰吗?
4) I'd like you to meet my friend, Joe.
我想让你认识一下我的朋友乔。
5) I feel I have met you before.
我感到我以前见过你。
6) Didn't you teach in Wuhan University, China?
你以前没有在中国的武汉大学教过书吗?
7) That must be my twin brother.
那一定是我的双胞胎兄弟。
8) It's a small world, isn't it?
这是个很小的世界,是吧?
9) You look alike as two peas. How is he?
你们看起来一模一样,他好吗?
10) Very nice to meet you. Larry has mentioned you several times.
很高兴见到你,拉瑞多次提到过你。

Meeting New Friends

11) By the way, are you a representative of this congress?
    顺便问你一下,你是这个会议的代表吗?
12) I feel honored to get you as my friend.
    有你做我的朋友,我感到荣幸。

背景知识

英美人姓名:出国在外,认识了不少朋友,可总觉得名字很难记住。这其中有几点可以共同分享。

(1) 姓名的起源:英美人姓名的起源和我们大致类似,有的来自于生活环境和大自然,如 Laura(月桂)、Floral(花朵)、Viola(紫罗兰)等;有的来自于动物,如 Tiger(老虎)、Lion(狮子)、Fawn(幼鹿)等;有的来源于职业,如 Fisher(渔夫)、Smith(铁匠)、Carpenter(木匠),等等。

(2) 姓名的构成:这一点与我们的不同,一般的结构是"名(first name/given name/Christian name) + 姓(family name/last name/surname)",在两者之间可能还有一部分叫做中间名(middle name),不很固定,往往是母姓或者祖辈的名字。

(3) 称呼的使用:对于同一个人在不同的时候称呼不同,如 Mary Smith 在一般场合称作 Mary Smith,在熟人之间称作 Mary,在比较正式的场合称作 Miss Smith,在正式场合称作 Miss Mary Smith,如果成了公众人物则称作 Smith。

(4) 常用的名字:记住一些使用频率最高的名字很有用。下表列出一些重复率高的名字。

女子名		男子名	
Ashley	阿什利	Michael	迈克尔
Jessica	杰西卡	Christopher	克里斯托弗
Amanda	阿曼达	Matthew	马修
Sarah	莎拉	Joshua	乔舒亚
Brittany	布里塔尼	Andrew	安德鲁
Megan	梅甘	Daniel	丹尼尔

Jennifer	珍妮弗	Justin	贾斯廷
Nicole	尼科尔	David	大卫
Stephanie	斯蒂法妮	Ryan	赖安
Katherine	凯瑟琳	John	约翰
Lauren	劳伦	Steven	史蒂文
Rachel	雷切尔	Robert	罗伯特
Samantha	萨曼莎	James	詹姆斯
Heather	希瑟	Nicholas	尼古拉斯
Elizabeth	伊丽莎白	Joseph	约瑟夫
Danielle	丹尼尔	Brian	布赖恩
Christina	克里斯蒂娜	Jonathan	乔纳森
Emily	艾米丽	Kyle	凯尔
Mary	玛丽	Sean	肖恩
Alice	爱丽斯	William	威廉

注 释

① **give a lecture** 意思是"做演讲",另外也可以表示为 **deliver/read a lecture**,但切忌使用 **give somebody a lecture**(训斥某人)。

② **alike as two peas** 的字面意思是"像两颗豌豆一样像",指非常像,几乎没差别。

③ 本科生几个年级的表达方法:

大一生: Freshman /newcomer

大二生: Sophomore

大三生: Junior

大四生: Senior/senior undergraduate

Reception Dinner
招待宴会

Topic Introduction
话题导言

不管是学术交流,还是商贸会谈,或者是官方访问,主办方或接待方总会在开始的时候招待客人。情况不同,招待的形式也往往不同,重要的官方招待会一般是正式的宴会,小型交流活动的招待会则多比较简单随意,但都是为了表示主人的热情和礼貌。

作为客人,参加主人举办的招待宴会这样的活动,要注意有什么具体要求,如是否要穿正式的服装、几点钟开始、是否需要致辞、餐桌上的位次安排等。初次出国参加这样的活动难免紧张,生怕出了什么洋相,有一个办法倒是可以克服这种担心,就是看主人做什么就跟着做什么,只比别人慢半拍就可以了。

照例,在接到宴会邀请时要表示乐意参加,如果一个代表团中有个别人因故不能参加则要表示歉意并明确说明理由。同样,在宴会结束时客人对主人的款待要表示感谢。

Situational Dialogs
情景对话

丁唐(Ding Tang)受到了接待方的热烈款待,既然是出席宴会,当然别忘记问清楚活动的细节和一些注意事项,诸如时间、地点、参加人员、人数、做些什么样的准备及所穿的服饰。

Dialog 1

Anne: Are you accustomed to① the weather here, Dr. Ding?
丁博士, 你对这里的天气还习惯吧？

Ding Tang: Yes, I'm an all-weather man. But we're fighting against the jet lag.
习惯, 我对各种天气都适应, 但我们正在克服时差问题。

Anne: I hope you're used to everything here. Our director would like to host a reception dinner tonight to welcome you and your colleagues to visit our institute.
我希望你们习惯这里的一切。我们主任想今晚举办一个招待宴会以欢迎你和你的同事们访问我们研究所。

Ding Tang: It's so kind of him to invite us to the dinner. We'd be glad to. Could you tell me when and where?
请我们参加宴会真是太客气了, 我们很高兴参加。能告诉我什么时间, 在哪里吗？

Anne: Six thirty, at the Banquet Hall of the University Inn. We'll send a van to pick you up.
6点30分, 在大学酒店的宴会厅。我们将派一个旅行车来接你们过去。

Ding Tang: You're so considerate. Thank you very much. By the way, should we dress② formally?
你考虑得这么周到, 非常感谢你。顺便问一下, 我们要穿得很正式吗？

Anne: Yes, please. This is a formal dinner party.
是的, 这是一个正式的宴会。

Ding Tang: Thank you for telling me about it and thank you for your invitation.
谢谢你告诉我, 谢谢你们的邀请。

Dialog 2

Director: The honored guests are welcome to our dinner. I suggest a drink for our future cooperation in research and all the guests present today. I wish everyone good luck and good health.
我们欢迎各位贵宾来参加今天的宴会。我提议为我们未来

Reception Dinner 24

招待宴会

	在研究方面的合作以及今天所有的来宾干杯,并祝大家万事如意,身体健康。
Anne:	Thank you for our director's suggestion and wishes, and now cheers! 谢谢主任的提议和祝愿,现在请干杯!
All:	Cheers!③ 干杯! …… ……
Ding Tang:	All the dishes are so delicious, and I like them very much! 所有的菜都这么美味,我很喜欢它们。
Anne:	It's kind of you to say so. Please help yourself to some fruit. 你这么说真是太客气了。请随便吃些水果吧。
Ding Tang:	Thank you. 多谢。 …………
Ding Tang:	This is a wonderful dinner party. I think we must be going now. 这真是一个不错的宴会,我想我们该走了。
Anne:	Would you stay a little while for a second④ cup of coffee? 再呆一会儿,再喝一杯咖啡好吧?
Ding Tang:	I've had enough. Thank you for your dinner. 我已经喝得够多了,谢谢你的晚餐。
Anne:	Thank you for coming. 多谢你的光临。
Ding Tang:	Good night. 晚安。
Anne:	Good night. 晚安。

141

1) Our director would like to host a reception dinner tonight.
我们主任想今晚举办一个招待宴会。

2) We'd be glad to.
   我们很高兴参加。

3) It's my pleasure to be invited to such a dinner.
   被邀请参加这样的宴会我感到荣幸。

4) It's so kind of him to invite us to the dinner.
   请我们参加宴会真是太客气了。

5) I'm so sorry one of us can't go to the dinner.
   真对不起,我们中有一个不能参加宴会。

6) Could you tell me when and where?
   能告诉我什么时间,在哪里吗?

7) By the way, should we dress formally?
   顺便问一下,我们要穿得很正式吗?

8) You're so considerate. Thank you very much.
   你考虑得这么周到,非常感谢你。

9) All the dishes are so delicious, and I like them very much!
   所有的菜都这么美味,我很喜欢它们。

10) Let's drink for our cooperation in the future.
    我们为将来的合作干杯吧。

11) This is a wonderful dinner party. I think I must be going now.
    这真是一个不错的宴会,我想我该走了。

12) I've had enough. Thank you for your dinner.
    我已经喝得够多了,谢谢你的晚餐。

背景知识

交际礼仪(III):

(18) 离开厕所要留门缝:在美国,公寓里的厕所和浴室都连在一起。到美国人家做客,如果想到洗手间,若看到浴室的门开着,表示里面没有人;若关着,表示里面有人使用。此外,还要注意一点,从厕所出来一定不要把门关得严丝合缝,要稍微留些空隙,特别是不

Reception Dinner

要把随手关门的习惯带到英美国家。

(19) 搭便车有危险:到英美各国旅行,千万不要贪小便宜而搭便车,特别是女性,如果为了省钱而搭便车,等于是自杀行为。搭便车吃了亏,也无处申告,同时还会受到警察的指责。

(20) 不卖烟酒给孩子:英国法律禁止未成年者饮酒和抽烟,英国的商店,绝对不把烟酒售给小孩子,即使大人托买,也决不例外。

(21) 烟酒自便:举杯祝酒,喝多喝少自己掌握,尤其不能强劝女宾干杯。频频敬酒,客人不但不会领情,反而会引起不愉快。吸烟有害健康是人们普遍的认识,吸烟自便,但必须主动先敬旁边的人,即便身边都是女士,也要先问一声,以表示自己的礼貌。如果对方不吸,还要礼貌地问一下:"我可以吸烟吗?"出席宴会要在正餐结束的时候方可吸烟,还要得到同座的许可。

(22) 请客不讲客套:在我国人们宴请宾客,即使美味佳肴摆满一桌,主人也往往会说:"今天没有什么好菜,大家请随便用!"至于赞美之词,应该留给客人去说。但在英美,宴席上主人一开始便会介绍:"这是本市最好酒家做的最有名的饭菜。"在家里待客,也总会说:"这是我太太(或厨师)最拿手的菜",其目的是表达对客人的尊重和诚意。

(23) 客气饿肚子:当客人恰逢吃饭时到中国人家里拜访时,主人一定热情地请你入座用餐,一次不成功,还会一请再请,直到把客人请上餐桌才肯罢休。英美则没有这种习俗,当英美主人听到推辞的话后,就不再请第二次了,就自顾自吃起来。如果你真的没有吃饭,那就只好忍饥挨饿了。

(24) 互不招待,各自付账:在英美,当几个人在一起吃饭时,若没有事先商定好,一般是各付各的账,称之为 go Dutch 或 AA 制。不管谁穷谁富,也不管付钱多少,从来都不替别人代付,这样他们认为才尊重对方,合乎礼貌。(李常磊《英美文化博览》)

注 释

① be accustomed to 和 be used to 是一个意思,都表示"习惯于",如:
I'm not accustomed to hot weather. (我不习惯炎热天气。)

② dress 在这里是动词"穿戴"的意思,如:
Dress yourself quickly. (你快点穿衣服。)
而 dress 还可以和 up/down 连用,构成短语,dress up 是"盛装"的意思,如:
She like to dress up for a party. (她喜欢把自己打扮得漂漂亮亮去参加晚会。)
dress down 是"穿着随意"的意思,如:
I dressed down for such a casual occasion. (在这样非正式的场合,我穿着随便。)

③ 喝酒时说 cheers 和中文的"干杯"意思是不同的,cheers 只是举杯敬酒的用语,有"祝你健康,成功"等意思,并不是"喝干一杯酒";而中文的"干杯"虽然也是祝酒用语,却含有"喝完杯中的酒"的意思。

④ a second 意思是"又一,再一",不定冠词和序数词连用,表示"又一次,再一个",如:
You'll have to do a third time if you fail again. (如果失败,你得再做一次。)

Visiting an Academia
访问学术机构

Topic Introduction
话题导言

专门从事科学研究的机构叫做研究所(research institute)、研究院(academe/academy)、研究中心(research center)等，这些机构有独立设立的，也有附属于政府和大学的。他们主要从事自然科学和社会人文科学的研究工作，为政府和社会承担研究项目。美国的大学教师很多人都在研究所任职，在教学之余从事研究工作。

当政府、企业、社会团体、军事机构等需要对某个课题进行研究的时候，就面向全社会发布课题招标项目，任何有能力的个人或研究机构都可以竞标。竞标要提供的主要文件就是研究方案 (research proposal)，然后由专家组成评议小组进行匿名评议(blind review)，而研究方案的作者姓名等内容是这些专家看不到的。这种竞标课题的研究经费比较可观，很多研究者都乐于从事这类工作。

Situational Dialogs
情景对话

李康(Li Kang) 今天的活动是参观研究所和看土豆试验田。

Dialog 1

Li Kang: Dr. Mayer, what're the activities for today?
迈耶博士,今天的活动是什么?

Dr. Mayer: Eh, we're showing you around[①] our research institute in the morning, and driving to the experimental potato field in the afternoon.
呃,我们上午带领你们参观整个研究所,下午开车去看土豆试验田。

Li Kang: Have you arranged someone to interpret everything we'll see?
你安排人给我们讲解了吗?

Dr. Mayer: Yes, before visiting the institute, we'll make a presentation to explain everything first and an interpreter will be with you during the visit.
安排了,参观研究所之前我们先有一个演示会介绍所有的东西,而在参观过程中有一个解说员和你们在一起。

Li Kang: Thank you very much for your consideration.
非常感谢你们周到的考虑。

Dr. Mayer: It's nothing.[②]
没有关系。

Dialog 2

Dr. Mayer: Next is the presentation of our institute and what we have done in the past ten years. Please let me know if you have any questions.
下面是我们研究所和我们过去十年所做的事情的介绍,如果有什么问题,请告诉我。

Li Kang: How many research projects will be included?
这包括多少个研究项目?

Dr. Mayer: Twenty-five projects. Ten years ago, our institute was established, and mainly funded by the Ford Foundations. For the first year we obtained the project about how to kill the potato pests from the Department of Agriculture of Idaho State.
25个项目。十年以前,我们研究所成立,主要得到福特基金会的资金支持。第一年我们就从爱达荷州农业厅得到了如

Visiting an Academia

何消灭土豆害虫的项目。
…… ……

Li Kang: Are the researchers doing their projects single-handedly or cooperating with others?
所有的研究人员都是独立工作还是相互合作？

Dr. Mayer: Everyone here has very good team spirits, but each person can undertake an independent project.
这里的每个人都有很好的团队精神，但是每个人都能独立承担独立的项目。

Li Kang: What's the role of these graduates?
这些研究生的作用是什么？

Dr. Mayer: Most of them do their own research, and some of them are the helpers for their major professors.
大多数人都做自己的研究，有些也是他们专业导师的帮手。

Dialog 3

Dr. Mayer: This is the advanced laboratory we have here. All the apparatuses are of great precision.③
这是我们这儿最先进的实验室，所有的仪器都有很高的精度。

Li Kang: Did you buy them yourselves?
你们自己买的吗？

Dr. Mayer: Yes, we did. But they were sponsored by research project tenderees. We haven't spent one penny on them.
是的，但都是研究项目的招标人赞助的。我们没有花一分钱。

Li Kang: How I wish we could have such advanced things!
我们要有这么先进的东西就好了！

Dr. Mayer: You will, I'm sure. ...And this is the show room.
我确信，你们会有的。……这是陈列室。

Li Kang: What's it for?
有什么用处？

Dr. Mayer: We bring forth all our previous research reports here, and every one has its own posters hanging up in the room.
我们把以前做的所有的研究项目报告都在这里展出，每个报告都有招贴悬挂在室内。

Li Kang: That's quite like an exhibition saloon.
这很像一个展览馆。

Dr. Mayer: Yes, correct.
是的，很对。

1) What're the activities for today?
   今天的活动是什么？
2) Shall we visit your research institute?
   我们今天要参观你们的研究所吗？
3) Have you arranged someone to interpret everything we'll see?
   你安排人给我们讲解了吗？
4) Is the institute part of the college?
   研究所是这个学院的一部分吗？
5) Please let me know if you have any questions.
   如果有什么问题，请告诉我。
6) How do you win these research projects?
   你们是怎么赢得这些研究项目的？
7) How many research projects will be included?
   这包括多少个研究项目？
8) Where can you find these funded projects?
   你们从哪里找到这些有资助的项目的？
9) Everyone here has very good team spirits.
   这里的每个人都有很好的团队精神。
10) Did you buy them yourselves?
    你们自己买的吗？

11) How I wish we could have such advanced things!
我们要有这么先进的东西就好了!
12) We bring forth all our previous research reports here.
我们把以前做的所有的研究项目报告都在这里展出。
13) Are these projects very competitive?
这些项目竞争激烈吗?

背景知识

美国的科研机构体系：美国的研究开发工作是分散在联邦政府实验室、私人工业公司、高等院校和其他非赢利机构这四大类研究机构中独立进行的。联邦政府通过研究合同、采购合同和其他政策，可以在某种程度上影响政府以外的科研机构，使全国科技工作成为一个整体。自上世纪80年代以来，各州政府为发展本州经济也开始关心和参与本州重大科技计划的管理，但一般并不直接成立研究机构。

(1) 联邦政府研究机构：联邦政府各部门所属的研究单位共有750多个。这些研究机构的人员均为政府雇员，但这些机构的行政管理却由政府以合同形式交由高等院校、私人工业企业或非赢利机构来负责。这些研究机构一般规模庞大、经费充足，主要从事高风险的、长远的研究和开发。联邦政府的科研经费实际上只有三分之一拨给自己所属的研究单位(其中的四分之一以上又拨给联邦资助研究发展中心)，另外三分之二则以不同形式，主要是以研究合同和研究资助的形式，拨给政府以外的研究单位。

(2) 工业企业研究机构：据不完全统计，美国私人工业企业目前有不同规模的实验室大约2万个。它们的研究开发活动大致有两类：第一类是联邦政府通过研究合同或采购合同委托企业进行的研究。第二类是工业企业本身投资进行的研究，范围较为广泛，主要集中在化工、医药、电子、工业仪器和科学仪器等领域。

(3) 高等院校研究机构：美国高等院校的研究工作主要集中在125所研究型大学，其中前40名大学的研究经费占全国高等院校研究经费的52%。美国大学的研究机构大体上可分为：①教学与研究相结合的各院系实验室,全美约有六千多个;②拥有众多专职研究人员的独立研究所,全美约有5000个;③政府在大学中设立的各种研究中心;④工业部门与大学的合作研究机构。目前在美国高等院校共有19个联邦资助研究发展中心,其中能源部所设最多,以研究经费计算,占75%左右。

(4) 其他非赢利研究机构:此类机构既不隶属于政府部门,又不设在大学或由大学管辖,也不像工业企业那样以赢利为目标。这主要是指各种私人非赢利研究所或公司、博物馆、动物园、植物园、医院以及某些学会和私人基金会等。据不完全统计,美国年经费预算在200万美元以上的非赢利研究机构目前大约有二百多个,其中有的年度经费预算高达近亿美元,比较著名的有:国际斯坦福研究所、德拉皮尔实验室、巴特尔研究所、兰德公司、米特公司、麻省总医院等。此类研究机构虽然数量不多,但对美国科学技术的发展很有影响,是其他三类研究机构的有益补充。

注 释

① show someone around 是"带领某人参观"的意思,如:
Could you show me around the campus?（带我们参观一下校园,好吗？）
其他常见的类似短语还有:

show off（卖弄,炫耀）

show of reason（似乎有理）

show oneself（出现,露面）

show one's cards（摊牌,公开自己的计划）

show one's hand（表明自己的计划或意图）

show one's teeth（发怒）

show sb. the door（逐出,拒绝要求）

Visiting an Academia 25

show out (送出客人)
show sb. over (领某人参观)
show up (到席,露面,暴露)

② "It's nothing."是对"Thank you."等表示感谢的话的回答,意思是"没有什么值得谢的"、"不用谢"。

③ are of precision 相当于 are precise,即 be + of + n. 相当于 be + 该词的 adj。

Visiting a University
参观大学

Topic Introduction 话题导言

出国到大学访问或参加学术研讨会或进行教育合作项目往往都会参观大学校园,有时候可能还是其中的一项活动。美国的大学校园有几个特点,一是总面积都比较大,而实际的教学区域则比较小;二是多数校园历史悠久,各种建筑物点缀其中;三是环境优雅,特别是绿化做得很不错。

大学的校园大多数都以学校图书馆和公共活动中心(commons)为中心向四周展开,各个学院呈环形围绕着图书馆,一般每个专业性的学院都有一栋或几栋连在一起的办公教学楼,而文学院、理学院的各个系则比较分散。参观校园时注意校内的标志指向,一旦走错了路都可以沿指向找到回去的路。

Situational Dialogs 情景对话

出国到大学访问,少不了参观大学校园,国际合作办公室(International Programs Office)的秘书Christina今天带丁唐(Ding Tang)参观该校的大学校园。

Visiting a University 26

参观大学

Dialog 1

Christina: Now let me show you around the campus. I'll give you a brief introduction to① each key place. If you have any questions, let me know.
现在我带领你们参观校园，每到一个重要的地方我都会给你们做一个简介。如果有问题，就问我。

Ding Tang: How long will it take us to tour the campus?
走遍校园要多长时间？

Christina: About one hour and a half. We'll be back here 11:30.
大约一个半小时，我们 11:30 返回到这里。

Ding Tang: What's the area of the whole campus?
整个校园的面积多大？

Christina: It's 780 acres, but only one third② is used for academic activities.
有 780 英亩，但是只有三分之一用于教学活动。

Ding Tang: How about the rest two thirds?
其余的三分之二呢？

Christina: We have an experimental farm, an experimental forest park and some residence halls surrounding the core area.
我们有一个实验农场、一个实验森林公园和一些学生公寓环绕在中心区域周围。

Ding Tang: The campus tour is just in the central area?
校园参观只是在中心区域？

Christina: Yes. Let's go and please follow me.
对的，我们走吧，请跟着我。

Dialog 2

Christina: This new building is the Students Sports Center, and the students have access to all the sports equipments.
这座新建筑物是学生体育活动中心，学生们可以使用这里的所有运动设施。

Ding Tang: Do they have to pay for this?
他们要为此付钱吗？

Christina:	Yes, at the beginning of each semester they have to pay a kind fee called sports fee. So, they have to show their student ID. 要的,每个学期开始他们都要交纳一种叫做运动费的杂费。所以,他们要出示他们的学生证。
Ding Tang:	Do the students enjoy playing here? 学生们喜欢在这儿玩吗?
Christina:	Yes, they do. This is a very good place to exercise. 喜欢,这是一个锻炼的好地方。
Ding Tang:	Do you have any other sports establishments on campus? 校园内还有其他运动设施吗?
Christina:	Yes. There's another sports complex③ near the residence halls. 有,在学生公寓附近还有一个运动中心。

Dialog 3

Christina:	This is the oldest building of our university, and it was built in 1819. 这是我们大学最为古老的建筑物了,建于 1819 年。
Ding Tang:	Is it still the original appearance? 这是不是还是原来的样子?
Christina:	No, it was destroyed by a thunderbolt in 1889 and rebuilt in 1896, and the eastern wing was added in 1945. 不是,1889 年被雷电烧毁过,1896 年重建,而东翼是 1945 年扩建的。
Ding Tang:	What's it used for? 现在是做什么用的?
Christina:	Now it's the office building for president, vice presidents and provosts. The College of Arts is also housed④ here. 现在是校长、副校长和教务长的办公室,文学院也在这里。
Ding Tang:	Was it funded by the State Government? 当时是州政府出资的吗?
Christina:	Yes, the State decided to establish a college of agriculture. 是的,州政府决定建一所农学院。
Ding Tang:	But they hadn't expected it would have become so large a university. 但是他们没有想到会发展成为一个这么大的大学。

Visiting a University

Typical Sentences
典型句型

1) How long will it take us to tour the campus?
   走遍校园要多长时间？
2) Is this the bird's-eye view of the whole campus?
   这是整个校园的鸟瞰图吗？
3) What's the area of the whole campus?
   整个校园的面积多大？
4) How about the rest two thirds?
   其余的三分之二呢？
5) How many colleges and departments are there in your university?
   你们大学有多少个学院、多少个系？
6) How many students are there in this university?
   这个大学有多少个学生？
7) Are the computer labs open round the clock?
   计算机室24小时开放吗？
8) Do the students enjoy playing here?
   学生们喜欢在这儿玩吗？
9) Do you have any other sports establishments on campus?
   校园内还有其他运动设施吗？
10) Is it still the original appearance?
    这是不是还是原来的样子？
11) Was it funded by the State Government?
    当时是州政府出资的吗？
12) The State decided to establish a college of agriculture.
    州政府决定建一所农学院。

Background 背景知识

美国大学简介 (Colleges and Universities in the United States)：
美国是世界上教育事业最发达的国家之一，目前全美共有3700多所高等院校。2002年美国高校在校本科生和研究生达1578万人，授予准学士学位58.5万，学士学位126.5万，硕士学位45万，博士学位4.8万，专业学位9.5万。美国还是全球拥有外国留学生最多的国家。2002年在美国各类高校学习的各国留学生达到50万人。

美国是世界上第一个实现高等教育大众化的国家。2002年美国高中毕业生的大学升学率高达68.6%，还有相当一部分将在日后接受各种形式的高等教育。同时，美国的高等教育体系还被公认为全世界最具竞争力的。据国际权威机构的评估，全世界排名在前10位的大学中，美国就有6所。美国的高等院校形式多样，公立私立院校各具特色，互为补充，适应了社会发展的不同需要。

美国高等教育最初是从欧洲移植而来的传统教育，国家的独立和经济的发展使高等院校注重农工技艺教育，之后加强了理工结合、文理渗透、基础和应用并重的全面教育。第二次世界大战以来，美国高等教育发展更加迅速，层次结构逐步完善，学校类型和学科专业日趋多样化，横断学科和交叉学科不断涌现，成人教育和教育方式终身化突飞猛进。与此同时，高等教育进一步走向国际化，海外大学和科研机构纷纷建立，国际间大学的学术交流也大大加强。

大学校园常用词汇 (Commonly-Used Words and Expressions)：
下面是大学校园常用的一些词语。

amphitheater 阶梯教室
assembly hall 礼堂
assignment 作业
Bulletin Board 公告栏
Bursar's Office 财务办公室
Business School 商学院
cafeteria 食堂
campus network 校园网
Career's Office 就业指导办公室
class participation 课堂活动
classroom/lecture room 教室
commons 公共活动中心
computer lab 计算机室
coordinator 协调员

Visiting a University 26

参观大学

dean 学院院长
department/division 系
department head 系主任
faculty 系, 全系教师
Graduate School 研究生院
Health Center 保健中心
ISO 国际学生办公室
Language Center 语言中心
library 图书馆
off-campus 校园外
office hour 办公时间
on-campus 校园内
orientation 说明会
playground 操场
presentation 演示会
president's office 校长办公室
professor 教授
provost 教务
reading theater/room 阅览室
registrar 注册主任
registration 注册
Research Center 研究中心
Research Institute 研究所
residence hall 学生公寓
school/college/institute 学院
Sports Center 运动中心
Scholarship Committee 学术委员会
Students Center 学生中心
Students Union 学生会
tuition waiver 学费减免
tutor/mentor 辅导教师
thesis defense 论文答辩
University Bookstore 大学书店
university campus 大学校园

注 释

① a brief introduction to 是"某事物的简介", 如 a brief introduction to our research project(我们研究项目的简介)。

② 分数词是英语中容易错的一个词类。分数词是由基数词和序数词合成, 即分子用基数词表示, 分母用序数词表示, 当分子超过 1 时, 分母就要加 s 了, 如 two thirds(三分之二)、three fourths(四分之三)、four fifths(五分之四)等。

③ complex 在这里做名词, 意思是"综合场所", 如 an iron and steel complex(钢铁联合企业)。complex 作形容词时表示"复杂的, 综合的", 如 a complex argument(复杂的论证)。

④ house 也可以用作动词，意思是"提供住处，供给房子用"，如：
Those caves may house snakes or some other wild animals.（那些洞里也许有蛇或者其他什么野兽。）
He is trying hard to feed and house his family.（他努力设法赡养和安置他的家属。）

Attending a Dissertation
听学术演讲

Topic Introduction
话题导言

出国到大学或研究机构访问都有机会听到学术演讲,这种演讲活动往往是学术研讨会的一部分内容。英美等西方国家的学术活动异常频繁,经常性的学术研讨会是相互交流的好机会。学术演讲会之前,一般主办方都会散发一些演讲大纲、演讲者的介绍等。现在人们都用电脑设备演示演讲的主要内容,图文并茂,生动有趣。

在学术研讨会上,美国的研究人员一般阐述其观点、方法和结论,也谈研究的局限性和需要进一步研究的方面,并喜欢把研究过程中的逸闻趣事也展示给听众。演讲之后,往往留有时间供听讲者提问,他们很愿意和同行讨论有关的学术问题。

情景对话

学术研讨会是互相交流学习的好途径,碰巧该大学邀请了一些学术权威来做演讲,丁唐(Ding Tang)当然不会错过这个好机会。

Dialog 1

Christina: Will you go to today's meeting?
你去参加今天的会议吗?

Ding Tang: Yes, I will. What's the agenda for today?
去,今天的议程是什么?

Christina: The University has invited some academic authorities[①] with great scientific attainments to make speeches this morning.
这个大学邀请了一些具有很高学术造诣的学术权威今天上午来做演讲。

Ding Tang: That will widen our view. I think it'll benefit our research.
那将开阔我们的视野,我觉得会对我们的研究有益处。

Christina: The convener will give some handouts about those VIPs'[②] dissertations. So, please be punctual.
会议召集人将散发一些那几个重要人物学术演讲的资料,所以,要准时到。

Ding Tang: Yeah, thank you for telling me.
好的,谢谢你告诉我。

Dialog 2

Ding Tang: You have made a very outstanding presentation, Dr. Williams.
威廉斯博士,你做了一个非常好的介绍。

Dr. Williams: Thank you. You're from China?
谢谢,你从中国来吗?

Ding Tang: Yes, and we are doing some research related to your field. But I can't have a very clear idea about the analysis methods you used.
是的,我们也在做一些与你的领域相关的研究,但是我对你的分析方法还没有一个清晰的认识。

Dr. Williams: Have you looked through[③] my handout?
看了我散发的资料了吗?

Ding Tang: Yes, but I need to know more about it. Could you spare me some minutes to discuss this question with you?
看了,但是我需要知道得更多一些。你能给我几分钟和你一起讨论这个问题吗?

Attending a Dissertation 27

Dr. Williams: Sure, can we deal with it at the end of this morning's meeting?
当然可以,我们今天上午会议结束的时候来讨论,好吗?

Ding Tang: All right, thank you.
好的,谢谢了。

Dialog 3

Christina: How do you like the dissertations by these VIPs?
你认为这些重要人物的学术演讲怎么样?

Ding Tang: Great. But the moderator gave them very limited time to expound their viewpoints.
好极了,但是主持人给他们阐述观点的时间很有限。

Christina: Yes, they all brought forth leading concepts in this domain. Most important of all, they improved some research and analysis methods.
是的,他们都提出了这个领域处于领先地位的观念。重要的是,他们改进了一些研究和分析方法。

Ding Tang: Yeah. Now we can apply their improved methods to our research projects.
是啊,现在我们可以把他们的先进方法应用到我们的研究项目中了。

Christina: You are right.
你说的没错。

Ding Tang: I'd like to invite them to China to make some speeches for Chinese scientists, so that all of us can learn something from them.
我想邀请他们到中国去给中国的科学家们做些演讲,这样我们所有人都可以从他们那里学到一些东西。

Christina: That's a good idea.
那是个好主意。

161

Typical Sentences
典型句型

1) Will you go to today's meeting?
   你去参加今天的会议吗?
2) What's the agenda for today?
   今天的议程是什么?
3) Their researches will widen our view.
   他们的研究将开阔我们的视野。
4) We can learn their methods so as to benefit our research.
   我们可以学他们的方法以有益于我们的研究。
5) You have made a very outstanding presentation, Dr. Williams.
   威廉斯博士,你做了一个非常杰出的介绍。
6) We hope to read more of your research papers.
   我们希望看到你的更多的研究论文。
7) We are doing some researches related to your field.
   我们也在做一些与你的领域相关的研究。
8) Could you be our consultant in our present project?
   你能在我们目前的研究中担任顾问吗?
9) I can't have a very clear idea about the analysis methods you used.
   但是我对你的分析方法还没有一个清晰的认识。
10) Have you looked through my handout?
    看了我散发的资料了吗?
11) How do you like the dissertations by these VIPs?
    你认为这些重要人物的学术演讲怎么样?
12) They've made great achievements in this field.
    他们在这个领域做出了很大成就。

Attending a Dissertation

Background 背景知识

　　研究报告(Research Report)：研究报告通常是学术演讲会上散发的重要材料，但大部分情况下只是散发研究报告的提纲。美国学术界对科学研究有一套大家认可的规范，研究报告的撰写一般也是按照这个规范去做。就结构而言，研究报告主要包括：

　　(1) 内容提要(abstract)：概括性地介绍全文的主要内容。

　　(2) 引言(introduction)：简要说明选择该课题进行研究的重要性和必要性，对理论研究、科学应用等的重要意义。

　　(3) 文献综述(literature review)：通过文献检索的方法介绍前人在该课题相关内容的研究方面已经取得了哪些成就，还存在什么问题，需要继续完善哪个方面，为该课题的研究提供了哪些可供借鉴的理论、方法和有参考价值的数据和结论。

　　(4) 研究问题(research questions)：列举出应该研究清楚哪些具体的问题。一个课题一般包括一个或几个主要问题，为了研究这些主要问题，又有哪些次要问题(sub-questions)需要研究。

　　(5) 研究方法(research methods)：非常具体地说明应用哪些研究方法，如问卷法、访问法、实地勘测法等，什么时间、什么地点、样本如何选取等都要说明得非常详细，并有非常具体的附属材料(问卷、访问提纲、勘测工具等)。

　　(6) 研究过程(research procedures)：叙述按照研究方案进行的具体活动步骤，获取资料和数据的详细情况，还包括遇到不能按照原方案实施的时候，采取了什么样的补救措施。

　　(7) 分析方法(data analysis methods)：说明对研究过程取得的资料和数据进行了什么样的分析，以及这样分析的科学依据是什么，在分析过程中使用了哪种计算机应用软件（比如 Microsoft Excel / SigmaPlot）。

　　(8) 分析结果(analysis results)：说明经过分析，得到了什么样的结果，以及对这些结果作了哪些必要的校正，依据是什么。

　　(9) 结论(conclusion)：说明经过对分析结果和整个研究过程的概括，得出的结论。

(10) 局限性(limitations)：虽然有了这样的研究结论,但由于方法、技术、分析、时间、地点等的影响,这样的研究结果还有什么局限性,哪些方面是不完善的,并说明以后的研究方向。

(11) 附录(appendix)：主要包括问卷的全文、访问笔记、外文资料的原文等等。

(12) 参考文献(references)：列出在整个报告中参考、使用过的文献资料,常见的是 APA 格式。与此相对应的是文中的注释,报告中的任何一条注释都要和参考文献相对应,如果引用了别人的观点、材料、数据等而不加注释,可能受到侵权指控。

注 释

① authority 在这里指"权威,威信",也可指"当局,官方",如：
the local authorities （地方当局）

② VIP 是 very important person 的缩写形式,指很重要的人物。英文中这样的缩写还有很多,如：MVP 是 most valuable player 的缩写,意思为"最优秀选手",VP 是 vice president 的缩写,意思为"副总裁"。

③ look through 是"浏览,从头到尾看一遍"的意思,如：
Have you looked through the report? （你看了报告了吗？）
表示"看"的词语英语中有很多：look 是常用词,指"注意或有意识地看",如：
He looked but saw nothing. （他看了,但什么也没看见。）
gaze 指"由于惊讶、好奇、喜悦、同情或感兴趣而目不转睛地看",如：
What are you gazing at? （你在凝视什么？）
stare 指"睁大眼睛、目不转睛地盯着看",如：
It's rude to stare at people. （盯着看人不礼貌。）

Attending a Dissertation

glare 指由于"羡慕、恐惧、惊讶或愚蠢而用恐吓、凶狠或愤怒的眼光看",如:
He glared at her.(他向她瞪眼。)
peek 指"偷看"、"通过孔隙窥视",如:
You must not peek while you are counting in such games as hide-and-seek.
(像捉迷藏一类游戏中,你数数时绝对不能偷看。)
peer 指"细看",如:
He was peering down the well.(他细看下面的井。)

About Research in Cooperation
关于合作研究

Topic Introduction
话题导言

中国的科研人员出国进行科学研究和外国的科研人员到中国来参与研究的情况越来越多，尤其是近些年中国的科研人员出国进行合作研究的情况增长很快，形式也多样，如访问学者、博士后研究、项目合作等，为中国科研人员的成长和培养的国际化开辟了新的途径。

据笔者所知，很多出国研究人员的英语口语能力亟待提高，对不同的文化环境也感到无所适从，尽管这较少影响他们所从事的自然科学研究项目。

Situational Dialogs
情景对话

刘杭(Liu Hang)希望有人与她合作研究武夷山自然资源项目，也要帮朋友打听博士后的事情。李康(Li Kang)也与美国同事谈起了自己的项目。

Dialog 1

Liu Hang: I hear you're recruiting a post-doctoral fellow. What're the requirements?
我听说你在招聘一个博士后研究人员，有什么要求？

About Research in Cooperation 28

Dr. Smith: Yes, we need one person to cooperate with. You want to apply for that position?
是的,我们需要一个人合作,你想申请吗?

Liu Hang: No, Dr. Smith. One of my friends is a scientist in Chinese Academy of Sciences and he holds a Ph. D. degree in Building Materials Science.
不是的,史密斯博士。我的一个朋友是中国科学院的科学家,有建筑材料科学专业方面的博士学位。

Dr. Smith: If so, he's qualified to apply for that position. You may ask him to download and fill in the application and submit it with other needed qualifications and certifications.
如果是这样,他有资格申请这个职位。你可以要他下载并填写申请表并和其他资格证书一起交来。

Liu Hang: All right. How long is the cooperation duration?
好的,合作期限是多长时间?

Dr. Smith: We can employ him by a one-year contract, but it can be extended to another year.
我们可以签一年期的雇佣合同,但是可以延长一年。

Liu Hang: How about the fellowship for one year?
一年有多少研究津贴?

Dr. Smith: It's 27,500 dollars, and he has to work 40 hours a week. He may check our website for more information.
27,500美元,每周工作40小时,他可以从我们的网上查阅更多信息。

Liu Hang: Thanks a lot. Your information is very useful.
谢谢,你的信息很有用。

Dialog 2

Dr. Hall: How is everything going with your research project?①
你的研究项目进展如何?

Li Kang: Very well. I think I can finish the first phase at the end of this month?
很好,我想我可以在这个月底完成第一阶段的研究。

Dr. Hall: As planned,② you should make a presentation for your research progress some day next month.
按照计划，你要在下个月的某一天对你的研究进展作一个汇报。

Li Kang: Yes, I remember that. Can I use the projector to present it?
是的，我记得这事。我可以用投影仪演示吗？

Dr. Hall: Sure, you can. Just tell the institute office ahead of③ two days.
当然可以，提前两天告诉研究所办公室就可以了。

Li Kang: I mean I'd like to apply PowerPoint documents to my presentation, so that I can state everything more clearly.
我是说我想用幻灯片文件进行说明。

Dr. Hall: Nothing is better than that.
那再好不过了。

Dialog 3

Liu Hang: I have a brainchild, Professor Lee.
李教授，我有一个想法。

Prof. Lee: Let's hear it.
说来听听。

Liu Hang: We have a project about the visitors' impacts to the natural resources of Wuyishan Mountains, and we hope to cooperate with someone.
我们有一个关于游客对武夷山自然资源影响的项目，希望能有人合作。

Prof. Lee: Have you begun it yet?
你们开始了吗？

Liu Hang: No, we've just won the project from the Chinese Academy of Sciences. The project will last two years. I'm wondering if someone is interested in such a project.
还没，我们刚刚从中国科学院拿到这个项目，该项目的研究期限是两年。我不知道是否有人对这个项目感兴趣。

Prof. Lee: Do you need money or manpower?
你们是需要资金还是人力？

About Research in Cooperation 28

关于合作研究

Liu Hang: Both, I think.
我想都需要。

Prof. Lee: It's a coincidence that I have some fund in hand④ for international projects. I will bat around⑤ the details about the Wuyishan Mountains and we can discuss it several days later.
碰巧,我手上有国际项目的资金。我要详细了解武夷山的具体情况,我们几天后再谈吧。

Liu Hang: Good. It's just what I thought.
好的,这就是我所想的。

典型句型

1) I hear you're recruiting a post-doctoral fellow.
我听说你在招聘一个博士后研究人员。

2) What're the requirements of your future cooperator?
你对未来的合作者有什么要求?

3) The Ph.D. degree in microbiology is a must.
必须具有微生物学博士学位。

4) Where can I download the application forms?
我可以在哪里下载申请表格?

5) How long is the cooperation duration?
合作期限是多长时间?

6) How about the fellowship for one year?
一年有多少研究津贴?

7) Can I take a paid holiday in summer?
我夏天可以休带薪假期吗?

8) How is everything going with your research project?
你的研究项目进展如何?

9) Can I use the projector to present it?
我可以用投影仪演示吗?

10) We hope to cooperate with someone.
    我们希望能有人合作。
11) I'm wondering if someone is interested in such a project.
    我不知道是否有人对这个项目感兴趣。
12) I hope you can fund my research in China.
    我希望你能资助我在中国的研究。

背景知识

文化冲突(cultural conflict)：当一个人离开自己熟悉的文化氛围走进另外一种截然不同的文化环境中时，会自然而然地把自己在原来文化背景下养成的文化意识、思维习惯和个性品质带到新的文化环境中,这在英语中被称作 Culture Baggage，这等于是说"文化"是一件甩不掉的行李,时刻背在身上。在异国他乡从事科学研究,就要克服这种由不同文化带来的冲击。

(1) 留心观察:不同的文化背景往往为这个社会存在的事物提供了不同的规则和标准,理解一定文化环境中自己接触到的语言的和非语言的信息,首先要细心观察。

(2) 不轻易判断对错:在美国看见许多与自己的文化不同的事情,不要简单地因自己的习惯把任何东西都分为"好"或"坏"。这样你将会造成许多误解,当你有更完全的信息时再作判断也不迟。

(3) 敢提问题:任何人都不能懂得世界上的一切,当有不明白的问题时应大胆发问,大多数美国人都会非常耐心地解答问题。提问题的方式很多，可以就现象提问，也可以问一些事情发生的背景，或重复听到或见到事物，以便清楚准确理解。

(4) 换位思考:文化环境的不同，可能对相同的事物产生不同的理解。试着把你

About Research in Cooperation

自己放在别人的位置,并且从别人的角度来考虑问题,以便更快地适应文化的差异。

(5) 积极参与:适应新的文化氛围的最好途径就是参与其中,经历的事情越多,学到的东西也就越多。努力认识周围的人,多结交朋友,参与他们的社交活动,了解他们的文化。

(6) 敢于嘲笑自己:处于新文化环境中时,不可避免地会出现错误或尴尬的场面,嘲笑自己的错误是一种解脱的妙计,也是在鼓励其他人在一种友好的氛围中进行交流。

(7) 接受挫折:在新的文化环境中工作不是容易的,挫折是在所难免的,一时的焦急忧虑都是很正常的反应,承认自己受到的挫折有利于尽快认识新的世界。

注 释

① How is everything going with...? 是用来询问事情进展状况的一个问句,如:
How is everything going with your assignments? (作业做得怎么样了?)

② as planned 可以看作是 as it is planned 的省略形式,英语中的状语从句多可以这样省略,如:when the time is permitted 可以省略为 time permitted; if it is necessary 可以省略为 if necessary; whether it will be raining or snowing 可以省略为 whether raining or snowing 等。

③ ahead of 是"在……前面"的意思, ahead of time 意思是"提前",还可以说成 ahead of schedule 等。

④ in hand 是"在控制之中"的意思,如:
The project is well in hand. (这项计划控制得很好。)

⑤ bat round 在这里是"探讨,琢磨"的意思,也有"到处寻乐"的意思。

About Students Exchange
关于学生交换

Topic Introduction 话题导言

国际教育交流与合作的重要内容就是学校之间学生的交换。中国的大学经常有校方代表团出国与对方学校探讨有关交换学生的问题，如经费问题、学分问题、签证问题、学生的选择等都是探讨的内容。美国大学里负责这方面事务的部门多半是国际项目办公室(International Programs Office)。

一般情况下，关于学生交换的问题都是在多次商谈之后才能确定下来的，最初的可能是电话、书面、电子邮件或者网上会议等形式，最终走向"签约"这一步。本话题选择初次意向提出、细节询问和签订合同三个场景来设定会话场面。

Situational Dialogs 情景对话

大学之间的学生交换十分平常，这有利于互相之间取长补短。丁唐(Ding Tang)所在的大学就决定和美国的大学建立合作关系，双方就一些细节和需要注意的事项做了一些讨论。

About Students Exchange 29

Dialog 1

Ding Tang: Our University is very interested in your students exchange program, Dr. Whitman.
惠特曼博士,我们大学对你们的学生交换项目很感兴趣。

Dr. Whitman: We're glad to do such a project with any qualified university, and now we're getting along well with① Seoul National University.
我们很愿意跟合乎条件的大学开展这样的项目,现在我们跟首尔大学合作得很好。

Ding Tang: What's a qualified university you refer to?
什么是你指的合乎条件的大学?

Dr. Whitman: It must be a four-year university and can confer at least bachelor's and master's degrees. Beyond all doubt②, your university is eligible.
必须是四年制大学,至少能授予学士和硕士学位。毫无疑问,你们大学是合格的。

Ding Tang: We hope to discuss with you about the details of students exchange program. Could you name a person to negotiate with us?
我们希望和你们探讨学生交换项目的具体细节。能安排人和我们谈一谈吗?

Dr. Whitman: Sure, I can give you a reply tomorrow.
可以,我明天就答复你。

Dialog 2

Dr. Whitman: We're very willing to cooperate with you in students exchange program. Let's discuss some material issues today.
我们很愿意和你们进行学生交换项目,我们今天讨论一些实质性的问题吧。

Ding Tang: That's what we need also.
那就是我们所需要的。

Dr. Whitman: Can you pick out some students whose English is enough for class participation in America?
你们能够挑出一些英语水平足够参与美国课堂活动的学生吗?

Ding Tang: Yes, we can. How about your ideas of tuition and fees?
能。你们对于学费和杂费的想法是什么？

Dr. Whitman: We award exchange students Full Tuition Waivers and necessary stipends, but they have to pay health insurance, various fees and textbooks.
我们授予交换学生"学费全免"奖学金并发给必要的生活津贴，但是他们要支付健康保险，各种杂费和课本费。

Ding Tang: We can also provide them with the equal terms. How about dorms?
我们也能提供同等的条件。宿舍怎么样？

Dr. Whitman: They may stay in any residence hall on campus, or they may rent apartments off campus if they like.
他们可以住在校内的学生公寓，或者在校外租房，只要他们愿意就行。

Ding Tang: That's good enough.
那足够好了。

Dialog 3

Dr. Whitman: Have you balanced everything, Dr. Ding?
丁博士，你们把一切都想好了吗？

Ding Tang: I think so. In my opinion, for one thing[③] we can sign a Letter of Intent about this students exchange program.
我想是的。我认为我们可以先就学生交换项目签一个意向书。

Dr. Whitman: I agree with you. And, both of the two parties may study more about the Cooperation Agreements, and we may sign them at the end of your visit to the United States.
我同意你的意见，而且我们双方都可以再研究研究合作协议，你们访问美国结束时我们再签字。

Ding Tang: Good idea. I think it better for the two presidents to sign the Letter of Intent and the two program directors sign the Agreements.
好主意，我认为双方校长签署意向书，而双方项目负责人签署协议书，是更好的。

About Students Exchange 29

关于学生交换

Dr. Whitman: I back you up④.
我支持你的意见。

Typical Sentences
典型句型

1) We're very interested in your students exchange program.
   我们对你们的学生交换项目很感兴趣。
2) What's a qualified university you refer to?
   什么是你指的合乎条件的大学？
3) We'd like to know the details of students exchange program.
   我们想知道学生交换项目的具体细节。
4) We're very willing to cooperate with you in students exchange program.
   我们很愿意和你们进行学生交换项目。
5) Let's discuss some material issues today.
   我们今天讨论一些实质性的问题吧。
6) The credits they get at your university will be part of their credits needed for their degrees.
   他们在你们大学取得的学分将是他们获得学位所需学分的一部分。
7) How about your ideas of tuition and fees?
   你们对于学费和杂费的想法是什么？
8) We award exchange students Full Tuition Waivers.
   我们授予交换学生"学费全免"奖学金。
9) Both of us may study more about the Cooperation Agreements.
   我们双方都可以再研究研究合作协议。
10) We're expecting a brilliant future of our cooperation.
    我们期待我们的合作有个光明的前景。

Background
背景知识

美国大学生的校园生活（Campus Life）：学生在大学学习期间，除了学问上的长进外，大学环境对学生的态度、信念、自信心、行为及未来的成就均有重大影响。美国的高等院校一般都允许学生有较大的自由来塑造自己的校园生活。

（1）参与学校事务：美国大学生的自治团体，主要目的是帮助校方维持同全体学生的有效合作，并为学生提供自我管理的直接经验。学生干部由学生自治会主持的选举产生。

（2）文娱活动：丰富多彩的课外活动是美国大学的传统，而且被视为大学教育有价值的组成部分。但大多数学生专业课程的负担较重，只能参加2—3项有组织的课外活动。课外活动的选择范围很广，通常有剧社、乐队、合唱队、辩论社、电影协会、法语俱乐部等等。

（3）体育活动：许多院校的校际运动会是由得到校方财政大力支持的高效率的体育部主办的。一些运动项目，特别是橄榄球和篮球，通常是商业化的，庞大的体育场馆往往座无虚席。目前越来越多的院校开始减少对只有少数学生可以参加的体育竞赛的偏重，而把注意力集中到推广有广泛参与性的体育活动。

（4）学生会：作为校园里的社区中心，学生会不仅为学生，也为教职员、校友和来访者提供社交和娱乐活动的机会。一栋典型的学生会楼通常有礼堂、餐厅、小吃部及一些可供跳舞、展览、音乐欣赏、电子游戏之用的游艺室。

（5）学生宿舍：如果学校提供宿舍的话，绝大多数美国大学生喜欢住校，这增加了社交和受教育的机会。许多院校对学生有住校的规定，除非他们的家就在学校附近。学校的一些宿舍有配套起居室和卧室，但一般只有卧室并附有公用的会客室、自修室、康乐室、厨房和洗衣设施等。学校通常聘用研究生或高年级本科生为宿舍顾问，负责管理宿舍并辅导学业和个人问题。

（6）男女大学生联谊会：校园里这种以两个或三个希腊字母命名的联谊会是从18世纪和19世纪初的各种文学社团或读书会发

展而来的,有的联谊会在遍及各地数以百计的院校设有分会,有的只有寥寥可数的几个分会,目前全国性的男大学生联谊会约有 150 个,女大学生联谊会约有 60 个。至于地方性的联谊会则数不胜数。

（7）荣誉学会：在许多院校,学生的最高荣誉就是被选入 Phi Beta Kappa,成员评选的主要标准是学习成绩,虽然也考虑其他条件。几乎所有的学科都有荣誉学会,优秀大学生可以经评选加入,如 Sigma Xi 专门挑选优秀的科学研究人员为成员,而 Phi Delta Kappa 则由教育界杰出人士所组成。

（8）同级会和校友会组织：目前几乎所有的院校都有自己的校友会。由各校校友会干事组成的美国校友会理事会旨在推动校友会的活动并促进对高等教育的支持。一年一度的校友返校活动是美国的一大社会风俗。各院校均在校友间积极展开筹款活动,校友的捐款占据了高等教育自愿捐款的相当大一部分。

注　释

① get along with 是"和某人打交道,相处；事情进展"的意思,如：
He is getting along well with his neighbors. (他和邻居的关系不错。)
② beyond all doubt 是"毫无疑问"的意思,还可说 out of question / past question / without question / beyond doubt 等。
③ for one thing 是"首先"的意思,如：
For one thing, people now enjoy a higher standard of living. (第一,现在人们的生活水平提高了。)
"首先"还可以说成 above all / first / first of all / firstly / in the first instance / in the first place 等。
④ back up 在这里是"支持"的意思,如：
The new evidence backed up my argument. (新的证词有助于我的辩论。)

About English Training
关于英语培训

Topic Introduction
话题导言

英语作为一种国际性的语言，受到我们的普遍重视是理所应当的。不仅国内的教育培训机构把英语培训作为生财之道，而且英语国家也把英语培训作为一种赚取非英语国家钱财的一种手段。

英语培训的国际合作可以说是如火如荼，英语国家的各个大学几乎都有语言培训中心，独立设置的英语培训学校数以千计，非英语国家每年从英语国家聘请的教师也是成千上万。英语培训的国际合作多数是在教育机构之间进行的，很多教育方面的代表团出访时都肩负着培训合作谈判、签约等任务。

美国各大学都在国际学生办公室（International Students Office / ISO）下面设立了一个语言培训机构，专门负责英语培训的有关事宜，开展的项目包括英语教师培训、外国留学生英语培训、选派教师出国任教、校际培训交流等。

Situational Dialogs
情景对话

英语作为国际性交流语言，被越来越多的非英语国家人士所重视，高卫平(Weiping)这次到美国的另一个任务是要同一家英语培训机构做一些英语培训的生意。

About English Training

关于英语培训

Dialog 1

Linda: You say you have something to discuss with me, Weiping. What's it?
卫平，你说你有事情和我讨论，是什么事情？

Weiping: I have an idea about English training, Linda.
琳达，我有一个关于英语培训的想法。

Linda: Let's hear it.
说来听听。

Weiping: I think we can organize some teachers of English from China to come here and you train them for two or three months.
我想我们能从中国组织一些英语老师来这里，你们培训他们两三个月。

Linda: That's a good idea. How many people?
好主意，多少人？

Weiping: Thirty teachers for this summer session. Could you give a price for each person who will stay here two months?
这个暑期30人，你能给出他们在这里呆上两个月的价格吗？

Linda: You mean everything, including room, food, textbooks, and tuition?
你是说所有的，包括住、吃、课本和学费？

Weiping: Yes, you'd better include nearby trips on weekends and transportation fares from and back to China.
是的，你最好也把周末在附近游览以及来回中国的交通费都算在内。

Linda: All right, and I'll ask the secretary to do the calculation right away.
好的，我马上让秘书计算一下。

Weiping: OK, thank you.
好的，谢谢。

Dialog 2

Weiping: There're many students who want to study English in the United States, Great Britain or any other English-speaking country.
有许多学生想到美国、英国和其他英语国家学习英语。

Linda: It's useful for them. But I know it's a big problem for Chinese students to get visas. Why not send our teachers to your country?
这对他们有用处。但是我知道对中国学生来说获得签证是个大难题,为什么不派些我们的老师到你们国家呢?

Weiping: That's a good idea, but they'd prefer① to study in the English context. We can organize a group first.
那是个好主意,但是他们宁愿在英语环境中学习,我们可以先组织一个小组的人。

Linda: You may have a try, of course. Do you need any help?
当然你们可以试一试,需要帮什么忙?

Weiping: I'm thinking if you and our company sign an agreement about training partnership, so that the students can show the document to the visa officials.
我在想我们公司和你们签署一个培训合作伙伴的协议,这样学生就可以把这个文件拿给签证官看了。

Linda: That's easy to do. Could you do a draft② of the agreement?
那很容易做,你能起草一个协议吗?

Weiping: Sure, I can.
当然,能。

Dialog 3

Linda: You need twenty people to teach English, right?
你们需要20个人去教英语,对吗?

Weiping: Yes, they need to teach forty days during the summer session in Shenzhen, China. Actually, we prefer university students.
是的,他们需要在暑期在中国深圳教书40天。其实,我们宁愿要大学生。

About English Training

Linda:	We can recruit qualified students. What're your requirements?
	我们可以招聘到合格的学生,你们的要求是什么?
Weiping:	First, they must be native English speakers. Their pronunciation and intonation of English are perfect and clear. They must be conscientious people and easy to cooperate with.
	首先,英语必须是他们的母语,语音、语调要正确清晰,他们必须是负责任的人并容易合作。
Linda:	I agree. We can put up③ posters on the bulletin boards on campus and around the whole city.
	我同意。我们可以在校园内和整个城市的布告栏内张贴海报。
Weiping:	An advertisement with the *University Daily News* is necessary.
	《大学每日新闻报》上登一个广告是必要的。
Linda:	That'll cost a lot.
	那要花很多钱。

典型句型

1) I have an idea about English training, Linda.
   琳达,我有一个关于英语培训的想法。
2) Some teachers of English from China want to come here for your English training program for two or three months.
   中国的一些英语老师想来这里参加你们两三个月的英语培训项目。
3) Could you give a price for each person who will stay here two months?
   你能给出他们在这里呆上两个月的价格吗?
4) Does the price include accommodation, food, textbooks, and tuition?
   这个价格包括住、吃、课本和学费吗?
5) Many students want to study English in any English-speaking country.
   许多学生想到英语国家学习英语。

6) It's a big problem for Chinese students to get visas.
对中国学生来说获得签证是个大难题。

7) They'd prefer to study in the English context.
他们宁愿在英语环境中学习。

8) Can we sign an agreement about training partnership?
我们能签署一个培训合作伙伴的协议吗？

9) The main purpose is that the students can show the document to the visa officials.
主要的目的是学生就可以把这个文件拿给签证官看了。

10) Could you do a draft of the agreement?
你能起草一个协议吗？

背景知识

　　培训课堂的规矩：不管是组织国内人员赴国外参加培训，还是聘请外籍教师来中国任教，课堂的一些规矩还是要明白的。

　　（1）称呼老师：最安全的方法是用"教授"（professor）。若知道老师的姓，可称呼为某某教授，但不要称老师为先生（sir）或女士（miss），尤其是对女老师，因为他们很可能会在意学衔、学位。也不要随便直呼老师的名字，除非老师告诉学生可以这么做。

　　（2）授课方式：讲授（lecture），即老师讲学生听；研讨（seminar），即学生先自行看书或做完功课后，再到课堂上和老师讨论，多为小组方式。

　　（3）课后作业：美国老师布置许多作业（assignments），几乎每堂课都有，有的老师也许一开始就告诉你这学期每堂课的进度和作业，有的则可能随堂才讲。

　　（4）课堂规则：尽量早几分钟进教室，如果迟到，可轻声说"对不起"，一切以不打扰旁人为原则；学生可自由选择自己喜爱的座位；美国人多半记不清拼音式的中文名字，事先取个西方名字是必要的；多提问题，让老师觉得你有参与感，知道你的存在，千万不要怕自己英文不好而不开口，也不要怕自己的意见有错而不问，问错总比不开口而一直错下去好;欲表达自己的意见时,可用询问的语气征询老师同意,以示礼貌;最好在上课前或下课后才去洗手间,如果要在上课时去,不必举手征求老师同意,只要静静地去再静静地回就可以了。

（5）不该做的:打哈欠及打瞌睡,和别人说话,吃东西,嚼口香糖,看其他书。如果想在课堂上录音,最好征求老师同意。

（6）考试形式:除了期末考(final exam)，期中考（mid-term exam）之外,还有随堂考(pop quiz)。题型可能有多项选择、简要回答、说明、对错判断等,考试时千万不要作弊,否则有被逐出校门的可能。

注　释

① prefer 是"宁愿,喜欢,选择"等意思,如:
Most Americans prefer coffee to tea.（多数美国人喜欢咖啡胜过茶。）
Which of these two dresses do you prefer?（这两套衣服你喜欢哪一套？）

② draft 在这里的意思是"草稿,草图。"也有"汇票,付款通知单"的意思,如:
a rough draft for a speech（讲话草稿）。

③ put up 是"举起,抬起,进行,提供,表现出,建造,提名,推举"的意思,如:
Put up your hands if you have any questions.（有问题请举手。）
A new elementary school will be put up here soon.（这里很快就要建一所小学了。）

About Chinese Training
关于汉语培训

Topic Introduction
话题导言

随着中外文化交流活动的增加,中国文化也在吸引着全世界的人们,在英美等西方国家学习汉语的人也越来越多。一方面,很多外国人来到中国学习汉语;另一方面,外国大学也非常重视汉语的教学与培训,而且很多大学都把汉语列为外语选修语种。

到外国去培训汉语,一般是中国大学派遣老师在外国大学开办短期或长期的培训班,也有中国赴外部分访问学者在外国大学开设汉语课或者中国文化课。不管属于哪一种情况,事先都是经过双方协商达成协议,这也是西方人喜欢"约定"的表现。

Situational Dialogs
情景对话

李康(Li Kang)和史密斯博士(Dr. Smith)正在讨论要开办的培训课程,但不管哪种情况,还是要先签好合约。

Dialog 1

Dr. Smith: As for[①] the training programs, we can do an exchange.
至于培训项目,我们可以做一笔交易。

About Chinese Training

Li Kang:	What do you refer to?
	你说的是什么？
Dr. Smith:	You need one teacher of English and we need one teacher of Chinese here. So, you give me a Chinese to exchange for② an American.
	你们需要一个英语教师，而我们需要一个汉语教师。所以，你给我一个中国人来换我一个美国人。
Li Kang:	Absolutely a good idea.
	这绝对是个好主意。
Dr. Smith:	You pay your person and we pay ours. So, you pay nothing to the English teacher and we pay nothing to the Chinese teacher.
	你们给你们的人付工资，我们给我们人付工资。所以你们不用付什么给英语老师，我们也不用付什么给汉语老师。
Li Kang:	No, I don't agree on③ that. You pay the Chinese teacher here and we pay the English teacher there.
	不，我对这一点不同意。你们在这里给汉语老师付报酬，我们在那里给英语老师付报酬。
Dr. Smith:	Let's see. ...Yours sounds more reasonable.
	我想想，……你说的听起来更合乎情理。

Dialog 2

Dr. Smith:	There're dozens of④ businesspeople who want to study some Chinese. Can you teach?
	有几十个商人想学些中文，你能教吗？
Li Kang:	Yes, I can. How many?
	能教，多少人？
Dr. Smith:	Around twenty-two or twenty-three.
	大约22或23人。
Li Kang:	How long do they want to study and what do they need?
	他们想学多长时间，要学什么？
Dr. Smith:	One month. They're businesspeople doing business with Chinese. They often go to China and need to know how to speak some daily-used sentences and read some public signs.
	一个月，他们是生意人，在和中国人做生意。他们经常去中

Li Kang:	That's easy for me. I think no problem for me. How about the pay? 对我来说很容易做，我想我没有问题。报酬呢？
Dr. Smith:	Twenty-four dollars an hour plus an allowance of 1200 dollars for one month. 24美元一个小时，加上一个月1200美元的津贴。
Li Kang:	Good. I'll take it. 好的，我同意做。
Dr. Smith:	All right. Let's make it certain. Can you come again tomorrow and sign the contract? 好的，我们就敲定了这件事。你明天能再来签合同吗？
Li Kang:	No problem. 没有问题。

Dialog 3

Li Kang:	I hope to give a course about Chinese culture, Dr. Smith. What do you think about it? 我希望开设一门关于中国文化的课，史密斯博士。你怎么看？
Dr. Smith:	Good. This week is the deadline for you to apply for a new course. Have you prepared the syllabus? 很好，这个星期是申请开课的最后期限，你准备好了课程表吗？
Li Kang:	Yes, here it is. I need your comments and recommendation. 准备好了，给你看。我需要你的意见和推荐。
Dr. Smith:	Sure, I can recommend you to the Department Chair. How many hours are you planning to give each week? 可以，我会向系委员会主席推荐的。你打算每个星期教授几个小时的课？
Li Kang:	Two hours a week. The students can get two credits if they complete my course successfully. 每周两小时。学生成功完成了这门课就可以得到两个学分。

About Chinese Training 31
关于汉语培训

Dr. Smith: You are a great person. Wish you success.
你是个了不起的人，祝你成功。

Li Kang: Thank you very much.
非常感谢。

Typical Sentences
典型句型

1) We can send excellent teachers of Chinese here to teach.
我们能够派遣优秀的汉语老师来这里任教。

2) Can we do an exchange of sending teachers?
派遣老师的事情，我们可以做一个交易吗？

3) You give me a Chinese in exchange for an American.
你给我一个中国人来换我一个美国人。

4) Your idea sounds more reasonable.
你的想法听起来更合乎情理。

5) Can you run a class of Chinese for those businesspeople?
你能为这些生意人开设一个汉语班吗？

6) There's no problem for us to do this.
对我们来说是没有问题的。

7) How long do they want to study and what do they need?
他们想学多长时间，要学什么？

8) Can you give a course about Chinese culture, Dr. Zhou?
周博士，你能不能开设一门关于中国文化的课？

9) Must I prepare the syllabus within this week?
我必须在本周内准备好教学大纲吗？

10) I need your comments and recommendation.
我需要你的意见和推荐。

11) How many hours are you planning to give each week?
你打算每个星期教授几个小时的课？

12) The training class will last one semester.
这个培训班将开设一个学期。

Background
背景知识

汉语水平考试(HSK)简介:HSK是测量母语非汉语者(包括外国人、华侨和中国国内少数民族学员)的汉语水平而设立的国家级标准化考试,由北京语言文化大学汉语水平考试中心设计研制。

(1) 汉语水平考试(HSK)是统一的标准化考试,实行统一命题、考试、阅卷、评分,并统一颁发证书。

(2) 中国国家教育部在北京语言文化大学设立国家汉语水平考试委员会,全权领导汉语水平考试,并颁发汉语水平证书。汉语水平考试委员会负责汉语水平考试的咨询工作。

(3) 汉语水平考试(HSK)每年定期在国内外举行。目前,已在新加坡、日本、韩国、菲律宾、马来西亚、泰国、澳大利亚、加拿大、美国、法国、德国、英国、意大利、俄罗斯、越南等国家设点举办HSK。

(4) HSK是以测量一般语言能力为目的的标准化考试,它不以任何特定教材或特定教程的内容为依据,所以考生无需按特定教材的内容准备考试。

Notes
注释

① as for 是"至于"的意思,如:
I don't know anything as for the others. (至于其他,我一无所知。)

② exchange for 是"交换,互换"的意思,如:
He exchanged the blue trousers for a red pair. (他把蓝裤子换成红色的。)

③ agree on / upon 是"达成一致意见"的意思,如:

About Chinese Training

They quarreled one day and could agree on nothing.(他们争吵了一天,没有达成任何协议。)

④ dozens of 是"若干,许许多多,几十个"的意思,如:
There're dozens of people surrounding the police car.(有几十个人围着那辆警车。)

About Academic Cooperation
关于合作办学

Topic Introduction
话题导言

中外合作办学在近几年的发展可以说是轰轰烈烈,有些是经过国家教育部正式批准的合作办学项目,有些却是在打政策的擦边球、钻法律的空子。虽然有些问题已经暴露出来,如一些境外的"野鸡"大学飘洋过海来赚中国人的钱,学生毕业得到的洋文凭却不能被承认等,但出国寻求合作办学的机构和个人仍然很多。

出国寻求合作办学需要和境外的大学就合作方式、费用分担、师资派遣、文凭颁发等问题进行磋商和谈判。合作办学的代表团对外国大学的资质和国内的认可程度一定要事先研究清楚,才能在合作办学中学到真正的经验,赚到踏实的钱。

Situational Dialogs
情景对话

丁唐(Ding Tang)和主管 Mary 就合作办学进行了一些讨论,包括合作方式,费用支付等。

About Academic Cooperation 32

关于合作办学

Dialog 1

Mary: I'm very interested in offering our MBA program with the joint① efforts of your university. The key is how to select students.
我对和你们大学一起开设工商管理硕士学位项目这件事很感兴趣。问题是如何选拔学生。

Ding Tang: I understand your worry. You're expecting that every student can follow the professors from your university.
我理解你的担心。你是期望每个学生都能听得懂你们学校教授的课堂教学。

Mary: Yes, they must be excellent in English. Do you have any idea to solve the problem?
是的,他们的英语必须很优秀。你有什么解决这个问题的主意吗?

Ding Tang: In my opinion, we can carry out② an intensive English course, such as reading, listening, speaking and academic writing.
我认为,我们可以开设英语强化课程,如阅读、听力、口语和学术写作。

Mary: That's a good way. Can your professors give some courses in Chinese for the first semester while the English course is going?
那是一个好办法。第一个学期英语课程进行的时候,你们学校的教授能用中文开一些课吗?

Ding Tang: Of course, this is under our consideration③.
当然,我们正在考虑这点儿。

Dialog 2

Mary: The second important question is about the tuition and professors' salary, traveling fares and allowance.
第二个重要的问题是关于学费和教授们的工资、旅费和津贴。

Ding Tang: Our purpose of this program is not for money. The tuition should not be too high, 3000 dollars per year at most.
我们这个项目的目的并不是为了赚钱。学费不能太高,每年

191

	最多3000美元。
Mary:	That can't cover the expenses if in the United States. How much is the balance when we finish the program within two years? 如果是在美国，这还不够开支呢。两年内这个项目完成的时候，能有多少结余？
Ding Tang:	We've calculated all possible expenditures in this list. If we pay professors' salary and bonus, traveling fares and allowance according to the standards there, the balance should be fairly good. 我们计算了所有可能的开支，这里有一个表。如果教授的工资和奖金、旅费和津贴按照我们那里的标准，余额还是可观的。
Mary:	Let me see, …Good, but the salary is a little less than we think. 我看看，……好的，但是工资比我们想象的少了些。
Ding Tang:	No, I don't think so. The professors will have free apartment, and that'll save a lot. 不，我不这样看。教授们住免费公寓，那要省很多钱。
Mary:	I thought they would have to pay rent. 我原来以为他们要付房租呢。

Typical Sentences
典型句型

1) I'm very interested in the joint MBA program efforts at your university.
   我对在你们大学合作开设工商管理硕士学位很感兴趣。

2) The admission officers will interview every prospective student.
   招生工作人员将对每个报名的学生进行面试。

3) Do you have any idea to solve the problem?
   你有什么解决这个问题的主意吗？

About Academic Cooperation 32

关于合作办学

4) Our professors can give some courses in Chinese for the first semester.
   第一个学期我们的教授能用中文开几门课。

5) How much is the tuition each semester?
   每个学期的学费是多少？

6) Our purpose of this program is not for money.
   我们这个项目的目的并不是为了赚钱。

7) We've calculated all possible expenditures in this list.
   我们计算了所有可能的开支，列了一个表。

8) The professors will have free apartment.
   教授们将会住免费公寓。

9) The degree will be co-issued by both universities.
   学位将由两个大学共同颁发。

10) The professors will teach the same thing as they do in the United States.
    教授们将教他们在美国教的一样的东西。

11) This program will be involved in the same texts, syllabus, class formats and assignments.
    这个项目将使用同样的课本、大纲、课堂形式，以及作业。

背景知识

　　美国的公立和私立大学：美国高等院校分为公立和私立两大类，公立院校是指由联邦政府、州政府和地方政府资助建立的学校；私立院校则是由个人及私人团体(如教会或企业等)资助建立的学校。

　　公立院校的主要经费来源：州政府的税收拨款；联邦政府对图书馆和其他设施、专门的学术研究项目及援助学生的拨款；地方政府部门的拨款，大部分是针对两年制社区学院和市立院校的；为弥补财政开支而收取的学费，学费通常比私立院校低得多；为政府部门、基金会及企业等开展研究提供服务签约所得款项；来自校友、

193

企业界、基金会等方面的赠款及从这些款项累积而成的捐赠基金所得的收益。

私立院校的主要经费来源为：向学生收取的学费通常比公立院校高，在经费来源中所占的比例也较大；地方、州及联邦政府提供的用途指定的补助（教会学校通常得不到这些补助）；来自校友、企业界、基金会等方面的赠款及从这些款项累积而成的捐赠基金所得的收益（这种来源在私立院校比在公立院校远为重要）；与政府部门、基金会及企业等签订的研究和服务合同。

然而，两类院校在经费来源方面的差异正在逐步缩小，公立与私立院校之间的实质性区别在于控制学校的是政府还是私人团体。

美国公立院校又可进一步分为国立、州立、市立三类。联邦政府对教育机构不直接实行控制和管理，因此除少数几个联邦政府直属的院校如军事院校外，其他公立和私立院校一样受各州法律的制约。联邦政府只在国防领域直接创办高等院校，其他领域则很少。州立高等院校通常由各州议会通过立法而建立，通常属州高等教育董事会管辖，董事会成员往往由州长任命。市立高等院校是根据州法律或特许状建立的，由当地的董事会管辖，董事会成员往往由市长、市教育局或市政会任命。美国有的城市还举办庞大的综合性大学，如纽约市立大学拥有校园20个，学生18万，规模上在美国高等学府中排行第三。

注 释

① **joint** 是"共同的，联合的"意思，如：**joint venture**（合资企业）。
② **carry out** 是"进行，贯彻，执行"的意思，如：
We should carry out the spare plan.（我们应该启用备用方案。）
③ **under consideration** 是"在考虑中"的意思，注意另外几个短语 **in consideration of**（报答；由于）、**take into consideration**（顾及，考虑到）

Attending an International Conference
出席国际会议

Topic Introduction
话题导言

对外开放 30 年以来，我国的科技人员、大学教师、政府官员出国参加各种各样国际会议的机会越来越多，而国际性的交流不仅使人增长见识，开阔眼界，更让国人学到了国外先进的技术，了解了科学的前沿。全世界每年召开数以千次的国际会议，政府的、学术的、国际组织的、文化交流的等等各种主题、各种形式。

举办会议的单位和形式不同，种类和名称也很多，有代表会议(conference)、专题座谈会(symposium)、学术讨论会(colloquium)、研讨会(seminar)、定期召开的应届会议(session)、全体大会(general assembly)、代表大会(congress)等。所以，参加会议一定要弄清楚是哪一种，是否要提交论文，是否要进行大会发言。

Situational Dialogs
情景对话

刘杭(Liu Hang)参加了世界自然资源与旅游研讨会，并作了一个成功的发言，得到了与会人员的一致称赞。

Dialog 1

Liu Hang: Dr. Steven, I'm very interested in the World Nature-based Tourism Seminar. Would you please tell me how to apply for it?
史蒂文博士，我对世界自然旅游研讨会非常感兴趣，你能告诉我如何申请吗？

Dr. Steven: Sure. Download the application form, fill it in as required and wait for the formal notice.
当然可以，下载申请表，按照要求填好，就等待正式通知了。

Liu Hang: Can I receive the notice as long as I submit the application?
我只要交了申请表，就能收到通知吗？

Dr. Steven: Not necessarily, and it depends on your qualifications.
不一定，这要看你的资格。

Liu Hang: What specific requirements do you have on the attendants?
你们对参加这个会议的人有什么特定的要求吗？

Dr. Steven: The attendants should be experts in the related field and everyone must understand English.
与会者应该是相关领域的专家，每个人都应该懂得英语。

Liu Hang: I see. What other requirements do you have?
我明白了，你们还有别的要求吗？

Dr. Steven: Every attendant should give a 10-minute presentation at the seminar. Have you prepared any article in accordance with[①] the seminar topics?
每个与会者应该在会上发言10分钟。你写了与会议主题相一致的文章了吗？

Liu Hang: Yes, I have.
写了。

Dr. Steven: Then you'll have a good chance to be[②] accepted.
那么，你参加会议的可能性较大。

Liu Hang: I hope so. Thank you so much.
希望如此，谢谢。

Dr. Steven: My pleasure.
不客气。

Attending an International Conference

Dialog 2

Mr. Chairman: Congratulations, Miss Liu. Your presentation was a real success.
刘小姐,祝贺你。你的发言真是成功。

Liu Hang: Thank you, Mr. Chairman. I'm so grateful for your hospitality. I can't find words to express my gratitude.
谢谢,主席先生。谢谢您的盛情,我不知道如何表达我的谢意。

Mr. Chairman: That's all right. Thank you for your effort. I believe everyone present thinks you have made a wonderful job.
不用谢。谢谢你的努力。我相信每个到会的人都认为你做得很不错。

Liu Hang: That caps the climax. I feel very pleased to have such a good resound.
那出乎我的意料,有这么好的反响我感到很高兴。

Mr. Chairman: You deserve it. I'm planning to discuss your research topic after this afternoon's assembly.
这是你应该得到的。我计划在今天下午的会议之后讨论你的研究课题。

Liu Hang: Thank you for your arrangement.
谢谢您的安排。

Dialog 3

Chairman: I hear you won the first award. Congratulations, Miss Liu.
我听说你获得了一等奖,刘小姐,我祝贺你。

Liu Hang: Thanks a lot. I had to omit the details for the presentation, and I have been worrying about it. I wish I had made myself understood[③].
多谢。我发言必须省略细节,我一直在担心。我希望大家都听懂我的发言了。

Chairman: I think so. We were talking about your research project. You really deserved the award.
我也这样想。我们一直在谈论你的研究项目,你得这个奖当之无愧。

Liu Hang:	Thank you. I am very glad it was received so well.
	谢谢,我很高兴受到如此好的欢迎。
Chairman:	Could you spare me thirty minutes to discuss it in detail?
	你能给我 30 分钟详细讨论一下吗?
Liu Hang:	It's my pleasure. How about this evening? I'll have to attend another discussion in five minutes.
	很乐意,晚上如何? 我 5 分钟之内要参加另一个讨论会。
Chairman:	It's good for me. Thank you in advance[④].
	这对我很好,提前谢谢你了。
Liu Hang:	See you this evening.
	今天晚上见。

典型句型

1) I'm very interested in the World Nature-based Tourism Seminar.
   我对世界自然旅游研讨会非常感兴趣。
2) Would you please tell me how to apply for it?
   你能告诉我如何申请吗?
3) Can I receive the notice as long as I submit the application?
   我只要交了申请表,就能收到通知吗?
4) What specific requirements do you have on the attendants?
   你们对参加这个会议的人有什么特定的要求吗?
5) What other requirements do you have?
   你们还有别的要求吗?
6) Your presentation was a real success, Dr. Wang.
   王博士,你的发言真是成功。
7) I hear you won the first award, Dr. Ding.
   我听说你获得了一等奖,丁博士。
8) I had to omit the details for the presentation.
   我发言必须省略细节。
9) I wish I had made myself understood.
   我希望大家都听懂我的发言了。

ATTENDING AN INTERNATIONAL CONFERENCE

10) You really deserved the award.
    你得这个奖当之无愧。
11) Could you spare me thirty minutes to discuss it in detail?
    你能给我 30 分钟详细讨论一下吗？
12) I'll have to attend another discussion in five minutes.
    我 5 分钟之内要去参加另一个讨论会。

背景知识

参加国际会议的礼节：参加国际会议有一些惯常的礼节要遵守，否则就会显得失礼。

(1) 申请：要准确及时地填写申请表格，注意姓名要按照英语的行文习惯，职务要遵守国际惯例，论文题目要醒目，摘要要行文流畅且简明扼要，还要尽早缴纳报名费和会议费。

(2) 入会：认真倾听别人的发言，因为都是行家，肯定都有独到的地方；轮到自己发言也要讲自己独立思考的观点和研究成果，注意语言一定要清晰明白，最好使用多媒体演示系统，图文并茂，并遵守会议限定的时间。

(3) 称赞：会上、会后称赞别人的发言、研究、演讲是一种礼貌的表现，接受别人的称赞也是一种礼貌，千万不要像在国内一样受到称赞时回答"哪里，哪里"、"一点都不好"、"还很不成熟"等之类谦虚的话，如果这样说西方人会认为你虚伪，或者感到不自在。

(4) 语体：国际会议属于正式的交际场合，使用的语体要正式、严谨。对有学术头衔的人要称呼"博士"、"教授"，不要称呼官职。

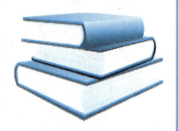

(5) 准时：西方人都比较守时，准时出席是很重要的一项礼节。

注 释

① in accordance with 的意思是"与……一致,与……契合(指见解、观点等)",如:
What you have just said is not in accordance with what we have learned from the witnesses. (你刚才说的和我们从目击者们那里了解到的不一致。)

② have a good chance to do 的意思是"做……的可能性很大",如:
You have a good chance to be made mayor. (你被选为市长的可能性很大。)

③ make oneself understood 中 understood 宾语补足语,字面意思是"使某人自己被听懂",就是"让别人听懂",如:
You should make yourself understood at the meeting. (你应该让别人在会上听懂你的话。)

④ in advance 是"提前,预先"的意思,如:
You must pay for the book in advance. (你必须预付图书的钱。)

Paying a Visit to a Government Office
访问政府机构

Topic Introduction 话题导言

我们到美国去参观、访问、旅游,如有机会,不妨去看看美国的政府机构。一般来说,美国州、县、市政府没有森严的警卫;而联邦机构如总统府、国防部、国会、联邦最高法院和情报机关等的安全检查还是很严格的。所以,到州及州以下政府和立法机构去参观都很随意,去联邦机构只要按照规定接受安全检查就可以了。

一般地,美国联邦政府机构的参观都要排队,分批由接待人员带领参观;而地方各级政府可以随意出入,进门处有秘书负责安排与有关官员见面。如只是想看看,你就直接说想参观一下(I'd just like to look around.)就行了。

Situational Dialogs 情景对话

刘杭(Liu Hang)在朋友 Tommy 的带领下参观了市政府,并对市政某些部门的职责有了初步了解。

Dialog 1

Liu Hang: What're these buildings for, Tommy?
汤米,这些建筑物是做什么用的?

Tommy: This is the city hall. Would you like to stop here to look around?
这是市政厅,想要停下来看看吗?

Liu Hang: Yes. Are all the city departments inside?
是啊,城市的所有部门都在里面吗?

Tommy: Almost. The Department of Health is at this end, and the Department of Utilities is in the western wing....
几乎,卫生局在这头儿,公用事业局在西边……

Liu Hang: How many departments does the city hall have in Bowling Green?
鲍灵格林的市政厅有多少个部门?

Tommy: About ten, barring the federal agencies and the courts. All right, let's go inside to have a look.
大约十个,不包括联邦机构和法院。好了,我们到里面去看看吧。

Dialog 2

Tommy: This is the Office of Permits and Licenses. You've got to have contact with① them if you want to run② a business.
这是许可证办公室,如果你要经商就要和他们打交道了。

Liu Hang: For example, if I want to open a restaurant, what kind of permits do I have to get?
例如,如果我要开餐馆,我需要什么样的许可证呢?

Tommy: You should get a building permit if you need to remodel a building into a restaurant, and after that you need a business permit.
如果你要把一个房子改造成餐馆,需要建筑许可证,然后你需要一个营业许可证。

Liu Hang: Easy to get them?
很容易弄到吗?

Paying a Visit to a Government Office 34

Tommy:	Easy, of course, as long as your business meets the law and their requirements after their inspection. 当然容易，只要经过检查，你的生意符合法律和他们的要求就可以。
Liu Hang:	Does this School Board take charge of③ schooling affairs? 这个教育局是负责学校教育事务吗？
Tommy:	Yes, this department administers all the elementary, junior high and high schools in this school district. 是的，这个部门管理本学区内的所有小学、初中和高中。

Dialog 3

Liu Hang:	What's the cubic building for? 这座方形的建筑物是做什么的？
Tommy:	This is the federal building. Some federal agencies are inside, such as the Federal Regional Court, the Social Security Administration and the Immigration and Naturalization Service District Office. 这是联邦大楼。一些联邦机构在里面，如联邦地区法院、社会安全局和移民局地区办公室。
Liu Hang:	That's another government system, different from the city departments. Right? 那是另一个政府系统，跟市政府部门不同。对吗？
Tommy:	Yes, they're responsible for the federal affairs. I'm thirsty. Let's go to the reception desk for a cup of coffee, shall we? 是的，他们负责联邦事务。我渴了，我们到接待处去喝杯咖啡，好吗？
Liu Hang:	Sure, is it free? 当然，不要钱吗？
Tommy:	No, ten cents for a cup, but the water is free. 要钱，一杯十美分，而水是不要钱的。

Typical Sentences
典型句型

1) What's the cubic building for?
   这座方形的建筑物是做什么的？
2) Some federal agencies are located inside.
   一些联邦机构在里面。
3) These agencies are responsible for the federal affairs.
   这些联邦机构负责联邦事务。
4) Is this Governor's Office here?
   这儿是州长办公室吗？
5) Could you tell where the city hall is?
   能告诉我市政厅在哪里吗？
6) What're these buildings for, Tommy?
   汤米,这些建筑物是做什么用的？
7) Would you like to stop here to look around?
   想要停下来看看吗？
8) Are all the city departments inside?
   城市的所有部门都在里面吗？
9) How many departments does the city hall have?
   市政厅有多少个部门？
10) You'll have contact with them if you want to run a business.
    如果你要经商就要和他们打交道了。
11) Does this School Board take charge of schooling affairs?
    这个教育局是负责学校教育事务吗？
12) Why not go to check the reception desk over there?
    我们怎么不到那边的接待台去问一下呢？

Paying a Visit to a Government Office

Background 背景知识

访问政府机构

美国的政治体制(political system)：美国是联邦制国家，政权组织形式为总统制，实行三权分立与制衡相结合的政治制度和两党制的政党体制。

(1) 政权组织形式：采用总统制，总统为国家元首和政府首脑。实行分权与制衡的原则，立法、行政、司法三种权力分别由国会、总统、法院掌管，三个部门行使权力时，彼此互相牵制，以达到权力平衡。国会有立法权，总统对国会通过的法案有权否决，国会又有权在一定条件下推翻总统的否决；总统有权任命高级官员，但须经国会认可，国会有权依法弹劾总统和高级文官；最高法院法官由总统任命并经国会认可，最高法院又可对国会通过的法律以违宪为由宣布无效。

(2) 国家结构形式：1787年的《美利坚合众国宪法》规定国家结构形式为联邦制，在建立统一的联邦政权的基础上，各州仍保有相当广泛的自主权。联邦设有最高的立法、行政和司法机关，有统一的宪法和法律，是国际交往的主体；各州有自己的宪法、法律和政府机构；若各州的宪法和法律与联邦宪法和法律发生冲突，联邦宪法和法律优于州的宪法和法律。美国宪法列举了联邦政府享有的权力，如征税、举债、铸币、维持军队、主持外交、管理州际和国际贸易等。不经宪法列举的其他权力，除非宪法明文禁止各州行使者外，一概为各州保留。州的权力主要是处理本州范围内的事务，如以地方名义征税、管理州内工商业和劳工、组织警卫力量和维持治安，等等。

(3) 选举制度：美国总统选举实行间接选举制。首先由各州选民投票选出本州选举人(人数与本州国会议员人数相等)，再由各州选举人同时在各州首府投票选举正、副总统。议员选举实行直接选举制。众议员、参议员由各州选民直接选举；州长、议员和某些州的法官、重要行政官员都由选民选举产生。

(4) 政党制度：采用两党制。美国宪法虽然没有规定政党地位，但政党是美国政治制度的重要组成部分，其影响渗透于其他各种

政治制度。两党的主要职能是操纵和包办选举,特别是总统选举。民主党和共和党两党长期轮流执政,其他一些政党都无法影响两大党轮流执政的地位。

（5）公民权利制度：美国宪法和法律规定,政府的权力来自人民,最终属于人民；政府的权力不是绝对的,而是受宪法和法律限制的。联邦宪法和法律一方面规定公民享有人身保护、言论、出版、集会、宗教信仰自由,私有财产权和选举权等权利；另一方面规定,国会不得制定剥夺公民的言论、出版、和平集会和请愿等自由的法律,公民的人身、住宅、文件和财产不受非法的搜查或扣押,非依法定正当程序,不得剥夺任何人的生命、自由或财产。此外,各州宪法和法律对公民的权利也有规定。

注释

① contact with 是"打交道"的意思,能够和很多动词连用,如：be in contact with（和……接触、有联系）, be out of contact with（脱离接触,失去联系）, bring into contact with（使接触,使与……联系）, throw in contact with（使接触,使与……联系）, come into (in) contact with（接触,碰上）, have contact with（接触到,和……有联系）, lose contact with（和……失去联系,离开）, make contact with（和……接触）。

② run 原意为"跑,奔驰",这里的意思是"经营",如：run a company（经营公司）。run 还可构成以下短语：
run away（潜逃）
run down（停掉,用完；筋疲力尽）
run into（达到；偶然碰见）
run over（碾过；浏览）
run out of（耗尽,用完）

③ take charge of 和 in charge of 都是"对……负责"的意思,如：
The chief engineer was in charge of directing the building of the subway.
（总工程师负责指挥地铁的建造工程。）

A Visit to Law Courts
参观法院

Topic Introduction
话题导言

各国的法律体系不同,法院的组织系统和审判制度也不同。出国留学、定居,乃至出国访问都涉及到各种法律问题,到法院去参观不仅能够增长见识,而且能够了解不同的司法体系。如果以后要在那里生活,与法院打交道是免不了的事情。

与政府机构一样,司法机关也是对公众开放的,不管是谁都可以参观,也可以旁听法院的审判,电视节目有时也直播法院的审判活动。

Situational Dialogs
情景对话

除了政府机关,美国的司法机构也是对外公开的,刘杭(Liu Hang)和朋友一起去参观了当地法院。

Dialog 1

Tommy: Today, we'll arrange you for① a visit to the local court.
今天我们将安排你们参观当地的法院。

Liu Hang: That's a good chance for us to know more about the United States. What kind of court are we going to visit today?

那是我们更多了解美国的一个好机会，我们今天要参观的法院是个什么样的法院？

Tommy: It's a federal regional court.
是一个联邦地区法院。

Liu Hang: It's said that the United States court systems are very complex.
据说美国的法院系统很复杂。

Tommy: Yes, the whole country has two court systems, one is the federal system, and the other is the state system.
是的，整个国家有两个法院系统，一个是联邦法院系统，一个是州法院系统。

Liu Hang: Are all the federal courts for appeals?
所有的联邦法院都是上诉法院吗？

Tommy: No, the federal court system has its own court of first instance, court of cassation and Supreme Court, and so does the state system.②
不是，联邦法院系统有它自己的初审法院、上诉法院和最高法院，州法院系统也一样。

Liu Hang: What's the difference of jurisdiction between the two systems?
两个系统的管辖权区别是什么？

Tommy: The difference is great, very great. The federal system exercises③ jurisdiction over law cases related to federal laws, international treaties, foreign governments, and interstate affairs, whereas the state system only deals with in-state law cases.
区别很大，非常大。联邦法院系统管辖涉及联邦法律、国际条约、外国政府和州际事务的案件；而州法院系统只管辖本州内的案件。

Liu Hang: That's really complicated.
那真是很复杂。

Dialog 2

Tommy: Here we are at the Lake Charles Federal Regional Court.
我们到了查尔斯湖联邦地区法院。

Liu Hang: It doesn't look very arresting, and I've noticed that almost all the federal buildings are of the same pattern and style.

35 A Visit to Law Courts

看起来不是很显眼，而且我注意到几乎所有的联邦建筑都是一个样子和风格。

Tommy: I agree. Please watch your steps. The western wing is the criminal court and the eastern wing is the civil court.

我也这样认为。请注意台阶。西翼是刑事法庭，东翼是民事法庭。

Liu Hang: Is a jury always necessary for a trial?

每次审讯都要组织陪审团吗？

Tommy: Not necessarily, it depends on the complexity and importance of the case. Most of the times, only one judge can hear④ a lawsuit.

不一定，得看案件的复杂性和重要性。多数时候，只有一个法官审案。

Liu Hang: What if either party thinks that the judgment is a miscarriage of justice?

要是有一方认为判决审判不公，怎么办？

Tommy: He may lodge an appeal to the Federal Court of Cassation in his district.

他可以上诉到本地区的联邦上诉法院。

典型句型

1) It's said that the United States court systems are very complex.
据说美国的法院系统很复杂。

2) What kind of court are we going to visit today?
我们今天要参观的法院是个什么样的法院？

3) It's a federal regional court.
这是一个联邦地区法院。

4) What's the difference of jurisdiction between the two systems?
两个系统的管辖权区别是什么？

5) This case falls within the competence of the court.
这个案件在这个法院的管辖之内。

6) Is the attorney very important in a trial?
   律师在审讯中很重要吗?

7) What kind of law cases should be judged in camera?
   什么样的案件应该秘密审判?

8) Is a jury always necessary for a trial?
   每次审讯都要组织陪审团吗?

9) What if either party thinks that the judgment is a miscarriage of justice?
   要是有一方认为判决审判不公,怎么办?

10) I believe that witnesses, evidences and procedures are the most important factors to receive a favorable judgment in a lawsuit.
    我认为,证人、证据和诉讼程序是获得诉讼有利判决的最重要的因素。

背景知识

美国法院组织(Court System of the United States):美国是英、美法系国家。美国司法制度的主要特点有:贯彻三权分立的原则,实行司法独立;法院组织分为联邦和地方两大系统;联邦最高法院享有特殊的司法审查权;等等。

美国法院组织划分为联邦和各州两大系统,名称和审级不尽相同,管辖权限错综复杂。法院一般是民事、刑事兼理。联邦系统的法院包括:

(1) 联邦地方法院(Federal Regional Court):是普通民事、刑事案件的初审法院,设在各州的联邦地方法院只审理属于联邦管辖的案件,设在首都哥伦比亚特区和领地的联邦地方法院,则兼理联邦管辖和地方管辖的案件。

(2) 联邦上诉法院(Federal Court of Cassation):分设在全国 11 个司法巡回区,受理本巡回区内对联邦地方法院判决不服的上诉案件,以及对联邦系统的专门法院的判决和某些具有部分司法权

A Visit to Law Courts

的行政机构的裁决不服而上诉的案件。

（3）联邦最高法院（Federal Supreme Court）：是美国联邦法院系统的最高审级和最高审判机关。法官均由总统征得参议院同意后任命；只要忠于职守，可终身任职，非经国会弹劾不得免职。美国宪法规定，联邦最高法院对涉及大使、其他使节和领事以及一州为诉讼一方的案件有初审权；对州最高法院或联邦上诉法院审理的案件，有权就法律问题进行复审；有权颁发"调审令"，调审下级联邦法院或州法院审理的案件。联邦最高法院还拥有司法审查权，审查联邦或州的立法或行政行为是否违宪。不论是初审案件，还是复审案件，都是终审判决。

（4）美国最高法院（United States Supreme Court）：是全国最高审级，由总统征得参议院同意后任命的9名终身法官组成，其判例对全国有约束力，享有特殊的司法审查（judicial review）权，即有权通过具体案例宣布联邦或各州的法律是否违宪。

联邦法院系统还有各种专门法院，如索赔法院、关税和专利权上诉法院；地方法院也有关税法院、征税法院等专门法院。

州系统的法院名称各州不一，一般分3级，其下还设有各种不列为审级的小型法院。（1）基层法院：一般称州地方法院、州巡回法院、州高等法院或州普通诉讼法院，为属州管辖的一般民刑事案件的初审法院，多数州规定须召集陪审团审理。（2）州上诉法院：大部分州设有州上诉法院，作为中级上诉法院。（3）州最高法院：州的最高审级是州最高法院，有的州称为最高审判法院、违法行为处理法院。也有的州分设民事最高法院和刑事最高法院。纽约州的法院组织比较特殊，其初审法院称为州最高法院，内分家事庭和遗嘱验证庭等。上诉级为上述法院的上诉庭，不另设法院。最高审级称州上诉法院。

Notes 注释

① arrange for 是"安排"的意思,如:
I have arranged for a car. (我已经准备好了一辆汽车。)

② "so + 助动词"这个结构是说明另外一个人或事物和前述的情况一样,如:
You were on time and so was I. (你很准时,我也一样。)

③ exercise 这里是动词"行使,运用"的意思,如:
What others think exercises great influence on most of us. (别人的想法对我们多数人产生很大的影响。)
exercise 还有"使(人)担忧,使(人)忙碌"的意思,如:
I am very much exercised about the future. (我对未来大伤脑筋。)

④ hear 是"审理,审讯"的意思,如:
The judge heard the case. (法官审讯了这件案子。)

Visiting a Corporation
到公司参观

Topic Introduction
话题导言

经常有国内的行业代表团前往欧美国家进行实地考察,他们往往会被安排到这些国家的某个公司去参观。这样做的目的主要是开阔视野,也确实比读很多有关国外公司介绍的书籍还来得管用。这正应了"百闻不如一见"那句话。

不同的公司有不同的业务范围,公司有大有小,名称也不同,Co.是 company 的缩写,多指商业公司(company);Inc.是股份有限公司(Incorporated);Corp.指的是 corporation(公司、财团法人);而 Div.只是公司的一个部分或部门(division);Establishment 是商业机构的营业处所;还有 firm 也是指公司,多半是合伙商号。到公司参观,谈论的话题或行为不要涉及到商业秘密和个人隐私,如不要翻阅非公开展示的资料,不要询问员工的工资等。

Situational Dialogs
情景对话

俗话说"耳听为虚,眼见为实",关于国外公司的书读得再多,也比不上实地考察管用。高卫平(Weiping)一行在接待方的安排下参观了国外公司。

Dialog 1

Alice: Our Company occupies① these two stories. The fourth floor is office area for staff, and the fifth floor is a showroom and some conference rooms.
我们公司使用了两层楼。四层是工作人员办公区,五层是陈列室和会议室。

Weiping: All the offices are very neat and orderly. You have a very good management.
所有的办公室都很整洁,秩序井然。你们管理得很不错。

Alice: Did you happen② to know our company in your country?
在你们国家的时候,你知道本公司吗?

Weiping: We often hear about③ your company, for it's a world-famous one. How many people are working in this division?
我们常常听说贵公司,因为是世界闻名的。你们这个分公司有多少人?

Alice: We have about 1200 employees, three hundred in the office and nine hundred in the plant.
我们大约有1200名员工,办公室有300名,工厂有900名。

Weiping: Where is your head office?
你们的总公司在哪里?

Alice: The headquarters of the Group Corporation is in Detroit, but the head office of the laptop computer manufacture is in Seattle.
集团公司的总部在底特律,笔记本电脑生产的总部在西雅图。

Dialog 2

Weiping: When was your company established?
你们公司是什么时候建立的?

Alice: This division began its business in 1996, but the head office was established in 1950s.
这个分公司1996年开始营业,但是总公司在20世纪50年代就成立了。

Visiting a Corporation 36
到公司参观

Weiping:	What line of business are you in?
	你们主要从事哪方面的行业？
Alice:	The Company supplies a wide range of④ office automation devices and we're also a manufacturer and seller of quality fabrics.
	本公司供应多种不同的办公室自动化设备，而且我们还是高级布料的制造商兼售卖商。
Weiping:	Do you invest overseas?
	你们在海外有投资吗？
Alice:	Yes, we have twenty branches outside the United States, and we've recently opened a new one in Bangkok.
	有，我们在美国之外有二十家分公司，最近在曼谷新开了一家。
Weiping:	That's great. You don't have any branches in China, do you?
	那真是了不起。你们在中国还没有分支机构，是吗？
Alice:	No, not yet. We're investigating Chinese market. Would you like to have a look at our showroom?
	还没有呢，我们正在调查中国市场。你们想看看我们的展览室吗？
Weiping:	Sure.
	当然了。

典型句型

1) When was your company established?
   你们公司是什么时候建立的？
2) Did you happen to know our company in your country?
   在你们国家的时候，你知道本公司吗？
3) You have a very good management.
   你们管理得很不错。
4) All the offices are very neat and orderly.
   所有的办公室都很整洁，秩序井然。

5) How many people are working in this division?
   你们这个分公司有多少人？
6) Where is your head office?
   你们的总公司在哪里？
7) What line of business are you in?
   你们主要从事哪方面的行业？
8) Do you invest overseas?
   你们在海外有投资吗？
9) You don't have any branches in China, do you?
   你们在中国还没有分支机构，是吗？
10) Would you like to have a look at our showroom?
    你们想看看我们的展览室吗？
11) Shall I show you our product information sheet?
    要不要看看我们的产品说明书？
12) We're very eager to learn something of your latest products.
    我们很愿意了解你们的最新产品。
13) Is the system you have adopted original?
    你们所采用的系统是全新的吗？

在美国注册公司：在美国成立一家公司需要经过复杂的手续和程序，必须根据市政府、州政府和联邦政府的法规进行注册登记。现在，美国的各行各业都有其行业法规，每个行业的经营者都要遵循其法规运营行商。

（1）选择公司种类：注册成立美国公司有很多不同的选择，不同类型的公司享有不同的权利及负有不同税务责任，在决定成立公司之前，必须做好详细的研究分析及咨询。最常用的有 Sole Proprietorship（独资经营公司）、General Partnership（合股公司）、Limited Partnership（有限合股经营）、C Corporations（C 股份公司）、S Corporations（S 股份有限公司）、Limited Liability Companies（股

Visiting a Corporation

份有限公司)等。

（2）登记注册：美国五十个州设有专门的登记注册部门，各州在注册登记时有不同的要求，收费也有所不同。

（3）业务牌照：美国有些类型的业务或职业需要专门的牌照，如保险业、房地产经纪等等，各市政府，各州政府有其法规。需要预先向相关部门查询，可以了解到最新的信息，比如在美国纽约州可以提供有关的信息资料的是政府注册办公室（State Office of Business Permit and Regulatory Assistance）。

（4）公司名称：为了防止重复使用公司名称或盗用相同的公司名称，各州政府注册部门在受理申请公司注册表格时都要进行调查，在确认没有相同公司名称已注册的情况下，才会批准登记新公司的名称。

（5）商业招牌：所有公司只有在城市建筑房屋管理部门获取商业招牌许可证后，才能够公开悬挂或展示公司招牌，如霓虹灯或灯箱，这都需先申请许可证。

（6）无障碍设施：所有的商业建筑物必须符合当地的残障人士保护条例，如出入口、洗手间的设施等都需符合要求。

（7）销售税号：一般的零售、批发商及提供事业服务的公司都需向各州的财税部申请销售税号码（Sales Tax）并填写 DTF-17 表格。

（8）雇主识别：除 Sole Proprietorships（独资经营公司）外的所有商业机构必须向税务局（IRS）索取雇主识别号码（EIN）及填写 SS-4 表格。雇主识别号码又称公司税号，是开设银行商业账号，报税必须提供的资料之一。如 Sole Proprietorships 的雇主要为其员工报税或建立退休计划，也需先申请雇主识别号码。

（9）制造厂商出产的货品必须要取得货品条形码（bar code）以后才能在零售店出售。

注释

① occupy 在这里的意思是"使用房间,占据",如:
The house is occupied.(那房子有人住着。)
其常用意思为"占领,占据",如:occupy an important position(占重要地位)。

② happen 是"凑巧,碰巧"的意思,如:
She happened to be out.(她恰巧出去了。)

③ hear about 是"听说"的意思,和 hear of 是同义短语,如:
Have you heard about my friend O'Neal in Louisiana?(你听说过我的在路易斯安那的朋友奥尼尔吗?)

④ a wide range of 是"很宽范围"的意思,如:
We have a wide rage of temperature this season.(这个季节气温变化很大。)

Touring a Factory
参观工厂

Topic Introduction
话题导言

出国访问、旅行有时候要到工厂去参观,特别是出国进行生产技术交流、经济贸易合作等项目时,到他们的现代化工厂去看一看是很有必要的。一来可以增长见识,了解某种产品的生产流程;更重要的是可以看看人家的车间管理,学习他们的经验。

美国的大型工厂都有参观通道,参观者可以沿着参观线路观看整个生产过程,从原料到成品的整个流程都一览无余。很多企业都对外来参观者进行讲解,还可以随时向流水线上的人员提问。到工厂参观最重要的一点就是注意安全,特别是要跟着"导游"沿着线路走,不要随便触摸机器和仪器,也不要对某个东西过于关心,否则被认为是要窃取技术机密就不容易说清楚了。

Situational Dialogs
情景对话

在国外到工厂去参观是很有必要的。高卫平(Weiping)今天的行程是去参观现代化的工厂,这对于以后开展项目合作是非常有利的。

Dialog 1

Jenny: Hello, everyone, welcome to our factory.
各位好，欢迎来到我们工厂。

Weiping: We've been looking forward to seeing your factory, for it's very famous.
我们一直期待着参观你们的工厂，你们工厂很有名气。

Jenny: This is our brochure. It's a brief introduction to the workshops.
这是我们的小册子，是对我们各车间的简单介绍。

Weiping: Yes, it's so beautiful.
是啊，很漂亮。

Jenny: Before we go around the workshops, we'll watch a video introducing our factory and our main products.
在参观车间之前，我们看一个介绍本厂和主要产品的录像。

Weiping: Good, that'll give us a whole impression.
很好，那会给我们一个整体印象。

Dialog 2

Jenny: Please follow me into this workshop. Watch your steps, for the visiting path is narrow.
请跟我到这个车间来，注意台阶，参观通道很窄。

Weiping: Thank you for your consideration.
谢谢你的关照。

Jenny: Would you come this way, please? That's dangerous. Please keep off①.
请这边走好吗？那很危险，请勿靠近。

Weiping: All right. May I ask some questions?
好的，我可以问几个问题吗？

Jenny: Please feel free to② ask any questions.
请随意提问。

Weiping: What's your annual capacity?
你们的年产量是多少？

Jenny: We produced about 18,000 units last year. It's supposed to③ increase this year.
我们去年生产了 18,000 台。今年应该还会增加。

Touring a Factory 37

Weiping:	When was this workshop founded? 这个车间是什么时候建立的?
Jenny:	It has a history of forty years, but these equipments were bought home only three years ago. 有四十年的历史了,但这些设备只是在三年以前买回来的。
Weiping:	Could you tell me the cost price of each unit? 能告诉我这每台的成本价格吗?
Jenny:	I'm sorry but that's confidential. I can't answer your question. 很抱歉,那是机密。我无法回答您的问题。

Dialog 3

Jenny:	How about a coffee break④? 我们休息一下,喝杯咖啡如何?
Weiping:	Time passes quickly. Say, it's about lunchtime. 时间过得真快。嘿,差不多是午餐时间了。
Jenny:	What do you think of these workshops? 你们对我们的这些车间有什么看法?
Weiping:	They've given us a very deep impression, especially the equipments and the working environment. 给了我们很深刻的印象,尤其是设备和工作环境。
Jenny:	We've spent a great deal of money on⑤ equipments, but it'll benefit the whole factory over the long run. 我们在设备上已经投下巨额的金钱,但就长远看对整个工厂是有利的。
Weiping:	How long did you take to establish such a production line? 建立这样一条生产线,你们花了多长时间?
Jenny:	Around three months, from installing the equipment to debugging. 从安装设备到调试,大约花了三个月。
Weiping:	You have a very efficient factory. I have confidence in establishing a long-term business relationship with you. 你们是个很有效率的工厂。我有信心与你们建立长期的商业关系。

221

Typical Sentences
典型句型

1) We've been expecting to visit your factory.
   我们一直盼望着参观你们的工厂。
2) We hope to learn a lot from this tour.
   我们希望能从这次参观中学到很多东西。
3) Could you give us your brochure?
   能把你们的小册子给我们看看吗?
4) May I have a look at your pamphlets?
   我可以看看你们的小册子吗?
5) May I ask some questions about the equipment?
   我能问几个有关设备方面的问题吗?
6) Would you please explain it again?
   请再解释一下好吗?
7) When was the workshop founded?
   这个车间是什么时候建立的?
8) When were these machines made?
   这些机器是什么时候制造的?
9) Are these machines the most advanced in the world?
   这些机器是世界上最先进的吗?
10) I'd like to discuss a few details with your manager tomorrow.
    我想明天和你们经理讨论几个细节问题。
11) You certainly have a big operation with very fine facilities here.
    你们的经营规模实在很大,这儿的设备也相当好。
12) You have a very efficient factory.
    你们有个很有效率的工厂。
13) I have confidence in establishing a long-term business relationship with you.
    我有信心与你们建立长期的商业关系。

Touring a Factory

Background 背景知识

美国工业概况：美国工业以技术先进、门类齐全、资源丰富、生产实力雄厚、劳动生产率高而著称于世，石油、天然气、电力、汽车、飞机、微电子工业、计算机技术、激光技术、宇航技术、生物工程技术、核能利用和新材料等方面，在世界上均居领先地位。

20世纪80年代以来，美国工业发展呈现一种不平衡状态，一方面，传统工业面临国际上新兴工业国家的剧烈竞争，正呈衰落状态，被称之为"夕阳工业"；另一方面，以高科技工业为核心的新兴工业部门则呈现出蓬勃向上的趋势，在一定程度上抵消了整个工业水平下降的趋势。

自70年代中后期以来，美国工业虽面临来自多方面的挑战，但其在世界工业中所占的份额一直保持在25%至26%的水平。有两种工业很值得一说：

（1）汽车工业：美国汽车工业是上世纪初兴起的一个工业部门，美国经济的三大支柱之一。1978年，美国汽车产量达到1290万辆的历史最高点后逐年下降，美国三家最大的汽车公司（通用汽车公司、福特汽车公司和克莱斯勒汽车公司）都出现了10亿美元以上的亏损。为此，这三家大汽车公司都在80年代着手进行了企业调整和改革。经过80年代上半期的改造与调整，美国汽车工业到80年代后半期渡过了难关，使美国汽车产量连续几年保持在1100万辆的水平，三大汽车公司的汽车产量均居世界最先进行列。

（2）高科技工业：与美国传统工业普遍衰败的状况相反，美国的高科技工业则生机勃勃，呈现出高速发展的潜力。电子计算机和信息处理技术是现代高科技工业的核心，美国在这一方面一直处于世界领先地位。在现代通信技术方面，美国也具有绝对的优势。在卫星、运载火箭、空间试验站、航天飞机及太空科学试验装置方面，美国尚未遇到他国的有力挑战。

注释

① keep off 指"避开,不接近"。由 keep 构成的短语还有很多,如:
keep up with(跟上),keep to(坚持,保持),keep on(继续进行),
keep out of(维持,继续)等等。

② feel free to do something 是"随意做什么",如:
Please feel free to walk around the campus.(请随便在校园内走走。)

③ be supposed to 可以理解为"应该,必须"等,如:
We are not supposed to smoke here.(我们不能在这儿抽烟。)

④ break 可用于工间或课间的休息,如:a lunch / coffee break(午餐时间的/喝咖啡时间的休息)。

⑤ spend money on something 是"花钱买什么东西"的意思,如:
They spent all their creative resources on futile projects.(他们将所有的创造力浪费在无益的项目上。)

还有一个搭配也要注意,spend time (in) doing something 是"花时间做什么事情"的意思,如:
Now more and more city adults spend their leisure time trying to improve themselves at school or college.(现在城市里越来越多的成年人利用业余时间到学校或大学去深造。)

Visiting a Farm
参观农场

Topic Introduction
话题导言

牛羊成群、大型机械、单家独院、土地连片这样的词语可以很恰当地描述美国的农场。当然,不同地区的农村也有不同的景象,有的以牧业为主,但已不是游牧而是围栏圈养;有的以养殖业为主,但更像在工厂里养鸡养猪;有的以种植业为主,土地成片,机械化耕作。

参观农场给人的感觉与在大城市逛街决然不同,你可以在主人的带领下到周围看看,也可以征得主人同意后自己欣赏农村风光,你最终会得出一个结论:全世界的农民都很朴实厚道。

Situational Dialogs
情景对话

刘杭(Liu Hang)同朋友驾车出游,途中偶然看见一片果园,果园的主人 Jimmy 十分热情,他们这次又长了不少见识。后来他们又去了老师 Bill 家里。

Dialog 1

Liu Hang: There's an orchard ahead. Shall we stop to have a look?
前面有一片果园,我们停车看看吧?

Larry: Sure, I also want to know something about a US farm.
可以,我也想了解一下美国的农场。

Liu Hang: Ah, it's an apple orchard. Why have so many apples fallen on the ground?
啊,是个苹果园。怎么这么多苹果掉在地上?

Larry: I don't know, either. Let's ask the owner of the orchard.
我也不知道,我们去问问果园主人。

……

Liu Hang: Excuse me, sir. Why have so many apples fallen on the ground?
打搅一下,先生。怎么这么多苹果掉在地上?

Jimmy: Aha, you see the trees fructify too many and too many apples will consume too much nutrition from the trees, so that I cut off those small ones and keep the better ones.
啊哈,你看这些树结果实太多,而太多果实又会消耗太多树的养分,因此我就把那些小的给剪掉了,而留下了大的。

Liu Hang: You want the rest apples to grow better?
你是要让剩下的长得更好?

Jimmy: Yes, and doing this[①] is a way to protect the trees. Have a taste of my fruit over there?
是的,这样做也是保护果树的一种方法。到那边去尝一下我的水果,好吗?

Liu Hang: We'd like to, thanks a lot. We want to go around your orchard.
很愿意,谢谢。我们就想看看你的果园。

Dialog 2

Liu Hang: Jimmy you have a big forest.
吉米,你有一大片森林。

Jimmy: Yes, my house is just like a castle. I'll show you something special. Let's go into the woods.
是的,我的房子就像是城堡一样。我给你看点儿特别的东西,我们到树林里面去吧。

38 Visiting a Farm

参观农场

Liu Hang:	All right. Do you have some precious deposits underground[2]?
	好的,你的地下有宝藏吗?
Jimmy:	Yes, you're right. Be careful and don't trample my treasure. Look, here they are!
	是的,说对了。小心,别踩了我的宝贝。看,这些就是了。
Liu Hang:	What are these small plants? I cannot make them out[3].
	这些小植物是什么?我认不出来。
Jimmy:	They are my bank. Ginsengs, American ginsengs.
	它们就是我的银行——人参,美国人参。
Liu Hang:	I've heard of[4] that, and have eaten them as well. It's a kind of medicine, a very famous medicine. We have them in the Northeast China, you know.
	我听说过,而且还吃过。这是一种药,一种有名的药。我们中国东北有,你知道吧。
Jimmy:	Yes, but the most precious ones grow in the wilderness of Korean Peninsula.
	是的,但是最珍贵的是生长在朝鲜半岛野外的。

Dialog 3

Liu Hang:	Bill, you're a great man.
	比尔,你是个了不起的人。
Bill:	Why do you say so?
	这从何说起?
Liu Hang:	You're a professor at the university, and also you have so large a farm and so wide a forest[5].
	你是大学教授,又有这么大的一个农场,这么宽阔的一片森林。
Bill:	Perhaps. The wheat land is about 800 acres and the forest is more than 2000 acres with 150,000 pine trees.
	也许吧。麦地大约有800英亩,森林超过2000英亩,有150,000棵松树。
Liu Hang:	No wonder you built your house with pine logs. Your wheat seems different from ours in China.
	难怪你都用松树原木建造房子。你的小麦似乎和我们中国的不同。

Jimmy: We have a long winter here, so we sow the seeds in spring and harvest in late fall.
我们这里冬天很长,所以我们春天播种,秋末收割。

Liu Hang: Yours is spring wheat, the same with that of Northeast China.
你的是春小麦,和中国东北的相同。

Jimmy: Correct, and it's different from that of Central China.
正确,和中国华中地区的不同。

Typical Sentences
典型句型

1) What are the principal farm products in this area?
   这个地区的主要农产品是什么?
2) There's an orchard ahead. Shall we stop to have a look?
   前面有一片果园,我们停车看看吧?
3) We want to go around your orchard.
   我们就想看看你的果园。
4) I also want to know something about a US farm.
   我也想了解一下美国的农场。
5) What are these small plants? I cannot make them out.
   这些小植物是什么? 我认不出来。
6) In this flat country people grow rice and raise cattle.
   在这土地平坦的乡间,人们种植水稻,饲养牲畜。
7) Farmers plow their fields and sow in spring.
   农民在春天犁地播种。
8) You have so large a farm and so wide a forest.
   你有这么大一个农场,这么宽阔的一片森林。
9) Your wheat seems different from ours in China.
   你的小麦似乎和我们中国的不同。
10) On many farms you will find cows and chickens.
    在许多农场你都会看到奶牛和鸡。
11) Many modern machines have revolutionized farming.
    许多现代机器革新了耕作方法。

Visiting a Farm

Background 背景知识

美国农业概况：美国自然资源丰富，发展农业有着得天独厚的条件。全国大部分地区雨量充沛而且分布比较均匀，土地、草原和森林资源的拥有量均位于世界前列。土质肥沃，海拔500米以下的平原占国土面积的55%，有利于农业的机械化耕作和规模经营，美国的耕地面积约占国土总面积的20%，为18,817万公顷，人均接近0.8公顷。美国还有永久性草地2.4亿公顷，森林和林地2.65亿公顷。

农业专业化程度很高，形成了一些著名的生产带，如玉米带、小麦带、棉花带等。早在1914年，美国农业已经在很大程度上实现了种植专业化，这种格局保持至今。这种区域分工使美国各个地区能充分地发挥各自的比较优势，有利于降低成本，提高生产率。通畅的水陆运输网的建立更进一步促进了区域分工专业化的生产，而区域分工和专业化生产也有力地推动了附近地区相关产业的发展。

农产品经常出现过剩，对国际市场的依赖性很大。美国是世界上最大的农产品出口国，它的农产品约有1/5供出口之用。美国农业产值还不到国内生产总值的3%，但20世纪90年代初，农业出口却占总出口的9%以上。由此可见，美国农业十分依赖于国际市场。一旦国际市场上农产品供过于求，美国政府就会面临农产品过剩问题。最为典型的事件发生在20世纪30年代初，当时因农产品过剩而引起了严重的农业危机，曾使农业遭到毁灭性的打击。

美国种植业主要包括几个重要的种植带。(1)东北部和"新英格兰"的牧草和乳牛带，指西弗吉尼亚以东的12个州。(2)中北部玉米带，指"中北部"大湖区附近的8个州。(3)大平原小麦带，北从与加拿大接壤的北达科他州、蒙大拿州往南直到俄克拉荷马州以及得克萨斯州的北部，共9个州。(4)南部棉花带，东起大西洋沿岸，西至得克萨斯州东部。(5)太平洋沿岸综合农业区，受太平洋暖流的影响，气候温和湿润，宜于多种农作物的生长。

美国的畜牧业是高度发达的产业，也是资金和技术密集的产业。畜牧业的分布与种植带虽有一定的关系，但并不十分明显。美国的东北地区饲养的奶牛头数约占全国的1/3，生产的牛奶和奶制品几乎占全国的一半，肉鸡生产也占重要的地位。玉米带提供玉米、豆饼等饲料，为当地养猪业提供了良好的条件，这是美国最大的猪肉生产基地。美国西部的"草原带"以放牧为主，可以饲养牛、羊、马等。美国畜产品在世界上占有巨大的份额。

注 释

① 动名词、不定式以及从句都可以充当句子的主语，但切记谓语动词需用单数。如：

To see is to believe.（眼见为实。）

What I have said is right.（我说的话都是对的。）

② underground 在这里作形容词指"地下的"，作名词时意思是"（英国的）地下铁路"，美国则用 subway。

③ make out 是个多义短语，有"了解，写（支票、账目等），有（友好）关系，声称，伪装，把……说成，论证，证明"等意思，如：

He immediately sat down and made out a check.（他立刻坐下来开了一张支票。）

How did you make out with your classmates?（你和同班同学关系如何？）

He makes out he's younger than me.（他声称比我年轻。）

He's not such a good doctor as some people make out.（他不是某些人所说的那样好的医生。）

④ hear of 意思是"知道，了解"，多用于否定和疑问句中，如：

I have never heard of the place.（我从没听说过那个地方。）

另外需注意的短语还有 hear about something（听到关于某事的消

Visiting a Farm

息)，hear form somebody（收到某人的来信或者电话）。

⑤ so large a farm 和 so wide a forest 是以形容词为中心词的结构，相当于说 such a large farm 和 such a wide forest，如：
You are so beautiful a girl.（你是这么漂亮的一个姑娘。）

About China: Geography & History
中国地理和历史

Topic Introduction
话题导言

  普通的西方人对中国的了解非常有限,当他们知道你来自于中国的时候,很可能会向你了解一些关于中国的情况。笔者曾经翻阅过美国路易斯安那州的中学课本,关于中国的内容非常少,历史课本中只有一章的内容是介绍中国的。这是因为他们大部分是欧洲移民的后裔,重视欧洲的历史和地理是理所当然的。

  对于我们中国人来说,介绍我们自己国家的地理和历史应该不是问题,但用英语把问题说明白还是不简单,有些时候还要使对方有可以参照的对象,比如说,"中国面积有960万平方公里(China covers an area of 9,600,000 square kilometers.)"这句话中表达的"960万平方公里",普通的美国人是没有概念的,因为他们不使用"平方公里"而使用"英亩、公顷、平方英里、平方英尺"这样的单位来表达面积。如果这时候把整句话说成 China covers an area of 9,600,000 square kilometers, a little larger than the United States.(中国有960万平方公里,比美国略微大一点儿。)就表达清楚了。

About China: Geography & History

Situational Dialogs 情景对话

中国地理和历史

和中国人渴望了解西方一样,西方人同样对古老而神秘的中国充满了疑问,刘杭(Liu Hang)的同学 Bill 对中国充满了好奇。

Dialog 1

Bill: Hey, you're from China, right?
嗨,你从中国来的,是吗?

Liu Hang: Yes. Have you ever been[①] there before?
是啊,你以前去过了吗?

Bill: Not yet. What's the area of your country?
还没有呢,你们国家的面积有多大?

Liu Hang: China is very big, covering an area of 9,600,000 square kilometers, a little larger than the United States.
中国很大,有960万平方公里,比美国略微大一点儿。

Bill: Even larger than America?
比美国还要大?

Liu Hang: Yes. But the landform of China is different, more mountainous and hilly than the United States.
是啊,但是中国的地形不同,比美国的山地和丘陵要多些。

Bill: I hear you've built a huge dam on the Three Gorges. Where's it?
我听说你们在三峡上建了一座大坝,是在什么地方?

Liu Hang: It's in the central part of China, on the Yangtze River, and this is the longest river in China and one of the longest in the world.
在中国的中部,在长江上。长江是中国最长的河流,也是世界上最长的河流之一。

Bill: Do you have snow in winter?
你们冬天下雪吗?

Liu Hang: It snows a lot in the north and northeast, but it doesn't in South China. In winter, sometimes it's minus 20°F, but it may be over 80°F on Hainan Island.
北方和东北下雪很多,但华南地区不下雪。冬天北方有时是零下华氏20度,而海南岛却在华氏80度以上。

Bill: The difference is really big.
差别真是很大。

Dialog 2

Bill: Do you have very big cities, like New York City?
你们有很大的城市吗,像纽约这么大的?

Liu Hang: Yes, we do. The city population is larger than that of your whole country. Shanghai is the biggest city. Have you heard of this city?
有,城市人口比你们国家的总人口还多。上海是最大的城市,听说过吗?

Bill: Yes, it's on the seaside of the Pacific. Is Beijing also very big?
听说过,在太平洋的海滨,北京也很大吗?

Liu Hang: Yes, it's the second largest, and it's a very ancient capital.
是的,第二大,也是一个古都。

Bill: How many provinces or states in your country?
你们国家有多少个省或州?

Liu Hang: The country is divided into 23 provinces, 4 municipalities directly under the Central Government, 5 autonomous regions and 2 special administrative regions.
全国分成23个省、4个直辖市、5个自治区和2个特别行政区。

Bill: Where's Hong Kong?
香港在哪里?

Liu Hang: Hong Kong is in South China, facing South China Sea.
香港在华南地区,面向南海。

About China: Geography & History

Dialog 3

Bill: To us Americans, China is an ancient and mysterious country.
对我们美国人来说,中国是一个古老而神秘的国家。

Liu Hang: Yes, China is a great country with a history of more than 5000 years.
是啊,中国是一个有五千多年历史的伟大国家。

Bill: Was China made up of② many small states long before?
很久以前,中国是由很多小国家组成的吗?

Liu Hang: Yes, before the Warring States Period, there were many mini-states within China, but in 221 B.C. Emperor Qin Shihuang united all the mini-states as one.
是的,在战国时期以前,中国境内有很多小国家,但是在公元前 221 年,秦始皇把所有的小国家统一成为一个国家。

Bill: How many dynasties has China experienced?
中国经历了多少朝代?

Liu Hang: Around 20 dynasties. In the Tang Dynasty China was a superpower in the world and many other countries sent their envoys to be friends with③ China.
大约二十个朝代。在唐朝时候中国是世界上的超级大国,很多国家都派使节和中国交好。

Bill: Do you think Confucius should be the greatest thinker in history?
你认为孔子是历史上最伟大的思想家吗?

Liu Hang: Yes, he was a great thinker and educator.
是的,他是一个伟大的思想家和教育家。

Typical Sentences 典型句型

1) Have you ever been to China before?
你以前去过中国吗?

2) China covers an area of 9,600,000 square kilometers, a little larger than the United States.
中国的面积有960万平方公里,比美国略微大一点儿。

3) China is more mountainous and hilly than the United States.
中国比美国的山地和丘陵要多些。

4) The Three Gorges Project is in the central part of China.
三峡工程在中国的中部。

5) The Yangtze River is the longest river in China and one of the longest in the world.
长江是中国最长的河流,也是世界上最长的河流之一。

6) The city population is larger than that of your whole country.
城市人口比你们国家的总人口还多。

7) Shanghai is the biggest city. Have you heard of this city?
上海是最大的城市,听说过吗?

8) The country is divided into 23 provinces, 4 municipalities directly under the Central Government, 5 autonomous regions and 2 special administrative regions.
全国分成23个省、4个直辖市、5个自治区和2个特别行政区。

9) Hong Kong is in South China, facing South China Sea.
香港在华南地区,面向南海。

10) China is a great country with a history of more than 5000 years.
是啊,中国是一个有五千多年历史的伟大国家。

11) In 221 B. C. Emperor Qin Shihuang united all the mini-states as one.
公元前221年,秦始皇把所有的小国家统一成为一个国家。

12) China has experienced around 20 dynasties so far.
中国经历了大约二十个朝代。

13) In the Tang Dynasty China was a superpower in the world.
在唐朝时候中国是世界上的超级大国。

14) Confucius was a great thinker and educator.
孔子是一个伟大的思想家和教育家。

About China: Geography & History

Background 背景知识

中国的地理和历史: 向外国人介绍中国的地理和历史,下面的英语段落也许是个参考,当然远非如此简单。

(1) 概说: China, the "Central Kingdom", is the world's third largest country after Russia and Canada, covering 9.6 million square kilometers. It supports a population of more than 1300 million people, about 22% of the world total, with only 7% of the world's arable land. 59% of the country consists of mountain, forest and desert, and 31% consists of high grasslands and pasture.

(2) 地理: China is situated in eastern Asia on the western shore of the Pacific Ocean. China's land drops off in escarpments eastward to the ocean, letting in humid air current and leading many rivers eastward. Among the rivers, the Changjiang (Yangtze) River and the Huanghe (Yellow) River are world-known. China has beautiful scenery, with mountains and ranges, highlands, plains, basins, and hills. The highlands and hill regions account for 65 percent of the country's total landmass, and there are more than 2000 lakes. The highest mountain peak is Qomolangma (Everest), the highest in the world, 8844 meters above sea level; the lowest point is the Turpan Basin, 154 meters below sea level.

(3) 气候: China is characterized by a continental climate. The latitude spans nearly 50 degrees. The greater part of the Chinese territory is situated in the Temperate Zone, its southern part in the Tropical and Subtropical Zones, and its northern part near the Frigid Zone. Temperatures differ therefore rather strikingly across the country. The northern part of Heilongjiang Province has long winters but no summers; while the Hainan Island has long summers but no winters. The Huaihe River valley is marked by distinctive seasonal changes, but it is spring all year round in the south of the Yunnan-Guizhou Plateau. In the northwest hinterland, the temperature changes dramatically. China high tundra zone is situated in the Qinghai-Tibet Plateau, where the

temperature is low in all four seasons. Some desert areas are dry all year round.

(4) 历史: In the 21st century B.C., China entered slave society with the founding of the Xia Dynasty, thereby writing a finale to long years of primitive society. The Xia was followed by the Shang and Western Zhou Dynasty, which encompassed the Spring and Autumn and Warring States periods. In 221 B.C., Qin Shihuang established China's first centralized autocracy, the Qin Dynasty, thereby ushering Chinese history into feudalism, which endured in a succession of dynasties, such as the Han, Tang, Song, Yuan, Ming, and Qing, until the Opium War of 1840. The contributions to world civilization of ancient China's four inventions: papermaking, printing, powder, and the compass, as well as remarkable achievements in mathematics, medical science, astronomy, agriculture, and architecture, are universally recognized. The Chinese Bourgeois Democratic Revolution of 1911 led by Sun Yat-sen toppled the rule of the Qing Dynasty, put an end to more than 2000 years of feudal monarchical system and culminated in the establishment of the provisional government of the Republic of China. The People's Republic of China was founded on October 1, 1949.

注 释

① 注意 have been(to) 和 have gone(to) 的区别: have been(to) 表示"曾到过(现在已回来)", have gone(to) 表示"已去某地(在途中或已到达)"。

We have been to England. (我们去过英国。)

They have gone to England. (他们去英国了。)

② be made up of 是"由……组成"的意思, 如:

The committee is made up of seven members. (这个委员会由7个成员组成。)

③ be friends with 是"和……友好"的意思, 如:

We should be friends with the people over the world. (我们应该和世界人民友好。)

About China: Politics & Economy
中国政治和经济

Topic Introduction
话题导言

西方普通人对中国的印象主要来自于媒体的宣传,中国的政治和经济发展水平究竟如何,他们并不太了解,毕竟,来过中国的西方人确实太少。这就需要走出国门的中国人实事求是地予以介绍,让没有来过中国的人消除他们对中国的偏见。值得一说的是,有些人就认为中国是个混乱不堪的国家,对此该驳斥的就要驳斥,最好建议他们来中国看看再发表意见。

特别提到一点,就是西方人理解的"共产主义(Communism)和社会主义(Socialism)"等词,与我们的概念有很大的不同。只有以活生生的事实才能准确地介绍中国的政治和经济状况,如改革(reform)、选举(election)、私有企业(private business)、私人轿车(private cars)、电脑在各个领域的使用(computer application)、城市建设(urbanization)等都是谈论的话题。

Situational Dialogs
情景对话

外国朋友往往对中国的政治和经济发展状况十分感兴趣,幸好刘杭(Liu Hang)是个关心祖国建设的青年。她努力向美国朋友介绍一个真实的中国。

Dialog 1

Bill: Could you tell me something about China?
能给我谈谈中国吗?

Liu Hang: What are you interested in?
你对什么感兴趣呢?

Bill: I saw your national flag in Los Angeles. What does it mean?
我在洛杉矶看到你们的国旗,有什么含义?

Liu Hang: Oh, I know that. The red color of the flag symbolizes revolution. The larger star represents the Communist Party of China and the four smaller ones, the Chinese people. This expresses the great unity of the Chinese people under the leadership of the CPC①.
哦,我知道这个。旗帜的红色象征着革命,大五星代表中国共产党,四颗小五星代表中国人民,表示中国人民在中国共产党领导下的伟大团结。

Bill: That's how it is. The Communist Party of China is the ruling party, but which party is the Opposition?
原来如此。中国共产党是执政党,那哪个党是反对党?

Liu Hang: We don't have such a party. The other eight democratic parties also participate in② politics and government.
我们没有这样的党,另外八个民主党派是参政党。

Bill: Who legislate and who implement laws?
谁制定法律,谁执行法律?

Liu Hang: The National People's Congress with its Standing Committee is the supreme legislature, and the State Council is the supreme administrative organ.
全国人民代表大会及其常务委员会是最高立法机关,国务院是最高行政机关。

Bill: Oh, I see.
哦,我明白了。

About China: Politics & Economy   40

中国政治和经济

Dialog 2

Bill: Does your government control all enterprises in order to actualize communism in China?

为了在中国实现共产主义,你们政府控制着所有的企业吗?

Liu Hang: No, it's not the case③. The state encourages the development of private, individual and foreign enterprises, though the public-owned economy is still the main body of the national economic system.

没有,不是那么回事。国家鼓励私有、个体和外资企业的发展,尽管公有经济仍然是国民经济体系的主体。

Bill: No wonder the increase rate of GNP④ is so high.

难怪 GNP 的增长率这么高。

Liu Hang: Yes, the economic system reform and opening-up work efficiently in the economic development.

是啊,经济体制改革和开放在经济发展中很有效地起了作用。

Bill: You have ancient four inventions, and now you have sent up manned spaceship into the space recently.

你们有古老的四大发明,现在又把载人的太空船发射到了太空。

Liu Hang: Yeah, every Chinese is proud of that.

是啊,每个中国人都以此感到自豪。

典型句型

1) The Communist Party of China is the ruling party, and the other eight democratic parties also participate in politics and government.

中国共产党是执政党,另外八个民主党派是参政党。

2) The National People's Congress with its Standing Committee

is the supreme legislature.
全国人民代表大会及其常务委员会是最高立法机关。

3) The State Council is the supreme administrative organ.
国务院是最高行政机关。

4) The red color of the flag symbolizes revolution.
旗帜的红色象征着革命。

5) The larger star represents the Communist Party of China and the four smaller ones, the Chinese people.
大五星代表中国共产党,四颗小五星代表中国人民。

6) China is now implementing political reform so as to develop democracy.
中国正在推进政治体制改革,以发展民主。

7) The economic system reform and opening-up work efficiently in the economic development.
经济体制改革和开放在经济发展中很有效地起了作用。

8) The state encourages the development of private, individual and foreign enterprises.
国家鼓励私有、个体和外资企业的发展。

9) The public-owned economy is still the main body of the national economic system.
公有经济仍然是国民经济体系的主体。

10) We have our own forms of democracy and freedom.
我们有我们的民主和自由的形式。

11) China is now implementing political reform so as to develop democracy.
中国正在进行政治体制改革,以发展民主。

12) Everyone enjoys the freedom to express his ideas.
每个人都有发表意见的自由。

13) Anyone who tries to split our country shall be punished.
任何分裂我们国家的人都会受到严惩。

Background 背景知识

中国的政治和经济：中国的政治和经济，也是西方人感兴趣的话题，他们中的很多人并不了解改革开放后的中国是个什么样子。

（1）概说：Today, China is implementing reform and opening-up policies, and has established socialist market economy, thereby charting the course for socialist modernization with Chinese characteristics.

（2）常用的词汇：

党群关系 Party-masses relationship
党政机关 Party and government organizations
参政、议政 participate in the management of State affairs
多党合作制 multi-party co-operation in exercising state power
按成本要素计算的国民经济总值 GNP at factor cost
按劳分配 distribution according to one's performance
包干到户 work contracted to households
包干制 overall rationing system
奔小康 strive for a relatively comfortable life
待岗 await job assignment, post-waiting
待业 job-waiting
地区差异 regional disparity
地方保护主义 regional protectionism
对外招商 attract foreign investment
防止经济过热 prevent an overheated economy
防止国有资产流失 prevent the devaluation of state assets
防止泡沫经济 avoid a bubble economy
下岗人员争取再就业 redirect laid-off workers for reemployment
扶贫、脱贫 poverty reduction and elimination
保持国民经济发展的良好势头 maintain a good momentum of growth in the national economy
长期共存、互相监督、肝胆相照、荣辱与共 long-term coexistence, mutual supervision, sincere treatment with each other and the

sharing of weal or woe

达到或接近国际先进水平 reach or approach advanced international standards

注释

① CPC 是 the Communist Party of China（中国共产党）的缩写。
② the case 是"实情,情况"的意思,如：
If that is the case, you must work much harder.（果真如此的话,你就必须更加努力了。）
③ participate in 是"参与,参加"的意思,如：
Will you participate in the table-tennis match next month?（你下个月参加乒乓球比赛吗？）
④ GNP 是 Gross National Product（国民生产总值）的缩写词,而 GDP 是 Gross Domestic Products（国内生产总值）的缩写。

About China: Population & the People
中国人口和人民

Topic Introduction 话题导言

中国的人口问题为世界所关注,西方多数人也只是知道中国是世界上人口最多的国家,普通人并不知道中国究竟有多少亿人口。有些人对我们的计划生育政策很不理解,他们想不通国家为什么还管人们生孩子的问题。不少人可能会问到如果不遵守"一对夫妻一个孩子"的政策会受到什么样的处罚。

说实话,多数西方人是友好的,他们问你这方面的问题也只是出于好奇而已,只有少数人会不礼貌地、挑衅性地追问一些计划生育政策问题。遇到这种人,你可以根据我国的政策对他们进行驳斥。

情景对话

很多西方朋友都对中国的人口和民族问题十分感兴趣,刘杭(Liu Hang)的同学 Jim 就是其中一位。

Dialog 1

Jim: Hi, Liu Hang. China has the largest population in the world. What on earth① is its population?
你好,刘杭。中国的人口世界上最多,究竟有多少?

Liu Hang: It's about 1300 million, about 22% of the world total, but we have only 7% of the world's arable land.
大约是13亿,约占世界总人口的22%,但我们只有世界7%的耕地。

Jim: Everyone knows that this is a smashing success.
人人都知道这是个了不起的成功。

Liu Hang: But, the distribution is not a balance. About 70% live in the eastern part, and especially the Yangtze River Delta and the Pearl River Delta are most densely populated.
但是,分布不平衡,大约70%的人口生活在东部,尤其是长江三角洲和珠江三角洲的人口极其稠密。

Jim: How about the western provinces and regions?
西部省区呢?

Liu Hang: On the contrary②, the average population per square kilometer there are fewer than 10 people in some places.
正好相反,那里有些地方每平方公里的人口还不足10人。

Jim: Why not emigrate③ there?
怎么不移民到那里去呢?

Liu Hang: Who is willing to go there, with wicked climate and desolate wasteland?
气候恶劣,土地荒凉,谁愿意去呢?

Dialog 2

Liu Hang: Hi, Jim. What's going on tonight?
嗨,吉姆,今晚有什么活动?

Jim: We'll have a seminar about world population and races.
有一个关于世界人口与种族的讨论会。

Liu Hang: That's good. Can I go with you?
很好,我可以和你一起去吗?

About China: Population & the People 41

中国人口和人民

Jim:	Sure you can. Do you have all races of people in China, just like the United States? 当然。你们中国像美国一样，有各个种族吗？
Liu Hang:	No, just some minorities are white. They live in the northwest. 不是，只有一些少数民族是白种人，他们生活在西北部。
Jim:	How many minorities in your country? 你们国家有多少少数民族？
Liu Hang:	55 minorities, but their population only makes up⑤ about 9.44% of the whole population. 55个少数民族，但是他们的人口只占总人口的大约9.44%。
Jim:	Do they have different religions? 他们有不同的宗教吗？
Liu Hang:	Yes, most of them do. Everyone has the freedom to believe in⑥ any religion. 是的，他们大多数信仰不同的宗教。每个人都有信仰宗教的自由。

Typical Sentences 典型句型

1) China has the largest population in the world.
中国的人口世界上最多。

2) China has about 1300 million people, about 22% of the world total.
中国大约有13亿人，约占世界总人口的22%。

3) By now about 40% of the population live in cities.
现在约有40%的人生活在城市里。

4) China implements the family planning policy of one couple, one child.
中国实行"一对夫妻一个孩子"的计划生育政策。

5) You'll have to pay a fine of several thousand yuan.
你要支付好几千元的罚款。

6) China is a country accommodating 56 nationalities.

中国是个有 56 个民族的国家。

7) We have 55 minorities in our country.

我们国家有 55 个少数民族。

8) Their population only makes up about 9.44% of the whole population.

他们的人口只占总人口的 9.44%。

9) Everyone has the freedom to believe in any religion.

每个人都有信仰宗教的自由。

10) China is a multi-religious country.

中国是一个多宗教的国家。

11) Freedom of belief is a government policy, and normal religious activities are protected by the constitution.

宗教信仰是国家的一项政策,正常的宗教活动受到宪法的保护。

背景知识

中国的人口问题:

(1) 中国人口的有关数字:根据国家统计局 2008 年 2 月 28 日发布的"2007 年国民经济和社会发展统计公报",2007 年年末全国总人口为 132,129 万人,比上年末增加 681 万人。全年出生人口 1594 万人,出生率为 12.10‰;死亡人口 913 万人,死亡率为 6.93‰;自然增长率为 5.17‰。出生人口性别比为 120.22。

(2) 中国人口的特点:第一,当前中国人口社会抚养比较低,劳动年龄人口比重大,劳动力资源丰富,为经济快速发展提供了强大的动力,但庞大的劳动年龄人口也给就业带来了巨大的压力。

第二,2007 年,65 岁以上老年人口比重达 8.1%以上,根据国际标准,中国已经进入老龄社会。据预测,到 2020 年,65 岁老年人口将达 1.64 亿,占总人口比重 16.1%。中国老龄化呈现速度快、规模大、"未富先老"等特点,对未来社会抚养比、储蓄率、消费结构及社会保障等产生重大影响。

About China: Population & the People

第三，从人口性别结构看，2007年末男性人口68,048万人，占51.5%；女性人口64,081万人，占48.5%，总人口性别比为106左右。从20世纪80年代开始，出生人口性别比持续升高，第五次全国人口普查时为117，而在2007年为120.22。

第四，从城乡分布来看，2007年末全国城镇人口达到59,379万人，占总人口的44.9%，乡村人口为72,750万人，占55.1%。人口城镇化率每年增加1个百分点。与此同时，庞大的流动迁移人口对城市基础设施和公共服务构成巨大压力。流动人口就业、子女受教育、医疗卫生、社会保障以及计划生育等方面的权利得不到有效保障，严重制约着人口的有序流动和合理分布，统筹城乡、区域协调发展面临困难。

以下一些词语涉及中国人口及计划生育方面：各族人民 people of all nationalities (all ethnic groups)；人口负增长 negative population growth(NPG)；计划生育责任制 responsibility system of family planning；实行计划生育、控制人口数量、提高人口素质 promotion of family planning to control the population size and improve the health of the people；国家人口和计划生育委员会 National Population and Family Planning Commission 等。

注　释

① on earth 是"到底，究竟"的意思，如：
What on earth is the matter there?（那里究竟发生了什么事？）
No force on earth can hold back the progress of the society.（没有任何力量能够阻止社会的进步。）

② on the contrary 是"相反地"的意思，如：
On the contrary, we can afford the house.（正好相反，我们买得起这座房子。）

③ 注意 emigrate, immigrate, migrate 的区别：
emigrate 是"迁出"的意思，如：
He's decided to emigrate and start a new life in America.（他决定移居美国，开始新的生活。）

immigrate 指"迁入",如：

They plan to immigrate to Finland next year. (他们计划明年移居芬兰。)

migrate 指"迁移,移居",如：

Ducks migrate every fall. (鸭子秋天迁徙。)

④ at all cost 是"不惜一切代价"的意思,还可以说 at any cost,如：

We must win the match at all costs. (我们要不惜一切代价赢得这场比赛。)

⑤ make up 是"占有多大比例"的意思,如：

Girls make up two thirds of our class. (女生在我们班占三分之二。)

⑥ believe in 是"信任,信仰"的意思,如：

Do you believe in ghosts? (你相信有鬼吗？)

Some people believe in everlasting life after death. (有些人相信永生。)

Chinese People's Life
中国人的生活

Topic Introduction
话题导言

应该说，多数西方人对中国人生活状况的了解是很不全面的，其信息来源主要是本国的媒体和周围的中国人。他们可能会问，所有的人都有饭吃吗？是不是只有少数人享有社会福利？一个公社社员一天的工钱是几分钱？因为他们中很多人对中国的认识还停留在"文革"时期。也不知是为什么，许多的西方人对中国的印象还停留在那个时期。

如果我们有机会走出国门，就应该向世人介绍一个真实的中国社会，特别是让他们知道中国近几年经济的发展和人民生活的改善。这里有一个建议，出国时候带上一两本画册(像广东省人民政府每年出版的《广东》年刊)，是非常有用的，笔者就曾将这样一本画册送给一个美国的中学校长，他将其拆开展示，受影响的是整个学校。

Situational Dialogs
情景对话

丁唐(Ding Tang)受到霍尔教授(Prof. Hall)的热烈款待，教授还就中国人生活的现状和丁唐(Ding Tang)讨论起来。

Dialog 1

Prof. Hall: Hi, Ding Tang. Did you have a sound sleep last night?
嗨，丁唐。你昨晚睡得好吗？

Ding Tang: I've nothing to complain①, but I prefer to sleep on my own bed at home.
还可以，但我喜欢在家里睡在自己的床上。

Prof. Hall: Everyone likes his home. How is your Chinese housing in general?
人人都喜欢家。你们中国人一般的住房情况如何？

Ding Tang: Quite a few② rich people have bought villas in the suburbs, and in the countryside peasants built many new houses.
相当多的有钱人在郊区买了别墅，农村的农民也盖了很多新房子。

Prof. Hall: I hear great changes have taken place in your country.
我听说你们国家发生了很大的变化。

Ding Tang: Yes, that's true. All people, young and old, men and women, are far better dressed than ever, especially young girls are seen to wear fashionable dresses here and there③.
是的，那是不错。所有的人，男女老少，都比以前穿得好得多，特别是年轻女孩都穿着时髦的衣服。

Prof. Hall: That's quite different from what I saw in China 30 years ago.
那和我30年前在中国见到的有很大的不同。

Dialog 2

Prof. Hall: You have long holidays during the Spring Festival and National Day. Where do you spend these days?
你们在春节和国庆节有很长的假期，你们到哪里度假？

Ding Tang: Many people travel to resorts of interests, or even go abroad, but it was impossible in the past years.
许多人去旅游胜地，或者甚至出国，但这在过去是不可能的。

Chinese People's Life 42

中国人的生活

Prof. Hall:	That's just like our Easter and Thanksgiving breaks. We have nine days off④ for each vacation.
	那就像我们的复活节和感恩节假期，我们每个假日都有9天假期。
Ding Tang:	Last Spring Festival we flew to Hainan for a holiday, and all of us had a very good time there.
	去年春节我们乘飞机到海南度假,所有人都过得很愉快。
Prof. Hall:	Do a lot of people have cars?
	很多人有汽车吗？
Ding Tang:	Yes, it's not unusual to own private cars, to say nothing of⑤ computers, air-conditioners, and TV sets.
	是的,拥有私人轿车也不稀罕了,更不用说电脑、空调和电视机了。
Prof. Hall:	All this was unthinkable 20 years ago.
	所有这一切在20年前是不可想象的。

典型句型

1) As the country is stronger and richer, the people live a happier life.
   随着国家的富强,人民的生活更幸福了。
2) Quite a few rich people have bought villas in the suburbs.
   相当多的有钱人在郊区买了别墅。
3) In the countryside peasants built many new houses.
   农村的农民也盖了很多新房子。
4) Great changes have taken place in our country.
   我们国家发生了很大的变化。
5) All people are far better dressed than ever, especially young girls are seen to wear fashionable dresses here and there.
   所有的人都比以前穿得好得多,特别是年轻女孩穿着时髦的衣服。
6) Many people travel to resorts of interests, or even go abroad, but it was impossible in the past years.
   许多人去旅游胜地,或者甚至出国,但这在过去是不可能的。

7) More and more people take planes either on business or go home.
越来越多的人乘飞机出差或回家。

8) People often take part in all kinds of recreational activities.
人们经常参加各种各样的娱乐活动。

9) Economic development has reached a comfortable level of living for many people.
经济的发展使许多人的生活达到了小康水平。

10) All this was unthinkable 20 years ago.
所有这一切在20年前是不可想象的。

背景知识

流行词汇：反映人们某个时期的生活水平往往都有一些流行的词汇来表达，如何用英语把我们目前流行的词汇说出来呢？

安居工程 housing project for low-income urban residents
按揭购房 buy a house on mortgage
摆脱贫困 shake off poverty
包干到户 work contracted to households
边远贫困地区 outlying poverty-stricken areas
仓储式超市 stockroom-style supermarket
发展不平衡 disparate development
发展是硬道理 Development is of overriding importance.
分期付款 installment payment
复式住宅 duplex apartment
工薪阶层 salaried person
公费医疗 medical services at state expense
家族企业 family firm
宽带接入 broadband access
宽带网 broadband networks
旅行结婚 have a honeymoon trip
耐用消费品 durable consumer items (goods)

Chinese People's Life 42

中国人的生活

人均住房 per-capita housing
脱贫致富 shake off poverty and set out on a road to prosperity
温饱工程 bring-warmth fill-bellies project
消费信贷 consumer credit services
小康之家 well-off family; comfortably-off family

注　释

① I've nothing to complain. 是"我没有什么抱怨的"的意思,指的是"过得还可以"。
② quiet a few 是"相当多"的意思,如:
I have quiet a few friends in America. (我在美国有很多朋友。)
③ here and there 是"到处"的意思。
④ days off 指"不工作,休息",如:
three days off (休息三天。)
⑤ to say nothing of 是"更不用说"的意思,如:
I can lend you 2000 dollars, to say nothing of 100 dollars. (我能借给你2000美元,更不用说100美元了。)

Violating Traffic Rules
交通违章

Topic Introduction 话题导言

在美国几乎所有开车的人都接到过警察的罚款单(ticket)，特别是刚到美国去的人即使已经是老"司机"了，也往往有违章的时候。例如，在没有交通灯的交叉路口，即使没有其他任何车辆来往，也要停车了望，然后才能继续行车。这种情况我们很容易忽略，实际上就是个习惯问题。

超速行车、闯红灯、不按顺序穿过十字路口、违规超车、酒后驾车、随意停车、不按规定年检、不携带保险资料等都是违章行为，都有可能接到警察的罚单。遇到警察查车，一定要按照指示行事，否则会产生不可挽回的后果。但过后如果认为警察的处罚不当，可以向法院提起诉讼，撤销警察的不当处罚。

Situational Dialogs 情景对话

国内和国外的交通规则总是有很大不同，稍不留神就容易接到罚单。这次刘杭(Liu Hang)也接到罚单了。

Violating Traffic Rules 43

Dialog 1

Liu Hang: Is this street "no entry"? I couldn't see such a sign.
这条街道禁止进入吗？我没有看到这样的标牌。

Officer: Of course there's no such a sign. But the road is so narrow; you couldn't have missed the speed limit sign.
当然没有这样的标志。但这条路这么窄，您不会看不到速度限制牌。

Liu Hang: I think I was going at the regular speed①. What is the speed limit?
我认为我以正常速度行驶，速度限制是多少？

Officer: The limit is 30 miles but you were driving at 40 miles. Please sign here.
速度限制是 30 英里，但您的速度是 40 英里，请在这里签字。

Liu Hang: No, I will not. Because I don't think I was wrong.
不，我不签字。因为我认为我没有错。

Officer: Were you driving at 30 miles?
您的速度是 30 英里吗？

Liu Hang: Yes, of course.
是的，当然是。

Officer: Even so, you must sign here first and pay the fine, and you may propose your objection if you think we're on the wrong side.
即使如此，您首先必须在这里签字并缴交罚款。如认为我们错了，您可以申诉。

Liu Hang: OK. I have no other choice②.
好的，只有如此了。

Dialog 2

Officer: Hello, madam. Can you show me your driver's license?
你好，女士。请把你的驾驶执照给我看看，好吗？

Liu Hang: Sure, here it is. Anything wrong, officer?
可以，给你。有什么问题吗，警官？

Officer: Your inspection sticker is overdue, madam. You should have had your car inspected before April this year.
你的年检证明过期了，女士。你应该在今年 4 月之前把车检验一下。

Liu Hang:	I don't understand, sir. Can you explain it clearly? 先生，我不明白。你能解释清楚吗？
Officer:	OK. Your car should be inspected once a year, and this sticker shows the car was inspected in April of last year. 好的，你的车应该一年检查一次，这个检验票表明你的车是去年4月检验的。
Liu Hang:	I just bought the car this August, and I don't know anything about inspection. OK, where should I have it inspected? 我今年8月刚买的车，我对检验的事情一无所知。好的，我应该在哪里检验呢？
Officer:	We have two inspection stations in town, one is opposite the City Hall and another is beside Wal-Mart③. But first you have to pay the fine. 市内有两个检验站，一个在市政厅对面，另一个在沃尔玛旁边。但是，你得先付罚款。
Liu Hang:	OK. I understand now. 好的，我现在明白了。
Officer:	You may propose your objection at court if you think we're on the wrong side. 如果你认为我们错了，可以向法庭申诉。
Liu Hang:	All right. Thanks. 好的，谢谢。

1) Is this street "no entry"? I couldn't see such a sign.
   这条街道禁止进入吗？我没有看到这样的标牌。
2) You couldn't have missed the speed limit sign.
   您不会看不到速度限制牌。
3) I was within the speed limit.
   我的车是在限速范围内。

Violating Traffic Rules 43 交通违章

4) Because I don't think I was wrong.
   因为我认为我没有错。
5) Anything wrong, officer?
   有什么问题吗,警官?
6) I'm sorry my car broke down.
   对不起,我的车坏了。
7) Can you explain it clearly?
   你能解释清楚吗?
8) I don't know anything about inspection.
   我对检验的事情一无所知。
9) Where should I have it inspected?
   我应该在哪里检验呢?
10) Did I cross the street against the traffic signal?
    我违章横穿马路了吗?
11) I didn't notice there was a no-U-turn sign.
    我没有注意到有一个不能调头的牌子。
12) I don't think I should be responsible for it.
    我认为我不应该对此负责。

背景知识

在美国开车: 长途开车旅游往往会有许多的紧急情况发生。根据美国交通局的统计,自上世纪70年代以来,死于车祸的人口已经超越两次世界大战的阵亡人数。原因就是:美国太大了,美国人又爱开车旅行,开各式开样的车出游可以说是"全民运动",从学生到退休人员皆是如此;美国地属大陆型气候带,天气变化多端莫测,许多情况是不能料到的。

暴风雪: 暴风雪期间避免长途开车。雪地开车最重要的是随时试踩刹车,看看刹到什么样程度下车子不会打滑,随时踩刹车是因为路况会随时改变。万一真的打滑也不要惊慌,不要紧急刹车,应朝相反的方向紧握方向盘,试着感觉车子偏移的方向,以便改正。

当然这只是一个建议,最重要的还是要随机应变,小心加谨慎。

暴风雨:美国的部分地区的暴风雨是相当吓人的,既使把雨刷开到最快,还是看不到前面的车。这时最好的策略就是停在路边,等雨下小点再开,千万不要冒险硬开。

超速问题:美国大部分公路皆有行车限速,普通公路是40至55英里,高速公路为65至70英里,一般的惯例是可以加减10英里。在高速公路上执勤的州警通常是躲在行车线之间的回转道内以测速器测速,一旦有车子超速,警车会先开出来,开警示灯。如果有警车从后方接近,应换车道让其通过,如果在换道之后,警车跟着换道而且响起警笛闪着大灯,那就说明警察要抓的就是自己。此时应立即减速停车坐直身体,双手放在警察看得见的地方,遵照指示行动。切记不要有加速,或不服从指示的行为发生,不然可能被逮捕。

迷路:在美国开车迷路是很正常的。迷路时千万不要慌张,应该立即停车,拿出当地的地图,查对方向后再开车。如果迷路时间太晚,而且身处乡村地区,依照常识是不要到一般住家询问,因为美国人民有合法拥枪自卫的权力,而且有合法枪支两亿支,此时如果深夜越过人家庭院去敲门是相当不理智的。最好是找便利商店或加油站的店员,向他们问清楚方向。

注 释

① at the regular speed 是"以正常的速度"的意思,at the speed of 的意思是"以……的速度",如:
The train ran eastward at the speed of 200 kilometers per hour. (火车以每小时 200 公里的速度向东行驶。)

② 需注意 choice, alternative, 及 preference 的区别。三个词都有"选择的机会"或"被选择的东西"的意思。
choice 是最常用的普通用词,强调自由选择。如:full of choice in life (生活充满选择)。

Violating Traffic Rules 43

交通违章

alternative 多强调选择的可能性受限制，一般不指具体事物的选择。如：
Can you recommend an alternative? (你能推荐别的选择吗？)
preference 强调按自己的爱好所做的选择。如：
He has a preference for poem. (他特别喜欢诗。)
③ Wal-Mart 是美国最大的私人雇主和世界上最大的连锁零售商。

Baggage Damaged or Lost
行李损失

Topic Introduction 话题导言

出国旅行最令人气恼的事,莫过于行李遗失或损坏。一旦发生这样不幸的事,多数人的第一反应是心急如焚。在这种状况下,还要用英语向工作人员请求协助,着实是件困难的事。

不管是乘坐飞机还是长途汽车,行李遗失或损坏都要即刻报告给机场、车站的相关部门,以求尽快找到行李或得到赔偿。本话题提供在行李损失的意外状况下,旅客如何用简单而清楚的英语,向工作人员描述行李的特征,提供足够的资料,以便尽快找回失物,或者得到合理的赔偿。其间,行李的颜色、大小、牌子、标签情况、内装物品等都要向工作人员报告。

Situational Dialogs 情景对话

旅行途中,让丁唐(Ding Tang)最气恼的事情就是行李的遗失和损坏。丁唐找到了相关部门的工作人员,描述自己的行李特点,希望可以尽快找到,或者得到赔偿。

Baggage Damaged or Lost 44

行李损失

Dialog 1

Clerk:	Hello, may I help you?
	你好，要我帮你吗？
Ding Tang:	I can't find my baggage in the baggage claim area.
	我在行李区找不到我的行李。
Clerk:	How many pieces?
	几件？
Ding Tang:	Two, a trunk and a suitcase.
	两件，一个大箱子和一个衣箱。
Clerk:	Could you describe them for me?
	你能描述一下吗？
Ding Tang:	Sure. The trunk is very big, light blue, made of[①] nylon cloth, about 90 inches long, 60 inches wide, 30 inches thick.
	当然。大箱子很大，浅蓝色，尼龙布做的，大约 90 英寸长，60 英寸宽，30 英寸厚。
Clerk:	What's the brand of the trunk?
	什么牌子？
Ding Tang:	It's a Polo House with three tags with my name and phone number.
	是马球屋牌的，上面有三个标签，标签上有我的名字和电话号码。
Clerk:	How about the suitcase?
	衣箱呢？
Ding Tang:	This one is medium-sized but much smaller than the trunk, light green. It's also a Polo House, also with three tags.
	这个是中等大小，比大箱子小多了，淡绿色，也是马球屋的，也有三个标签。
Clerk:	Did you see them when you were transferring at Tokyo?
	你在东京转机时看到它们了吗？
Ding Tang:	No, I don't need to transfer baggage myself.
	没有，我不需要自己转运行李。
Clerk:	OK, thanks. We're tracing your baggage through our computer system. Once we've got any information, we'll let you know.
	好的，谢谢。我们要通过电脑系统追踪你的行李，一旦有什么消息，我们就通知你。

263

Dialog 2

Ding Tang: Excuse me. My suitcase seems to be broken.
抱歉,我的箱子好像破了。

Clerk: Which one?
哪一个?

Ding Tang: This blue one. When I checked it in at Hong Kong Airport, it was looking brand new.
这个蓝色的。我在香港机场托运的时候,看起来还像是崭新的。

Clerk: What's wrong with it?[2]
哪里的问题?

Ding Tang: The bottom is broken, and the handle is missing.
底部破了,把手也掉了。

Clerk: Would you please lift it, and let me have a careful look? ...All right, have you lost anything inside?
请你提起来,我仔细看看,好吗?……好的,你里面的东西丢失了吗?

Ding Tang: No, madam.
没有,女士。

Clerk: OK. You may choose to have a new suitcase now, or you'll be compensated.
好的,你可以要一只新箱子,也可以得到赔偿。

Ding Tang: OK, I need a new one to hold[3] all these stuffs.
好的,我还是要一只新箱子,好装我的这些东西。

1) I can't find my baggage in the baggage claim area.
我在行李区找不到我的行李。

2) My baggage seems to be missing.
我的行李好像遗失了。

Baggage Damaged or Lost 44

行李损失

3) One of my suitcases hasn't come.
   我的行李少了一件。

4) A medium-sized black suitcase with a yellow strap around it.
   一个中型的黑色手提箱,扎有黄色的带子。

5) Did you see them when you were transferring at Tokyo?
   你在东京转机时看到了吗?

6) My suitcase seems to be broken.
   我的箱子好像破了。

7) My baggage is damaged.
   我的行李破了。

8) The bottom is broken, and the handle is missing.
   底部破了,把手也掉了。

9) I'd like to be compensated for the damage to my bags.
   我的行李破损,想请求赔偿。

10) I need a new one to hold all these stuffs.
    我要一只新箱子,好装我的这些东西。

11) What happens if you can't find it?
    如果你们找不到怎么办?

12) Please contact me at the Hilton Hotel, Room 808.
    请在希尔顿酒店808房间找我。

背景知识

遗失行李:航空公司托运的大件行李都是在转盘上领取。由于数量多,很可能出现拿错、被盗或转机时行李转掉了的情形。发现找不到行李时,先不要慌乱,看看四周有没有类似的行李箱是被误拿的。若真的找不到,赶紧找航站人员帮忙,拿行李牌及机票到失物招领处登记。为避免行李遗失及托运物品损坏,有几个方法可避免意外的发生:(1) 行李上务必写上英文名字及地址。(2) 对于行李的描述越详细越好,若能指认出行李上有特殊的卷标,可让寻找的人较易找寻。(3) 凡持 Visa 及 MasterCard 卡购买机票的旅客,在到达目的地后超过六小时未找到行李,持卡人可获得250美元刷卡购买日用品,家属同行者可获得500美元的理赔。超过48小时未寻回行李,判定属于遗失,即使第49小时找到行李,依然可以申请理赔,但要持机票、登机牌申请理赔。

当在机场发现自己的行李遗失时,请先办理挂失手续:立即向机场"失物招领办公室(Lost & Found)"报遗失。

根据航空公司的"终站赔偿法则",多次转机的旅客,由搭乘终站的航空公司负责理赔。而赔偿的额度根据国际航空协会规定:托运行李之赔偿最高限额约为每磅9.07美元(每公斤20美元),随身行李之赔偿限额为每位旅客400美元。对全部旅程均在美国境内各点之间者,相关法令规定航空公司之赔偿限额,每位旅客不得低于1250美元。若干种类之物品不得申报超额价值。

行李损坏:行李若在货舱内损坏,应在行李转盘处或是在航空公司设的专设柜台处理行李损坏事项。旅客必须填写行李破损报告,航空公司会安排专人修行李,或由旅客自行送修,再将收据寄回航空公司,就能获得理赔。若毁损的程度到完全无法修理,有些航空公司会理赔一只新的箱子,有些则以一年10%的折旧率,根据行李购买的年份换算现金赔偿。

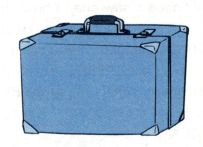

注 释

① made of 的意思是"由……做成",如:
This desk is made of wood. (这个桌子是由木头做成的。)

② What's wrong with it? 的意思是"出了什么问题?",如:
What's wrong with your computer? (你的电脑出了什么问题?)

③ hold 在这是"容纳;包含"的意思,如:hold the baby in one's arms (抱孩子)。

Robbed or Stolen
被劫被窃

Topic Introduction
话题导言

抢劫(robbery)和偷窃(theft)事件几乎在全世界都有发生,越是大城市,这样的案件越多。我们出国的时候,决不能对自己的物品放松警惕,贵重和紧要的物品一定要保管好,因为被偷走或被抢走的东西很难再找回来。俗话说,破财免灾。在美国,零钞的一大作用就是对付抢劫,遇到劫匪还是把钱给他们算了,以免他们伤人。

但是,遇到盗窃或抢劫,还是要报警,虽然你的物品可能找不回来,但如果警方掌握了罪犯的情况,对破案乃至整个社会的治安还是有作用的。美国的报警电话是911,可随时拨打。报警时一般要描述罪犯的体形、年龄、衣着、肤色等。

Situational Dialogs
情景对话

美国是全世界犯罪率最高的国家之一,在那里旅行一定要注意安全。尽管刘杭(Liu Hang)小心谨慎,但是还是被抢劫了。

Dialog 1

Robber: Hands up!
举起手来！

Liu Hang: What do you want?
你要干什么？

Robber: Shut up! Keep silent! Where's your money?
别说话！不许出声！钱在哪里？

Liu Hang: My wallet is in my backpack.
钱包在背包里。

Robber: OK. Move! Walk, and don't run and don't shout.
好了，走吧！走，别跑，也别喊。

(Liu Hang is calling 911.)

Liu Hang: Police! I've just been robbed here.
警察！我刚才被抢了。

Officer: Where are you now?
你现在在哪里？

Liu Hang: I'm at the corner of Smith Street and Parkinson Avenue, and I was going back to my school from Wal-Mart.
我在史密斯大街和帕金森大道的拐角处，我正从沃尔玛回学校。

Officer: Stay where you are. A patrol car will be there right away. What's your name please?
呆在那里别动，巡逻车马上就到。请问你叫什么名字？

Liu Hang: Liu Hang. I am an international student from China.
刘杭，我是中国来的留学生。

Dialog 2

Officer: May I help you?
我可以帮你吗？

Liu Hang: I want to report a case, officer.
警官，我要报案。

Officer: All right. Please go ahead①.
好的，请讲。

Robbed or Stolen 45

被劫被窃

Liu Hang: On my way home from the bank, someone came at② me all at once, and struck me on the head. My handbag was snatched away.
我从银行回家的路上，有人突然向我袭击，还打了我的头部。我的手提包被抢走了。

Officer: Can you give me a description of the assailant?
你能描述一下攻击者吗？

Liu Hang: He was a bit tallish and very strong, around③ twenty years old.
他有些高，很壮实，大约20岁。

Officer: Have you noticed his hair?
你注意到他的头发了吗？

Liu Hang: Yes, he was wearing blond hair. He was wearing a leather jacket and blue jeans.
注意到了，金黄色的头发。他穿着一件皮茄克和蓝色牛仔裤。

Officer: OK. Thanks a lot.
好的，谢谢你了。

典型句型

1) What do you want?
   你要干什么？
2) My wallet is in my backpack.
   钱包在背包里。
3) Police! I've just been robbed here.
   警察！我刚才被抢了。
4) Could you please call the police right now?
   请你打电话给警察好吗？
5) I'm a Chinese tourist and I want to report a burglary.
   我是一位中国游客，我要报一起入室行窃案。
6) I'd like to report a theft.
   我遭小偷了。

7) My pocket must have been picked.

   我的口袋被掏了。

8) I've been robbed.

   我遭抢了!

9) I'm at the corner of Smith Street and Parkinson Avenue.

   我在史密斯大街和帕金森大道的拐角处。

10) I am a tourist from China.

    我是中国来的游客。

11) I want to report a case, officer.

    警官,我要报案。

12) My handbag was snatched away.

    我的手提包被抢走了。

13) Someone stole my purse. I had some valuables in it.

    有人偷了我的手提包,我有一些贵重物品在里面。

14) He was a bit tallish and very strong, around twenty years old.

    他有些高,很壮实,大约20岁。

15) He was wearing a leather jacket and blue jeans.

    他穿着一件皮茄克和蓝色牛仔裤。

东西被窃:在国外常会碰到东西被偷的事件,尤其是在治安不好的国家或地区。抢劫者或盗窃者通常在下列几种情况中作案:(1) 假装前来搭讪;(2) 骑车强夺;(3) 趁旅客不注意时把放在地上的行李拿走;(4) 在人烟稀少的地方大胆行抢。若物品真的不幸被抢或被偷,你可以向当地警察局报案,若身上没有足够的钱,应当请求亲友汇钱过去,或者向驻当地使领馆求援。

被抢或被偷的物品要找回来的机率太小,最好的方法还是提高警觉,事先预防。如:(1) 养成检查门窗的习惯,并带好钥匙。(2) 现金、钱包、机票、护照等贵重物品,要随身携带。(3) 背包或旅行箱

Robbed or Stolen 45

等尽量不要离手。(4)居家或外出时若遇到巡员或警察盘问时,认清是否有正式凭证,以防冒充者。(5)避免夜归,避免夜晚到公园等场所。(6)对搭讪的人随时提高警觉。

注 释

① go ahead 是个多义词,具体的意思有"走吧,说罢,请进,前进"等,要看说话时的情景。

② come at 是"攻击,袭击"的意思,如:
The bear didn't come at the man lying on the ground.(那头熊没有攻击躺在地上的那个人。)

③ around 在这里相当于 about,意思是"大约,大概"。如:at around 5 o'clock (5点钟左右)。

Something Lost
物品遗失

Topic Introduction
话题导言

出国本来是件高高兴兴的事情，但丢了东西确实让人觉得扫兴。特别是丢了关键的护照、支票、金钱等物品，更是令人沮丧。当发现丢了东西时，要认真回想一下是在什么地方丢的，要及时报告以寻回失物。西方国家的交通系统、公园游览场所、市镇设施等都设有失物招领处(Lost and Found Office)。一般地说，工作人员要是拾到别人丢失的东西，都会交到那里去，所以要尽早报告。

报告时使用的英语比较简单，例如：I lost my umbrella on the subway train.(我的雨伞在地铁火车上丢了。) My handbag is missing.(我的手提包不见了。)失者要会描述所丢失物品的特征，就是在领取失物的时候，也会被要求说明特征才能得到。证件、支票的丢失会带来不便，因此自己的护照要备留复印件，以便尽快得到补发的旅行证件。

Situational Dialogs
情景对话

丁唐(Ding Tang)总是很不小心，这次又弄丢了东西，幸好这些公共场所都设有失物招领处。

Something Lost 46

物品遗失

Dialog 1

Clerk: May I help you?
有什么事吗?

Ding Tang: My passport is missing.
我的护照不见了。

Clerk: When did you notice① it was missing?
你什么时候知道护照不见了?

Ding Tang: Just a few minutes ago. I have searched everywhere, but I cannot find it. What should I do?
刚刚才发现的。我已经到处都找过了,可是都找不到。我该怎么办呢?

Clerk: First, we must file an official report at the police station. Then we will notify the immigration authorities.
首先,我们必须先到警察局作正式的笔录,然后我们会通知移民局的官员处理。

Ding Tang: Thank you for your help.
谢谢你的帮忙。

Dialog 2

Ding Tang: Excuse me. Has anyone found a watch around here?
对不起,有人捡到手表吗?

Clerk: No, sir. Not at the moment②.
先生,没有。现在还没有。

Ding Tang: Well, my watch is missing. Will you let me know if anyone finds it?
我的手表不见了。如果有人捡到,告诉我好吗?

Clerk: Sure. What's your room number, please?
当然,请问你的房间号码?

Ding Tang: Room 808. My watch is a brand new Rolex. Is it possible that anyone may come here with it?
是808房间。我的手表是崭新的劳力士,有可能有人会交到这儿来吗?

Clerk: Yes, if any personnel③ find it in the hotel. But frankly speaking, it is hard to say.

	会的,如果本酒店的职员捡到的话。但是,坦率地讲,这很难说。
Ding Tang:	I see. Thank you all the same. 我明白,还是要谢谢你。

Dialog 3

Clerk:	Hello, this is Yellow Cab. May I help you? 你好,耶洛出租车公司。能帮你忙吗?
Ding Tang:	I left my handbag on the back seat of the taxi about ten minutes ago. 我大约10分钟之前把手提包遗留在出租车的后座上。
Clerk:	Are you sure it's one of our taxis? 你确信是我们的出租车吗?
Ding Tang:	Yes, I think so. There was a big sign on top, and the taxi is yellow. 确信。车顶上有一个大牌子,车是黄色的。
Clerk:	Do you remember the license plate number? 你记得车牌号码吗?
Ding Tang:	No, I can't. 不记得。
Clerk:	Please tell me your name, address, phone number. 请告诉我你的姓名、地址和电话号码。
Ding Tang:	Ding Tang, Room 808 of Hilton Hotel and the phone number is 337-5386, extension 1808. 丁唐,希尔顿酒店808房间,电话号码是337-5386,分机是1808。
Clerk:	All right, Mr. Ding. Don't be worried, for I think the driver will come back soon. I will check him. 好的,丁先生,别着急,我觉得司机很快就回来,我问问他。
Ding Tang:	Thank you very much. 非常感谢。

Something Lost 46
物品遗失

Typical Sentences
典型句型

1) Where's the Lost and Found Office?
   失物招领处在哪里？
2) My handbag was lost. Can I have it reported?
   我的手提包不见了，我可以报告一下吗？
3) My passport is missing.
   我的护照不见了。
4) I lost my traveler's check.
   我把旅行支票丢了。
5) Where should I apply for reissue?
   我在哪里申请补发呢？
6) My watch is a brand new Rolex.
   我的手表是崭新的劳力士。
7) I left my wallet here about an hour ago.
   我一个小时之前把钱包丢在这里了。
8) Is it possible that anyone may come here with it?
   有可能有人会交到这儿来吗？
9) Has anyone found a watch around here?
   有人捡到手表吗？
10) My watch is missing. Will you let me know if anyone finds it?
    我的手表不见了。如果有人捡到，告诉我好吗？
11) I was told that my handbag had been found and handed in here.
    我听说我的手提包找到了，并且被交到了这里。

Background
背景知识

护照遗失：护照遗失的时候,补办的大致手续是报案、作废、重新申请。所以出国前应先将护照号码、发行年月日及国外大使馆等补发单位的电话另外抄录,并准备护照复印件及个人护照照片两张,以备不时之需。补发护照通常需要数周时间,若是紧急必须回国的人,可以申请"临时旅行证",两三天就可以办妥,但只能用于直接回国,不得再入境其他国家。

若护照丢失,首先要向国外警察机关报案,并取得遗失证明正本。然后向中国驻外使领馆申请补发护照,递交护照复印件、遗失证明、机票、照片两张、手续费。

旅行支票遗失：旅行支票是比现金安全的货币,必须有持票人的亲笔签名才能生效,所以当你买到旅行支票时,先在右上方签名,表示这张支票归你所有,其他人不得使用。因为有了签名,其他人较难模仿盗用,所以当旅行支票遗失时不必太担心,应尽快挂失止付,另外申请补发。由于补发迅速,所以不至于影响行程或计划。旅行支票的持有者必须记住支票号码。

出发前,在你购买旅行支票的银行询问清楚,万一遗失旅行支票,在境外应该向什么机构申请补发。例如,你买的是VISA,则必须找花旗银行。通常购买合约背书会有全球挂失止付电话及详细说明。

Something Lost 46

物品遗失

注 释

① notice 的意思是"注意到,留心到",如:
I didn't notice how he was dressed. (我没留心他穿什么衣服。)

② at the moment 的意思是"现在,此刻",如:
The number is engaged at the moment. (这个号现在占线。)
另外需注意的短语还有 for the moment (暂时,目前), in a moment (一会儿,立刻)。

③ personnel 在这里指"职员",同义词有 staff, employees;也可指"人事(部门)",如:personnel department (人事处)。

Suffering from Sickness
罹患疾病

Topic Introduction
话题导言

　　一个人难免生病。出国的时候又特别容易生病,主要是旅途的劳累、环境的变化、饮食的不习惯等因素都容易使人生病。这时候,令人着急的是,语言不通,又不知道在哪里看病,而且还有其他别的担心。

　　西方国家的医疗体系跟我们有很大的不同。一般感觉不适的时候,都是去私人开设的诊所(clinic)、大学的医疗中心(health center)或者是看家庭医生(family doctor),很少直接到医院(hospital)看病,除非得了急性病,需要看急诊(emergency)。如果诊所的医生认为需要手术或作进一步的检查,就会介绍病人到医院接受治疗。所以,西方国家都是各类专业诊所较多,而医院不多。

　　说自己生病了,英语有一个比较通用的句型 I have… / I feel… / I am…,加上症状就可以了。不要轻易判断自己得了什么病,因为这是医生的事情,只需要向他们说明症状就行。

Situational Dialogs
情景对话

　　出门在外,不管是环境的变化还是饮食的不适应,或者是旅途的劳累都容易引起疾病或不适,刘杭(Liu Hang)也不例外。

Suffering from Sickness 47

罹患疾病

Dialog 1

Doctor: What's wrong with you, madam?
女士,你怎么了?

Liu Hang: I sprained my ankle this morning when we climbed the mountain. I'm feeling sharp pain here.
我今天上午爬山的时候伤了脚踝关节。这里感到刺疼。

Doctor: Please put your foot on the stool. Well, let me have a look. It's a bit swollen. Can you feel pain here?
请把这只脚放到凳子上。让我来看看,有一些肿。感到这里疼吗?

Liu Hang: No, doctor.
医生,不疼。

Doctor: It's not so serious as it looks①. No fraction and you may set your heart at rest②.
没有看起来那么严重。没有骨折,你可以放心了。

Liu Hang: Perhaps the rugged trail gave the ankle a wrench.
也许是崎岖的山路把踝关节扭了一下。

Doctor: If I were you, I would stay in bed for some days. You'd better take some medicine for detumescence.
如果我是你的话,我就在床上躺几天。还是先吃些消肿的药吧。

Liu Hang: All right. Thank you, doctor.
好的,谢谢你,医生。

Dialog 2

John: Hi, Liu Hang. How's it going?
嗨,刘杭。还好吗?

Liu Hang: Hi, John. Not too well, I'm afraid.
嗨,约翰。不是太好,我恐怕。

John: Why, what's wrong with you today?
啊,你今天怎么了?

Liu Hang: I have a bad headache, and a fever perhaps.
我头痛得厉害,也许还发烧。

John: That's no fun. Why not go to see a doctor?
那就不好了。怎么不去看看医生呢?

Liu Hang: I'd prefer to take some medicine first. I brought much medicine from China when I came here.
我宁愿先吃些药吧。我来的时候从中国带来了不少药。

John: Possibly the medicine will work③. Maybe you should take a few aspirins.
可能这些药会有效果,也许你要吃些阿司匹林。

Liu Hang: All right.
好的。

John: Take a break first, for you look exhausted. If you need some help, let me know.
先休息,你看起来很疲劳。如果需要帮助,就告诉我。

Liu Hang: All right. Thank you.
好的,谢谢你。

Typical Sentences
典型句型

1) I have a high fever. 我发烧。
2) I have a headache. 我头痛。
3) I feel nauseous. 我想吐。
4) I have a griping pain. 我肚子痛。
5) I have a pain here. 我这里痛。
6) I have a sore throat. 我喉咙痛。
7) I am allergic to medicine. 我对药物过敏。
8) I have heartburn. 我觉得胸口很闷。
9) I have diarrhea. 我腹泻。
10) I am not feeling well. 我不太舒服。
11) I feel a little better. 我好一些了。
12) I feel much better. 我好多了。
13) What's wrong with me? 我患了什么病。
14) Is it OK for me to continue my journey? 还能继续旅行吗?

Suffering from Sickness 47

15) Is it OK for me to fly? 乘飞机没有问题吧?
16) How long will I have to stay in bed? 我需要卧床修养几天?
17) I have something wrong with my stomachache.
    我的胃有些不舒服。
18) I feel dizzy and I'm having terrible diarrhea.
    我头晕,腹泻得厉害。
19) I've had a bad headache and a high fever.
    我头痛发烧。

背景知识

出国常见病: 有些疾病是因为环境的改变而导致发病,气候、食物、劳累等都可能是病因。

感冒: 寒冷的冬季或气候突然变冷、变热时易使人感冒。症状较轻时会鼻塞、流鼻涕、打喷嚏、头痛。症状严重时会发烧、喉咙痛、咳嗽。感冒时要注意饮水及休息,用些药物减轻症状。

皮肤过敏: 一般容易皮肤过敏的人,应避免接触鲜花、坐卧草地或去蚊虫多的地方。从事激烈运动时应避免穿着紧身衣裤。有研究发现大量补充维生素C及每日适当的日晒能增加皮肤的抵抗力。汗疹、湿疹、顽癣是夏天常见的皮肤病,因此在炎热的夏季要及时防治皮肤病。

腹泻(Diarrhea): 腹泻的病原不一,大都是因为吃了不洁的饮食。有些人对某些食物过敏或消化不完全(如吃牛奶、生菜)也会腹泻。腹泻时服用对症的药物,并要大量补充盐和水份以防脱水。当有上吐下泻或有发烧时应去看医生。

便秘(Constipation): 便秘常是由于生活没有规律、饮食不当或胃肠蠕动不良引起的。因此平日多吃蔬菜、水果、高纤维食物及适度的腹部运动可起到预防作用。一般超级市场出售的 prune juice 可帮助肠子蠕动。

注 释

① so+adj.+a/an+n.(+as sb./sth.) 用于做比较,如:
He was not so quick a learner as his brother (他没他弟弟学得快。)

② set your heart at rest 是"放心"的意思,如:
I've done all the job, so you may set your heart at rest.
(我把这个活儿都做完了,你就放心吧。)

③ work 在这里起"有效,起作用"的意思。

Acknowledgements（致谢）

　　本系列能够以目前这种状态面世，得感谢很多人：德高望重的我国著名英语教育家、英语语法学界权威张道真教授，多年以来对笔者的教导和关心；广州乃至全国许多高校的前辈和同行，从他们身上笔者学到了很多东西，尤其值得一提的有恩师胡光忠教授、周力教授；美国爱达荷大学（the University of Idaho）的 Edwin Krumpe 博士、Steven Hollenhorst 博士和我的美国同学 Andrew Stratton、Natalie Meyer 以及路易斯安那州萨夫市 W. W. Lewis 中学校长 Oci McGuire 夫妇等都曾从不同方面给我以帮助；北京大学出版社外语编辑室的编辑们为本系列的选题、编校付出了辛勤的劳动；特别值得一提的是，本系列的部分前身是在广东语言音像出版社的有关领导及编辑的帮助下出版的，他们的约稿促使我编写了那个系列；还要提到的有广东涉外经济职业技术学院的刘乐老师，通读了全书初稿并提出了很多很好的意见和建议，还对人物的设计提出了独到的见解；更有其他许多朋友、领导和同事，对书稿的编写工作和出版从不同的侧面给我以支持和鼓励，如张婷婷女士、黄雨鸿先生、赵宁宁小姐、杜传贵先生、胡德奖先生、葛彬女士、何传春女士、王正飞先生等等，恕不一一枚举。

邱立志
2008 年 5 月 5 日